in and out of
Boston
with (or without) children

Other books by Bernice Chesler

Editor and Coordinator
The ZOOM Catalog
Do a ZOOMdo
People You'd Like to Know

Coauthor
The Family Guide to Cape Cod

Author
Mainstreaming through the Media
Bed & Breakfast Coast to Coast
Bed & Breakfast in New England
Bed & Breakfast in the Mid-Atlantic States

in and out of
Boston
with (or without) children

Bernice Chesler

Fifth Edition

Photographs by Stan Grossfeld

Old Saybrook, Connecticut

Maps by Deb Perugi and Steven Ackerman. Photo on page 95 by Deborah Schenck.
Photo on page 175 © Don Eaton, courtesy of Higgins Armory Museum. Poem on
page 183 reproduced by kind permission of the Arnold Arboretum and Tatsuya
Tamaoki. Map on page 249 based on information courtesy of The New England Ski
Areas Council (NESAC), Woodstock, Vermont. Fenway Park plan on page 251 ©
1991 Rand McNallly & Co.; reproduced by permission.

Library of Congress Cataloging-in-Publication Data

Chesler, Bernice
    In and out of Boston with (or without) children / Bernice Chesler; photographs
by Stan Grossfeld. -- 5th ed.
    p.   cm.
    Includes index.
    ISBN 1-56440-069-7
    1. Boston (Mass.)--Guidebooks. 2. Boston Region (Mass.)--Guidebooks. I. Title.
    F73.18.C5 1992
    917.44'61044--dc20   92-27680
                                              CIP

All coupon fees are paid directly to the author.

No one can pay or is paid to be in the text of this book.

Book and cover design by David Ford.

This book was packaged for The Globe Pequot Press by Editorial Inc.

Manufactured in the United States of America

Fifth Edition / Third Printing

To Benjamin

Preface

"Ten cents! Stop the presses! The Children's Museum has raised admission fees from fifty to sixty cents." The year was 1966. I was distraught. The first edition of this book, with the title of *In and Out of Boston with Children,* was being printed.

Shortly after the book was released, the owner of the swan boats called. "When are you going back to press? When you asked for a telephone number, I gave you our home phone. We have five children and the youngest is two years old. My wife thinks we should get an answering service."

Other feedback came from companies that gave tours to the public. "Your book has created more of a demand than we can handle." (It was the first such published list.)

And then readers/users suggested the title that has appeared on all subsequent editions: *In and Out of Boston with (or without) Children.*

Through each edition, the city's skyline has changed. And so have cultural, recreational, and historic resources in and around Boston.

But what about people? "People want adventure and fun," reports Polly Flansburgh, founding director of Boston By Foot, the pioneering walking tour organization. Everywhere, attractions have programmed accordingly for all ages, especially families. Museums and libraries have become major cultural centers. More than one place has lowered the minimum age "in response to parents' demand." More than one parent with grown children has declared that it is time to use this book "for what we want to do without children."

Because time seems to have become more precious for everyone, not just working parents, this silver anniversary edition includes more details to help with planning and realistic expectations. Because travelers often remember people as much as a place, sprinkled through the book are profiles of an artist, a sculptor, a bookseller. There are suggestions for nearby casual restaurants and picnic sites, and lots of cross-references so that you don't miss combination ideas—where do we go from the museum, the observation tower, the historic site. With this symbol ★, you can identify a place that can be rented for special occasions. Revised walking tours have incorporated the directions I have given to many out-of-towners who have one or two days to get a sense of the area. Information about handicapped accessibility has been expanded. And because you asked, there is information about Boston hotels with pools as well as a list of bed and breakfast reservation services.

In a phrase, herewith—a whole new book!

It has been rewritten with the help of hundreds of people. Recommendations and ideas have come from seemingly everyone I know or have ever met: longtime residents, short-term visitors from here or abroad, librarians, curators, administrators, historians, group leaders, tourists, teachers, counselors, television colleagues, newcomers (students, singles, and families), friends, neighbors, children, and relatives. Organizations and institutions have advanced decisions so that the very latest information would be available for press time.

My heartfelt thanks go to Jay Howland. As both editor and project director, she offered a welcome perspective, a sensitive ear, and creative coordination. Additional support and encouragement have come from my agent, Laura Fillmore, and the staff of Editorial Inc.

Comments are always welcome. Please address them to me at The Globe Pequot Press, P.O. Box 833, Old Saybrook, CT 06475–0833.

Happy exploring.

Bernice Chesler

The information in this book has . . .

. . . **distances** and **directions** calculated from Boston.

. . . **admissions** and **fees** that are subject to change. (Permanence is hard to come by.)

. . . **hours** that may change too. To avoid disappointment, check before you leave. Sometimes doors are closed for some special reason on a particular day.

Group leaders know that . . .

. . . **reservations** are either necessary or preferred. They are mutually beneficial.

. . . **special rates** are often available with advance notice. It's a good idea to make an **advance visit.**

. . . **transportation** involves expense, insurance, and parental permission slips—all details that take time.

. . . **spring bookings** fill early in the school year.

. . . **rainy summer days** bring a deluge of requests to the larger institutions. Details about less-obvious places are also included in this book.

. . . **advance materials** may be available. Orientation creates interest. Follow-up is follow-through. (Those with young children sometimes role-play before an excursion.)

. . . **supervision** is essential. A recommended ratio: one adult for every ten children. (One for every six is even better.) Sometimes groups separate and then meet at a specified time.

. . . it's hard to plan every detail.

Contents

Maps and Seating Plans

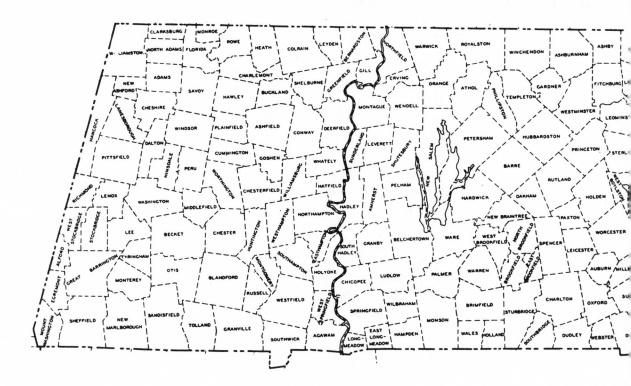

Massachusetts Cities and Towns

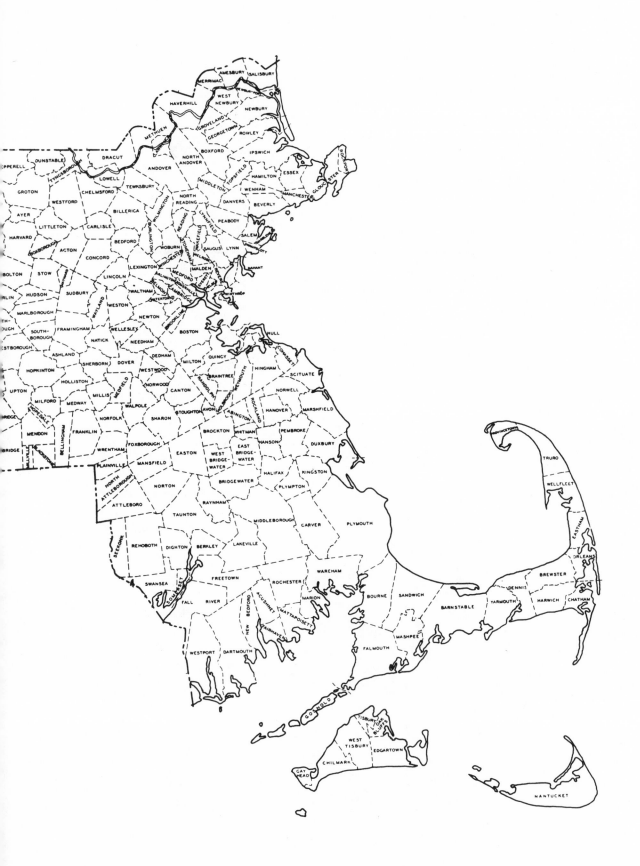

An Introduction
to the City

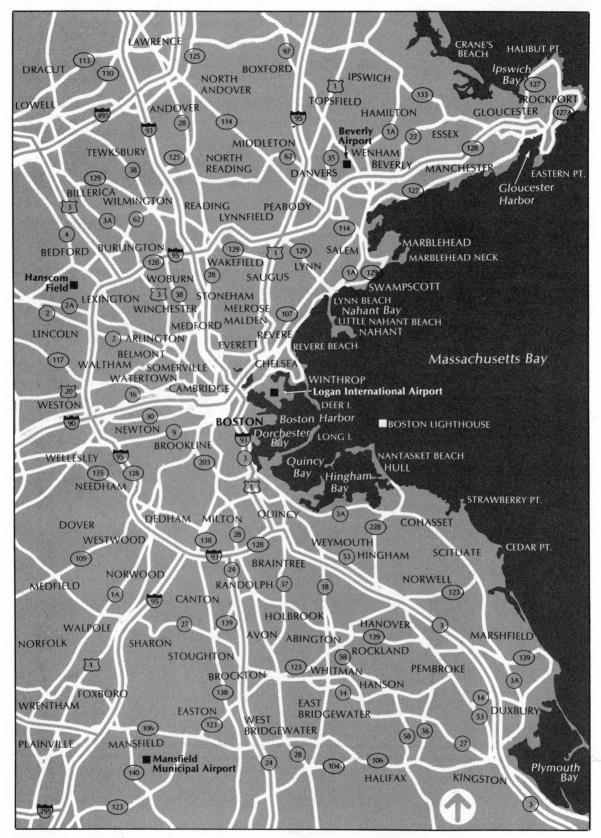

Boston Area Roads

A ONE-STOP INTRODUCTION

Where am I? How did Boston grow? The best introduction to the city: **John Hancock Observatory** (page 119).

Information

Boston National Historical Park Visitor Center 15 State Street, Boston 02109. **Phone:** 617/242–5642. (See page 97.)

Greater Boston Convention & Visitors Bureau, Inc. Prudential Tower, Suite 400, Boston 02199. **Phone:** 617/536–4100.

Recorded Information

Mass. Pike weather and road conditions: 617/237–5210.

Time and temperature: 617/637–1234.

Local weather: 617/936–1212.

National weather service: 617/567–4670.

Marine weather: 617/569–3700.

Harvard Center for Astrophysics–Smithsonian sky report: 617/491–1497.

Voice of Audubon (what birds have been seen where): 617/259–8805.

Events

Published listings are everywhere. Check local publications for what's around the corner. The most complete information can be found in

The Boston Globe: All Thursday editions have "Calendar," an event supplement.

The Boston Phoenix: A weekly issued on Fridays. "Summer Preview" supplement published in June.

The Boston Herald: All Friday editions have "The Scene," an event supplement.

The TAB: A weekly published in many communities.

Everything from radio programs to story hours are listed in **The Boston Parents' Paper,** a hefty monthly newspaper, available free in libraries,

Warmlines (206 Waltham Street, West Newton 02165): This parent resource center established in 1978, a private, nonprofit organization, has thought of everything. They provide much information and assistance, linking families with young children to community resources. Programming includes drop-in playgroups held in several locations; support groups; a computerized resource and referral service to child-care programs in Brookline, Needham, Newton, Waltham, Watertown, Wellesley, and Weston; lists of babysitters; a lending library; and workshops for parents. Publications include compilations of summer day camps, preschool programs, and children's activities. Office hours: Monday, Wednesday, Friday 9:30–3; Tuesday and Thursday 9:30–1. Phone 617/244–6843.

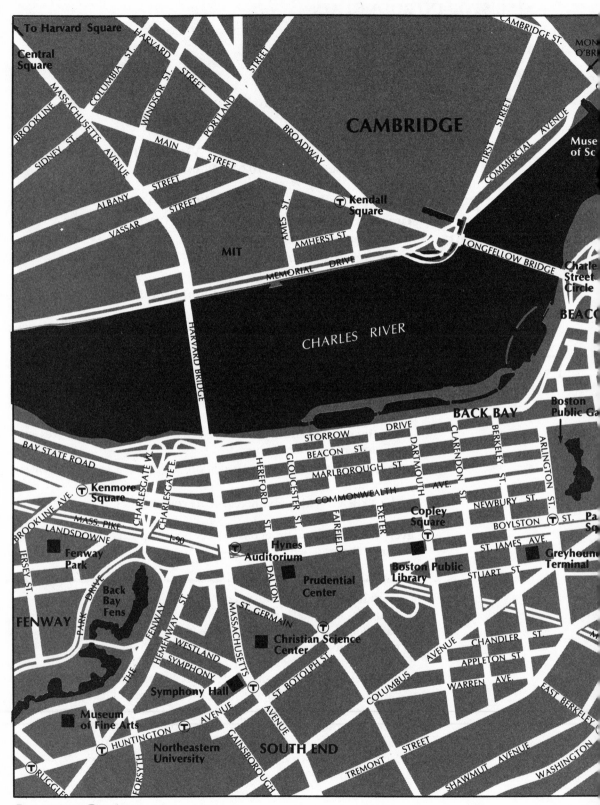

Downtown Boston

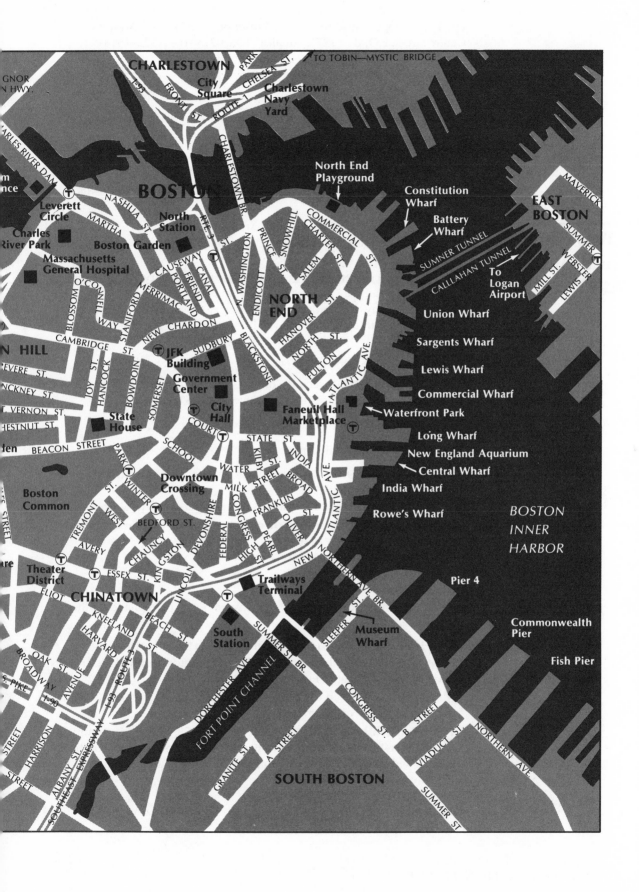

children's shops, day-care centers. Subscriptions available. Address: 670 Centre Street, P.O. Box 1777, Jamaica Plain, 02130 (617/522–1515).

Recorded Events Information:

Boston Garden: 617/227–3200.

Boston Jazz Line: 617/787–9700.

Harvard University: 617/495–1718.

"Great Dates in the Bay State" (Massachusetts Office of Travel and Tourism): 617/727–3201.

Museums: See page 149 for a list of recorded-information numbers.

Traveling In and Out of Boston

Through the 1990s, while the Central Artery is being depressed and the third harbor tunnel is under construction, there will be changes, detours, and possible delays.

Ⓣ **(The Massachusetts Bay Transportation Authority, or MBTA):** The nation's oldest subway had its first run from Park to Boylston in 1897. The system isn't always dependable—and it's very crowded at rush hours—but, when everything works the way it's supposed to, the Ⓣ is an efficient way to travel.

- **Phone:** 617/722–3200 or 800/392–6100. TDD: 617/722–5146.
- **Boston Passport:** Consecutive days of unlimited travel on all Ⓣ subway and local bus lines. Three days, $9. Seven days, $18.
- **Bicycle permits:** Please see page 222.

Air: Logan International Airport.

- **Phone:** 800/23–LOGAN (most answers on tape, 24 hours a day). Agents available 9–5, Monday–Friday.
- Ⓣ: Airport on Blue Line. Or water shuttle (page 233) between Rowes Wharf, Atlantic Avenue (downtown Boston), and Logan. Free shuttle buses between subway or dock and terminals. *Reminder:* No water shuttle service on Saturdays and some holidays.

Boat: See page 232.

Bus: If you do not know which company services a particular outlying community, call Greyhound.

- **Greyhound Bus Terminal.** Main terminal (617/423–5810) is at 10 St. James Avenue, near Park Square, between Arlington and Berkeley streets, two blocks from Boston Public Garden.
- Ⓣ: Arlington on Green Line. The Newton terminal (617/969–8860) is at the Green Line Riverside Ⓣ station.
- **Peter Pan Trailways**. Main terminal (617/426–7838) is at 555 Atlantic Avenue, across from Federal Reserve Bank and South Station. Ⓣ: South Station on Red Line. The Newton terminal (617/965–7040) is at the Green Line Riverside Ⓣ station.

Bicycling: For suggested routes, contact the Boston Area Bicycle Coalition, page 223.

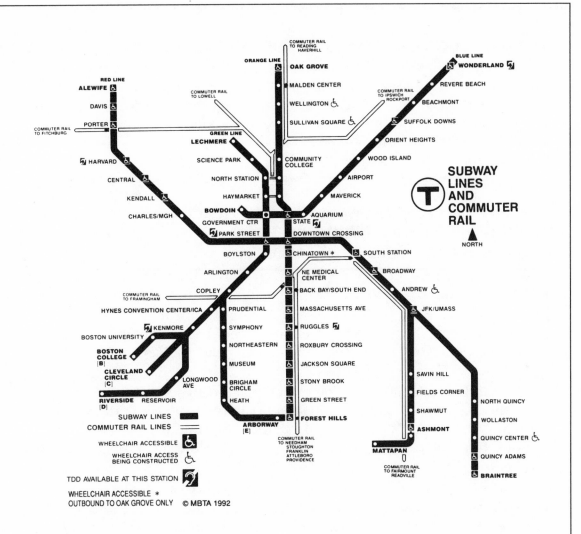

Hint: Bostonians know that you can change directions without paying an additional fare at Arlington or Hynes Convention Center/ICA stations, but not at Copley or Boylston stations.

Bikes on the Ⓣ: Permits are required. Please see page 222 for details. And note that bicycles are not allowed on the Green Line; on buses; or in Park Street, Downtown Crossing, Government Center, or Aquarium stations.

The Ⓣ

ONE, TWO, OR THREE DAYS IN BOSTON

Even a compact city can be too much to cover all at once. The Marketplace (page 134) is a magnet—historic, lively, fascinating, upscale and down, and a tourist mecca. The Freedom Trail (page 97) isn't arranged chronologically—each site stands on its own merit—so it doesn't have to be done in its entirety, all at once, or in any order. Some visitors concentrate on major museums; a visit to any one can easily absorb a half day.

These suggestions are intended to reduce a bountiful menu to edible size.

One Day, an Outside Overview with Inside Options (to Swallow the City Whole, on Foot)

John Hancock Observatory (page 119): Orientation.

Back Bay (page 126): Commonwealth Avenue, Newbury Street, the Public Garden, and the swan boats. Via Charles Street to

Beacon Hill (page 131): Historic district. Emerge on the top of Beacon Street at the State House. Follow Beacon Street on to School Street and by way of King's Chapel, the City Carpet (page 101), and Old City Hall to Washington Street. Jog right to Filene's Basement or left to

Faneuil Hall area (page 134): The marketplace with seats, food, entertainment, shops, people watching, old street patterns, and, on Fridays and Saturdays, Haymarket's produce pushcarts. (Warning: If you make some discoveries, have interesting conversations, shop, and/or peek inside, this may be as far as you get.)

The Waterfront (page 144): Harborwalk, open space, water views, revitalized historic buildings, the Aquarium.

North End (page 141): It's old. It's an ethnic neighborhood with plenty of restaurants and bakeries. Two Freedom Trail "inside" sites: Paul Revere House and Old North Church.

Option: Start at the North End and finish at the Observatory to see where you have been.

Two Days, Inside and Outside

Day 1:

Charlestown Navy Yard (page 107): USS *Constitution,* HarborWalk, tours. To get to Boston, walk over the locks of **Charles River Dam** (page 260); or take the ferry and then walk to the

North End (page 141): Good place for food shopping, lunch, a snack, dinner, listening, watching, looking up, stopping in to mom-and-pop places. Paul Revere House and Old North Church are inside; Copp's Hill Terrace is outside.

The Waterfront (page 144): The New England Aquarium and its views. If you missed the Navy Yard HarborWalk, be sure to explore at least part of the one here marked with a blue line.

Faneuil Hall area (page 134): A little bit of everything. Information booth is on south plaza of Marketplace. Year-round National Park Service Visitor Center is steps away (somewhat hidden) at 15 State Street.

Day 2:

Inside Freedom Trail sites: Old South Meeting House and the Old State House (pages 101 and 102): Two small museums in historic buildings dwarfed by sky-scrapers. Or start with

Back Bay (page 126): Newbury Street for shops, galleries, alfresco dining; Commonwealth Avenue for elegant townhouses, a green mall—and not one em-porium; Copley Square with Trinity Church and the Boston Public Library; the Public Garden and swan boats. Cross Beacon Street for a

Riverside walk, jog, or bicycle ride: From the Hatch Shell and Arthur Fiedler sculpture, go along the Esplanade and Storrow Drive, by the lagoon and playgrounds to Massachusetts Avenue. Cross to MIT on the right-hand side of the Harvard/Massachusetts Avenue Bridge, by Smoot markings that were first painted by a fraternity in the 1960s. (See plaque at Cambridge end of bridge.) Photographers detour to the right along Memorial Drive for the almost-famous shot of Boston and the State House in the background and sailboats in the foreground. Turn left along the river or take a bus along Massachusetts Avenue to

Harvard Square (page 137): Harvard Yard, walking tours, bookstores, museums (the glass flowers), shops, historic sights, performances, a hidden lane.

Three Days (to Savor)

Day 1: Follow the rough outline of Day 1 above.

Day 2: Recuperate with a change of pace.

A guided walk (page 125): Concentrate on one area.

A museum (page 149): See a program and exhibit. (Check the recorded-information numbers, page 149).

Or drive to Concord (page 55): If you haven't seen anything that fits your idea of real New England.

Day 3: Try Day 2 of Two Days with renewed energy and enthusiasm.

Commuting: Many radio and television stations carry traffic reports throughout the morning and late afternoon.

Train: Amtrak (617/482–3660 or 800/USA RAIL) leaves from **South Station** (Ⓣ: South Station on Red Line); from **Back Bay** (Ⓣ: Back Bay/South End station on Orange Line); and from **Route 128 in Westwood.**

Massachusetts Bay Transit Authority Ⓣ commuter rail service from **North Station** (Ⓣ: North Station on the Orange or Green Line): 617/722–3200 or 800/392–6100.

Recommended book: *Car-Free in Boston: The Guide to Public Transit in Greater Boston & New England.* Published every two years by Association for Public Transportation, P.O. Box 1029, Boston 02205; 617/482–0282. Sold for $5.75 in book and convenience stores or by mail; $7 includes postage.

Northeast Travelers Information

Canada

Newfoundland: 800/563–6353

Prince Edward Island: 800/565–0267

Nova Scotia: 800/341–6096

New Brunswick: 800/561–0123

Quebec: 800/363–7777

Ontario: 800/668–2746

Manitoba: 800/665–0040

Saskatchewan: 800/667–7191

Alberta: 800/661–8888

British Columbia: 800/663–6000

Northwest Territories: 800/661–0788

Yukon: 800/661–0494

New England

For camping, see page 237.

Connecticut: Department of Economic Development, 865 Brook Street, Rocky Hill, CT 06067–3405 (800/CT BOUND).

Maine: Publicity Bureau, P.O. Box 2300, Hallowell, ME 04347–2300 (800/533–9595, vacation kit; 207/582–9300, travel assistance).

Massachusetts: Office of Travel and Tourism, 100 Cambridge Street, Boston 02202 (800/447–MASS, vacation kit; 617/727–3201, travel assistance, Monday–Friday 9–5 Eastern time).

New Hampshire: Travel and Tourism, 172 Pembroke Road, Concord, NH 03301 (603/271–2666).

Rhode Island: Tourism Division, 7 Jackson Walkway, Providence, RI 02903 (800/556–2484 or 401/277–2601).

Vermont: Travel Division, 134 State Street, Montpelier, VT 05602 (802/828–3236).

Where to Stay

A full roster of places, complete with facilities and range of rates, is available from the Greater Boston Convention & Visitors Bureau (page 3). . . . Many hotels offer weekend rates that are family-friendly. Year round, some packages include tickets to Red Sox or Bruins games or to special museum shows. In summer, many vacationing families find a pool a practical asset, and at times, a major attraction for children. . . . Hotels and inns outside Boston are often less expensive than those in town. . . . Bed and breakfasts, page 15, in and out of Boston are extremely popular.

For all ages

Boston International AYH-Hostel 12 Hemenway Street, Boston 02115

Phone: 617/536–9455.

Ⓣ: Green Line B, C, or D car to Hynes Convention Center/ICA (formerly "Auditorium") stop; 1½ blocks to hostel.

Location: Within walking distance of Symphony Hall, Northeastern University, Christian Science Mapparium, New England Conservatory of Music.

Open: 7 a.m.–2 a.m.

Fees: Overnight: $12 AYH members ($12.75 July–September). $15 nonmembers. (Memberships may be purchased at the hostel.) $6 under 14, with parents. Reservations highly recommended—at least 3 weeks prior to arrival. MC/Visa accepted with 48-hour notice if there's room.

Bunks are in four- or six-bed rooms. Shared baths. Guests have use of kitchen, common rooms (one allows smoking), and dining and laundry rooms. Maximum stay: four nights. (Extensions may be possible.) Family room sleeps four in two bunk beds, when available, October–June. Linens may be rented or purchased. Personal lockers provided. Bicycle and baggage storage available. One building accommodates 110 year round; second building brings summer total to 220.

Hotels with Pools

A frequent summer request: "Please provide a list of Boston hotels that have pools." Herewith, together with some points of note:

- Use of pool is included with room rate.
- Day passes may be available at some hotel pools.
- Health club attendants are on duty.
- In most hotels, adult accompaniment and supervision is required.
- Suburban hotels with pools are popular year round. Boston area families have discovered them for reasonably priced family winter weekend getaways too.

Boston Harbor Hotel: 70 Rowes Wharf, Boston 02110. Children who are hotel guests or health club members are allowed in the 60-foot-lap interior pool on weekends and holidays. Special hours for children on weekdays. (In December, this hotel has Alice in Wonderland Tea Parties. See page 282.) Phone 617/439–7000 or 800/752–7077.

Boston Park Plaza Hotel: 64 Arlington Street, Boston 02116. Their year-round Cub Club, a package rate for one room with two double beds and two baths, includes free parking, swan boat rides, a daily story hour with milk and cookies in children's game room, an Eco-Tree in a cube that you bring home to plant, and discount tickets to attractions. Phone 617/426–2000 or 800/225–2008.

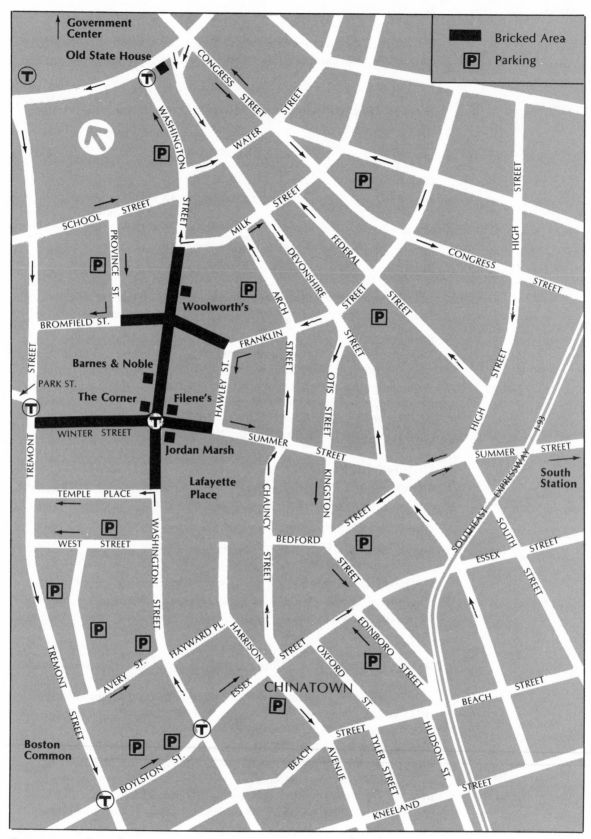

Downtown Crossing

Charles Hotel at Harvard Square: One Bennett Street, Cambridge 02138. Pool and exercise machines of on-site Le Pli Health Spa free to hotel guests. (Children's year-round membership available for use of pool, Monday–Friday 2–4:30 and weekends 12–4.) Phone 617/864–1200 or 800/882–1818.

The Colonnade: 120 Huntington Avenue, Boston 02116 (Back Bay). Open rooftop pool in summer. Rate includes free weekend parking, fitness facility. Outdoor cafe, children's menu. One or two children under 12, free in adults' room.

Four Seasons: 200 Boylston Street, Boston 02116. "Weekend with the Kids" offered year round. Rate includes use of 51-foot pool on eighth floor overlooking the Public Garden, VCR and children's movies, bedtime milk and cookies, feed for Garden squirrels and ducks, parking. Extra-large room. Children's menu in restaurants. Hotel babysitting available. Phone 617/338–4400 or 800/322–3442.

Guest Quarters Suite Hotel: 400 Soldier's Field Road, Boston 02134. All-suite hotel on Cambridge line. Various packages including family arrangement with windowed first-floor pool (on Charles River side), Jacuzzi, complimentary shuttle to downtown. Phone 617/783–0090 or 800/424–2900.

Hyatt Hotel: 575 Memorial Drive, Cambridge 02139. Health club atrium pool overlooks river. Games for children. Courtesy van to Boston and Harvard Square. Phone 617/492–1234 or 800/233–1234.

LaFayette Hotel: One Avenue De Lafayette, Boston 02111. Health club's 60-foot pool has glass doors that open onto large outdoor fourth-floor terrace. Lunch (children's menu available) served at the pool. Family memberships and day rate (includes towel, shampoo, blow-dryer) available. Phone 617/451–2600 or 800/621–9200.

Marriott Long Wharf: 296 State Street, Boston 02109. Next door to Aquarium. Pool, about half size of Olympic pool, with outdoor deck overlooking the harbor. Video games. Phone 617/227–0800 or 800/228–9290.

Meridien: 250 Franklin Street, Boston 02110. Health club with year-round use of small, pretty atrium pool. Former Federal Reserve Bank building. Elegant. Chocolate Bar (page 123). Phone 617/451–1900 or 800/543–4300.

Royal Sonesta Hotel: 5 Cambridge Parkway, Cambridge 02142. Summer special includes indoor/outdoor pool that has a retractable roof, health club facilities, complimentary Charles River boat ride, all-you-can-eat ice cream from lobby cart, free use of bicycles (junior and adult-sized; children's seats and helmets included), courtesy van to Boston and Cambridge points of interest. Year round, no charge for kids in room. Walk to Museum of Science. Phone 617/491–3600 or 800/SONESTA.

Sheraton Boston Hotel and Towers: 39 Dalton Street, Boston 02199. (Prudential Center). Has 60-foot-long indoor/outdoor (retractable roof) pool. Some family room weekend packages with crib, VCR, complimentary juices. Phone 617/236–2000 or 800/325–3535.

Hotels without Pools but with Something Special for Kids

The Bostonian: Faneuil Hall Marketplace, Boston 02109. Some rooms have working fireplaces and French doors that open onto small balconies. But there's only one Finch Suite; see page 135. Family weekend arrange-

ments include milk, cookies, and turndown service for kids. Phone 617/523-3600 or 800/343-0922.

Copley Plaza Hotel: Copley Square, Boston 02116. Boston's grand dame, page 129, has some suites with one or two bedrooms that are appropriate for families. Year round, children under 17 stay free. Guests have complimentary access to spa with pool at The Heritage, 3 blocks away. Phone 617/267–5300 or 800/826–7539.

The Ritz-Carlton: 15 Arlington Street, Boston 02117. Junior Presidential Suite, one of a kind, is an elaborate family suite with separate room for parents. Decorated children's room with lots of toys, arts and crafts, and TV with video games; bathroom with faucets shaped like dragons. Plus: You don't have to be a registered guest for chef's classes held for 8- to 12-year-olds from time to time. Phone 617/536–5700 or 800/241–3333.

A personalized style of travel

Bed and Breakfasts

B&Bs are in all downtown Boston neighborhoods—including Back Bay, Beacon Hill, and the waterfront—in brownstones and penthouses, in high-rise buildings and converted warehouses, and in restored South End Victorians. Many B&Bs are in private suburban homes, perhaps close to grandchildren, friends, a wedding or an appointment. The newest version: unhosted B&Bs where families can stay in a furnished apartment. Full details about hundreds of B&Bs are in my *Bed & Breakfast in New England* (The Globe Pequot Press). If you would like to host travelers or if you are a traveler who is looking for hosted or unhosted accommodations, the following B&B reservation services have Boston listings:

AAA Accommodations: 2218 Massachusetts Avenue, Boston 02140. Phone 617/491–6107 or 800/232–9989.

A Bed & Breakfast Above the Rest: 50 Boatswain Way, Suite 105, Boston 02150. Phone 617/884–7748 or 800/677–2262.

A Bed & Breakfast Agency of Boston, Inc.: 47 Commercial Wharf, Boston 02110. Phone 617/720–3540 or 800/CITYBNB.

Bed and Breakfast Associates Bay Colony, Ltd.: P.O. Box 57166, Babson Park, Boston 02157. Phone 617/449–5302 or 800/347–5008.

Bed & Breakfast Cambridge & Greater Boston: P.O. Box 665, Cambridge 02140. Phone 617/576–1492 or 800/888–0178.

Boston Bed and Breakfast, Inc./Boston Reservations: 643 Beacon Street, Suite 23, Waban 02168. Phone 617/332–4199.

Greater Boston Hospitality: P.O. Box 1142, Brookline 02146. Phone 617/277–5430.

Host Homes of Boston: P.O. Box 117, Waban Branch, Boston 02168. Phone 617/244–1308.

Free for All

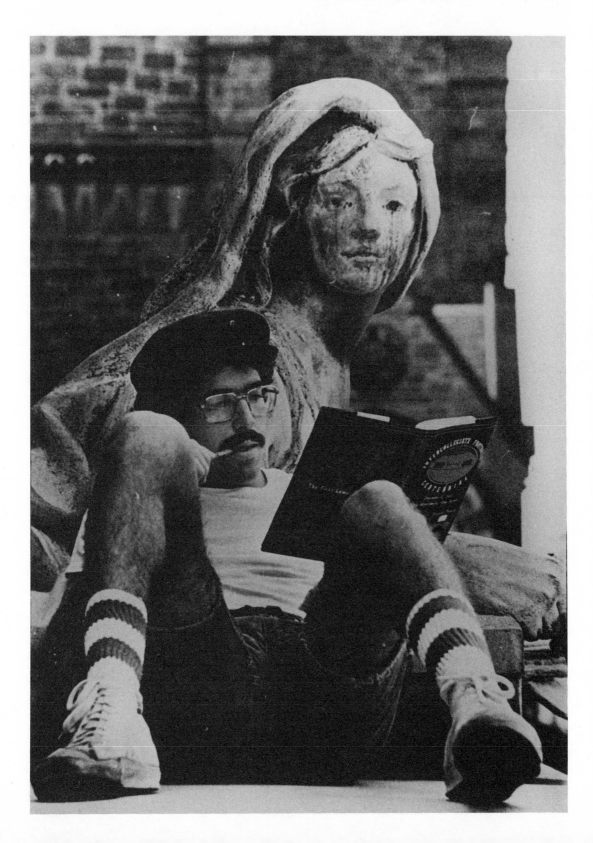

Free: 181 things to do and places to see in and around Boston.

Read a **newspaper published the day of your birthday** / page 129

See a **herring run** / page 274

Step inside a **glass globe** / page 120

Put yourself on the Arts/Mail **mailing list for discounted tickets** / page 50

Tour state-of-the-art **dance studios** and examine an elaborate gown worn by a professional ballerina / page 258

See **cows** being milked and then the **bottling process** while real glass bottles are being filled / page 31

Take a workshop at Longfellow's house and **wear an "I Am a Poet Too" button** / page 113

View **Wyeth murals** in an elegant recycled historic building / page 123

See the **world's first switchboards** in the reassembled garret workshop of Alexander Graham Bell / page 123

Get a fantastic view of **working locks** and waiting boats at the Charles River Dam / page 260

Take an **open-air 2-mile trolley ride** / page 70

Enjoy **outdoor entertainment** / pages 135 and 141

Watch **hot-air ballooning** / page 212

Feed ducks / pages 28 and 120

Go **birdwatching** with a guide / page 224

People-watch / pages 135 and 141

Bicycle with a group / page 223

Meet an **author or illustrator** / page 48

Browse in an **antiquarian book shop** / pages 102 and 141

See a **river otter** in action / page 167

Picnic and watch **harbor activity** / page 185

Visit a **national park,** hear a ranger's talk, and see an audiovisual program / page 69

Window-shop / pages 127, 134, and 137

Watch **maple sugaring** / page 274

Tour a **Boston Harbor island** / page 181

Fill a picnic jug from a **natural spring** / pages 92 and 196

Attend **live performances, lectures, or films** / page 50

Go to a **fish hatchery** / page 91

Look through a **telescope** in a university observatory / page 120

Listen to a **storyteller at a bookstore** / page 48

Count the number of countries represented by **trees and plants** along one path of the **Arnold Arboretum** / page 183

Meet a miller at work in a **gristmill** / page 93

Take an out-of-season **walk on a beach** / page 213

Visit **greenhouses** to see cacti, orange and lemon trees, orchids, ferns, and passion flowers / page 204

Dial-a-story / page 48

See **ship models** encased in glass; then step outside to see what is sailing in the harbor today / page 109

Jog, walk, or bicycle (up to 20 miles in one direction) on a **former railroad bed** / page 222

See the huge working gears and waterwheel at a rebuilt **350-year-old forge** / page 114

Under age 5? With adult accompaniment, take a free **train ride** from South Station to a stop near the **John Hancock Observatory** for an on-high look at Boston / pages 122 and 119

Under 17? For almost free (one dollar) you can **sail on the Charles River** all summer / page 229

Cross a marsh on a **boardwalk** / page 93

Borrow a library membership card to take **Boston By Foot's guided walking tour** / page 125

Observe the grooming and training of **Clydesdale horses** / page 29

Visit a **winery** and a nearby **horse farm** / page 268

Pose for the camera on **public art** that's made for sitting / page 135

Folk dance / pages 242 and 279

Walk, cycle, or cross-country ski along the Emerald Necklace with **Boston Park Rangers** / page 125

Play **hopscotch** on the Freedom Trail / page 97

Steady your footing in a half-mile-long **chasm** / page 203

Take a **company tour** / page 257

Go to a **museum.** Some are always free. Some are sometimes free; some have free programs. Culled list / page 149

On Boston's waterfront, enjoy a **ninth-floor view of the harbor** / page 145

Walk around Boston:

- **Back Bay:** Architecture, art galleries, church tours, the Mapparium, the Boston Public Library, exhibits / page 126
- **Beacon Hill:** Close-ups of architectural details, dramatic views of the city, and the Black Heritage Trail / page 131
- **Freedom Trail:** Most sites are free, and so are outdoor guided tours / page 97
- **Faneuil Hall Marketplace:** Browsing; street entertainment; Faneuil Hall; and, nearby, the Blackstone Block, Government Center, and City Hall / page 134

Comb the Thursday "Calendar" of the *Boston Globe,* the Friday "Scene" of the *Boston Herald*, the *Boston Parents' Paper,* or the *Boston Phoenix* for one-time events, free and open to the public.

To plan more than a week in advance, check the Calendar chapter, pages 273–283.

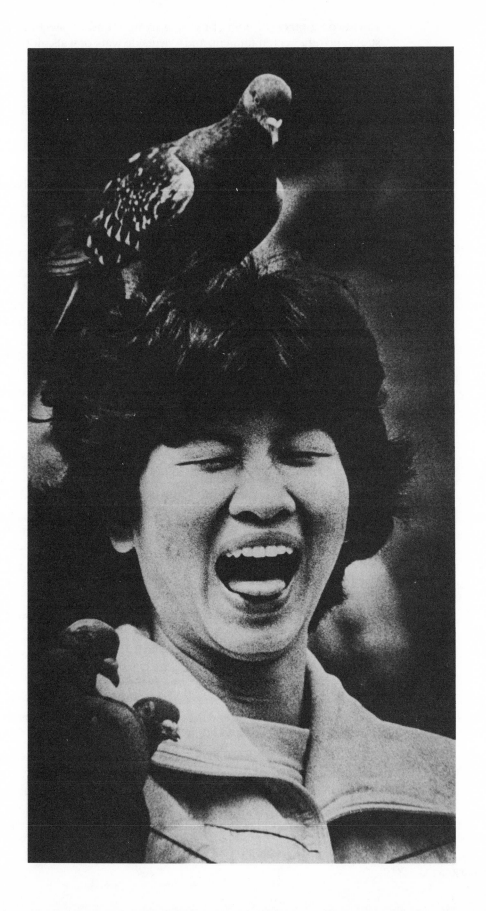

- **Harvard Square:** Museums, browsing, campus and architectural tours, street and other entertainment, and a riverside walk or walk along Brattle Street / page 137
- **North End:** Old North Church, an old burying ground, an ethnic neighborhood, food-oriented sights, a good library, and festivals / page 141
- **The Waterfront:** HarborWalk, the Aquarium plaza and walkway, and Waterfront Park / page 144

Custom-design your own freebie:

- **Plaque reading:** Look for plaques everywhere—on fences, embedded in buildings, and on statues too
- **Courthouse activity:** Local or state. Small-claim hearings or a trial. Check with the clerk for a schedule of open hearings
- **John Hancock Tower:** Focus on it from different points in the city. Does it ever have the same reflection?
- **Government in process:** Attend an open meeting at City Hall or at the State House
- **Combine familiar and unfamiliar:** Bring a visitor to a place you know well and see it with new eyes
- **Identification game:** Use one of the many photographic collections of Boston, and find the weathervane, doorway, or steeple
- **Meet people:** Shopkeepers, zookeepers, curators, politicians, artists, firefighters, bankers, road builders, and more may be available for interviews with advance arrangements

Explore a new (to you) open space area: Some have programs and guided walks.

- **Beaches:** Out of season more are available to nonresidents and are free / pages 194 and 213
- **Places in or very near Boston:** Arnold Arboretum, Boston Public Garden, MDC reservations, Mount Auburn Cemetery, and local parks / pages 183–189
- **Boston Harbor Islands:** Free admission and tours. A charge for the ferry, but not for island-hopping by water taxi / page 181
- **Cape Cod National Seashore:** Free except for parking fee at beach areas in summer / page 194
- **DeCordova Museum and Sculpture Park** / page 172
- **Great Meadows National Wildlife Refuge** / page 199

Take a day trip: All the cities and towns below (detailed on pages 55–94) have museums, shops, food, and historic sites and homes; but there's no charge for the following suggestions:

- **Cape Cod National Seashore:** Cedar Swamp Trail boardwalk, Great Island Trail, bicycle trails, programs / page 194
- **Concord:** Old North Bridge, Sleepy Hollow Cemetery, Walden Pond State Reservation (parking's free in winter) / pages 55 and 203
- **Gloucester:** Harbor activity, a coastal drive, Dog Bar Breakwater / page 61

- **Lexington:** Visitor center, picnic sites, Museum of Our National Heritage, walking trail, a farm with chickens / pages 66, 176, and 226
- **Lowell:** Guided walking tours (many)—to hydroelectric plant, mills, mansions, ethnic neighborhoods / page 69
- **Lynn:** Museum, audiovisual programs, concerts, boardwalk. Step into a "10-footer" and meet a turn-of-the-century shoemaker / page 71
- **Marblehead:** Ocean view dotted with sailboats and yachts, picnic sites, Old Town, an old burying ground, architecture, and charm / page 72
- **Newport:** Walking in town and along the cliff, a ride along Ocean Drive, kite flying in Brenton State Park / page 75
- **Plymouth:** Cranberry World (a museum), Plymouth Rock, Jenney Grist Mill / page 78; a winery tour / page 267
- **Portsmouth:** A revitalized area, a musical production under the stars, and experimental gardens / page 82
- **Rockport:** Shoreline views, artists at work, and lobstermen too / page 83
- **Salem:** Custom House, Chestnut Street, Salem Witch Trials Tercentenary Memorial / page 85
- **Sandwich:** The canal area, guided walks, and a glassworks tour / page 91
- **Sudbury** (Wayside Inn area): The Red Schoolhouse, lamplighters, a gristmill, picnic sites, a walk along a pond / page 93

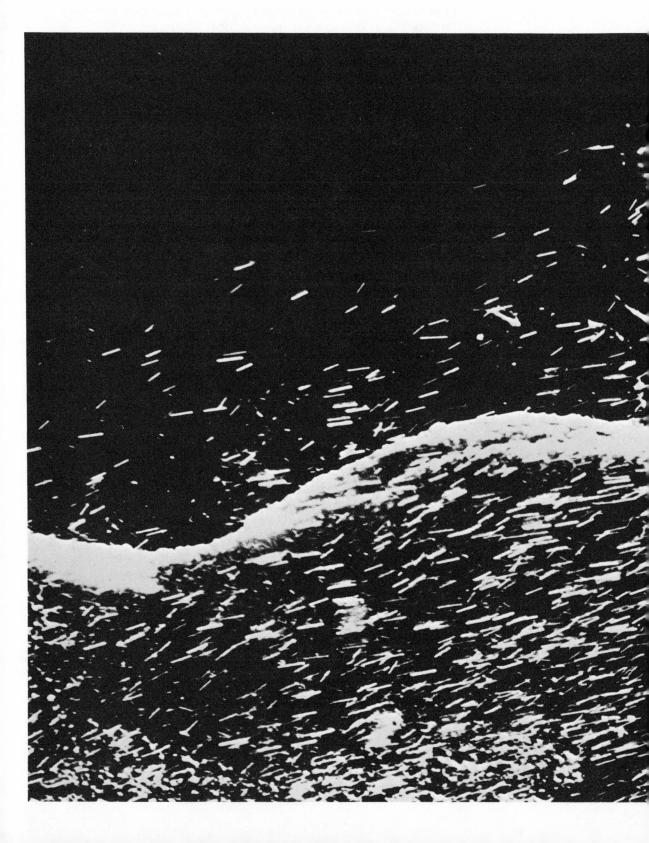

Animals

Places to Visit

Blue Hills Trailside Museum Page 167.

Drumlin Farm Education Center and Wildlife Sanctuary

(Massachusetts Audubon Society) South Great Road (Route 117), South Lincoln 01773

Phone: 617/259–9807.

Location: 22 miles west of Boston, ½ mile east of Route 126.

Directions: Mass. Pike to Route 128 (I–95) north to exit 49 (Route 20). Follow the signs to Route 117 west. Or Route 2 west to Route 126 south (toward Walden Pond). Left at the lights onto Route 117.

Train: 35-minute ride from North Station (617/722–3200 or 800/392–6100); 10 minutes less from Porter Square, Cambridge. From train, walk: Go left up the hill; at police station, left on Codman Road for a few minutes to Drumlin Farm property. Follow road in farm, crossing Route 117 to farm entrance.

Open: Year round, Tuesday–Friday 9–5. Closed Mondays except holidays; also closed Thanksgiving, Christmas, and New Year's.

Average stay: 1½ hours or longer, depending on programming.

Admission: $5 adults, $3.50 senior citizens and ages 3–15, free under 3. *Hay rides* (weather permitting), 1–3 p.m. weekends in winter, Tuesday–Sunday spring through fall; $1 per person.

Tours: For schools and other organized groups, and for special needs youngsters. Reserve early; spring and fall bookings fill quickly.

Rules: No picnicking. And please, no dogs.

Gift shop: They come from miles for it. Something for everyone.

Strollers: Paths can accommodate them.

Handicapped access: All buildings are accessible.

This large demonstration farm and sanctuary, located across from Massachusetts Audubon Society headquarters, is one of those places that you and the children will want to go back to again and again. It's particularly good for youngsters up to 12. Visitors see a typical New England farm garden, grapevines, horses, pigs, cows, owls, night animals, and chickens (see if you can find a freshly laid egg). There are fields to run in, tall grass to hide in, short trails to follow, and ponds to explore. Weekend family programs—informal

---

THE ANIMALS COME TO YOU

Staffers who like and know animals—and young people—bring a screech owl, a skunk or woodchuck, maybe a llama or snake to schools or other groups. For available animals, scheduling and fees, contact

Drumlin Farm, above, for Audubon Ark.
Franklin Park Zoo, page 28, for Wildlife on Wheels.
New England Alive, page 30, for Creature Coach.
Southwick's Wild Animal Farm, page 30, for Zoo Shows or Zoomobile.

with no registration required—are held at 11 and 2 and might include hands-on experience, a naturalist-led discussion about an animal, or a walk.

What else? Plenty. Workshops, clinics, forums, classes for all ages (preschoolers to adults), and a summer day camp.

Duck Feeding

In the **Boston Public Garden.** Or at a local lake or pond. Two close-to-Boston duck feeding destinations: **Larz Anderson Park,** page 188, and the designated place on **Norumbega Road,** along the Charles River in Newton, near Routes 30 and 128. Drive west on Commonwealth Avenue, Route 30, past the Marriott Hotel. Take first right after the Charles River Canoe and Kayak Center (page 231), next right down the ramp, and follow "Duck Feeding" signs. Year round, you get a noisy welcome here.

Franklin Park Zoo Franklin Park, Boston 02121

Phone: 617/442–2002.

Open: Spring through fall, weekdays 9–4 (Birds World opens at 10), weekends and holidays 10–5. Free flight cage is open May 1–September 15. Call for winter schedule.

Directions: From Boston, take Storrow Drive to Fenway/Park Drive exit to Route 1/Riverway to Route 203 east. Beyond Forest Hills overpass, go ¾ way around rotary (Arbor House Restaurant is on your right) onto Circuit Drive. Follow signs to Children's Zoo/Hooves and Horns/Blue Hill parking or to the Birds World/African Tropical Forest/Pierpont Road parking area. Both lots are monitored.

Admission (to the four exhibits, including the Children's Zoo): $5 adults; $2.50 ages 4–11, senior citizens, and students and military personnel with ID. Free for age 3 and under. Free for everyone Sundays 10–11 a.m. and Tuesdays 9–10 a.m. Group rates available. Parking is free.

Groups: Special tours and educational programs arranged.

Handicapped access: Accessible.

Sit next to a gorilla (with a glass wall between the two of you) and compare your outstretched hand to his or hers. Get an underwater eye-to-eye view of a hippopotamus. (You remain dry.) Take a walk with a llama. Travel through a small swamp, a rain forest, a desert, and a river. See birds building their nests—small; very big (storks); and with handles (black-headed weavers). Come in May, when the sheep are being shorn. Come in June, and there's a good chance you'll see a newborn zebra. Perhaps you will see a puppet show or an animal demonstration. Special events are regularly scheduled.

Indoors and out, it would take hours—maybe the whole day—to see everything in the four exhibits. There are lots of touch possibilities in the **Children's Zoo,** which has cows, rabbits, goats, chickens, donkeys, and sheep, along with some snow monkeys and ringtail lemurs plus a reptile house.

Last year two wallabies were born in the **Hooves and Horns** exhibit area. Each year for the past several years, a foal of an endangered species of zebra has been born. Now the staff is hoping that the camel's new companion will result in another birth.

It's about a half-mile walk along "the greeting," as Frederick Law Olmsted dubbed the meadow. Intended to be a place to socialize, the meadow connects the two ends of this enclosed 75-acre zoo, part of the larger, recently revitalized Franklin Park (page 188).

Baboons, antelope, dwarf crocodiles, and those gorillas and hippopotamus are among the animals in the **African Tropical Forest,** North America's largest freestanding enclosed tropical forest. In addition to four different habitats, **Birds World** features an elevated outdoor walkway and free-flight cage, an exoskeleton exhibit, and a waterfowl pond with flamingos, ducks, geese, and big goldfish.

In warm weather, bring a picnic and spend the day. In winter, there's plenty to see indoors.

For a Franklin Park Zoo visit, a perfect match

"Horse of Course," Boston Park Rangers   Boston Parks and Recreation Department, 1010 Massachusetts Avenue, Boston 02108
Phone: 617/522–2639 or 725–4505.
Age appeal: From 3 to senior citizens.
Location: Usually in an Emerald Necklace park in Boston.

In these one-hour sessions, members of the mounted unit of the versatile Boston Park Rangers, page 125, describe the training of the horse and its rider for urban duty. Grooming, shoeing, and types of tack are all part of the explanation. You are allowed to pat the horse and to feel the difference between the mane (not the tail—and you learn why) and the coat. Occasionally, if space permits, there is a demonstration of gaits. The program may be on the regular schedule of presentations offered to the public, or groups can make advance arrangements for a talk that is geared to their level and interests.

For **hay and sleigh ride** possibilities, see page 242.

Mega Clydesdale Farm Ltd.   155 Woodside Road, Sudbury 01776
Directions: From Wayland Center, Route 20 west about 3 miles to Landon Road on the left at an (unnamed at press time) gas station. Take Landon to Woodside Road on the right; continue a half mile to the only farm on the road.

Six Clydesdales are the pride and joy of Allan Clark, who has become a legend in the seven years since he acquired his first Clydesdale. If you would like to observe the grooming, harnessing, and training of these 6-foot-high, two-thousand-pound beauties, which have been seen on CNN, stop by on a Saturday or Sunday between 12 and 3. They may be pulling single or in a double hitch (side by side), a unicorn (two abreast and one in front), or tandem style (one behind the other). Allan Clark, a truck driver who talks about "stumbling into the horse-breeding business with these likable animals," has received awards for training several young people and adults to drive these prizewinning Clydesdales. Visitors spend an hour or two, watching and asking questions. One answer: "Each horse eats about half a bale of hay and about fifteen pounds of oats every day." Also here: Harry (the mascot), an English bulldog, and rabbits and chickens.

New England Alive 185 High Street, Routes 1A & 133, Ipswich 01938
Phone: 508/356–7013.
Open: April–November. Monday–Friday 10–5, weekends 9:30–6. After Labor Day 10–4.
Admission: $5 adults, $2 seniors, $3 ages 3–12. Under 3 free. Group rates available with advance reservations.
Picnicking: In a large shaded area.
Average stay: About 2 hours.
Classes: Single classes or series here for age 3 and up. Traveling educational programs (up to 150 miles) too.
Handicapped access: Accessible.

Children feed lambs, goats, and calves. They hold baby chicks. They walk along a wall and peer into twenty-five small aquariums. What else is here? "Yogi the bear." A bobcat. Some ponies, sheep, fox, snakes, turtles, ducks, turkeys, rabbits—among hundreds of animals. And it's all because a contractor turned naturalist/educator, Lyle Jensen, an area native who "knows woods inside and out," decided to open a farm and nature center featuring New England wildlife. It is a state and federally licensed rehabilitation center, a six-acre wooded place—except for the barnyard area—where you can see animals close up before they are released to the wild. (Some, because of injuries, are not released.) A running brook with waterfall ends up in a pond built on site. There are flower gardens. By next year, perhaps back trails will be cleared for walking.

"Charming setting. We all loved it."

—GRANDMOTHER OF FOUR

Southwick's Wild Animal Farm Off Route 16, Mendon 01756
Phone: 508/883–9182. Outside Massachusetts: 800/258–9182.
Location: 20 miles south of Worcester, 40 miles west of Boston.
Directions: Mass. Pike to exit 22 (I–495 south), to exit 19 (Milford), to Route 16 west, toward Mendon. Follow signs.
Open: The day before Easter until Columbus Day, 10–5.
Admission: $7 adults, $5 ages 3–12, under 3 free. Group rates available. In summer, $2 elephant ride, $1.50 pony ride. $1 each mechanical kiddie ride; $4 for ten. No charge for summer half-hour circus show or live animal presentations.
Average stay: At least 2 hours.
Picnicking: Small areas in grove.
Handicapped access: Accessible.

"We just had a baby zebra born here a month ago," declared Mrs. Southwick. And so it goes at this zoo, home to about 600 animals from more than 100 species. As you wind around on the wide paved paths, up hill and down dale, you see elephants; monkeys; rhinoceros; chinchillas; llamas; camels; lions; tigers; parrots; turtles; peacocks; flamingos; and, in the pond, some alligators. You mingle with deer in their unfenced acreage and walk with baby goats in the petting zoo. Sometimes the giraffes seem to get the most attention.

Walter D. Stone Memorial Zoo   149 Pond Street (next to Spot Pond Reservoir), Stoneham 02180

Phone: 617/442–2002, extension 0.

Open: At least spring through fall, 10–4 daily.

Admission: $2 adults, $1 seniors and ages 4–11; 3 and under free. (Playground, outside of admissions booth, is free.)

Picnicking: Some tables near the playground; others inside the zoo.

Handicapped access: Accessible.

A new beginning with a five-year plan. When the zoo was closed for about eighteen months for budgetary reasons, most of the animals were relocated. Recently reopened, the family-oriented zoo has a polar bear; four colobus monkeys; a waterfowl area; hoofed animals in the mountainside exhibit; and snakes, turtles, and lizards in the reptile exhibit. A highlight is the four-story aviary, where a hundred tropical birds are perched or flying around you. Some blend with the foliage; others are vividly colored. The simulated natural environment is complete with pools, plantings, and a waterfall. Interpretive signs are posted on a short, wooded waterside trail. On weekends there are fun and educational games and activities. Call for information about special events and weekend bus trips to the Franklin Park Zoo.

Shady Oaks Farm   38 Winthrop Street, West Medway 02053

Phone: 508/533–8905.

Directions: Follow Route 109 for about 2½ miles east of Interstate 495 to a left turn on Winthrop Street to a fork. Take left fork to farm, the fifth house on the right.

Groups: By advance arrangement; 12 maximum with adequate adult accompaniment.

Average stay: 30–60 minutes.

Fee: None.

Quick, get thee to this farm. Nationwide, such operations account for 1 percent of milk production. "There are probably fifteen of us in all of New England," says Robert Briggs; his father bought the farm in 1931, when the surrounding area was rural. "Yes, we still bottle here—using quart and half-gallon glass bottles and paper tops. We make our own chocolate milk with whole milk and syrup. That's why it's so thick."

In the summer the cows are outside except for milking time, which takes place every day—with six machines—between 4 and 5 p.m. (the best time to come) and between 6 and 7 a.m. The merry-go-round bottling equipment packages about 400 gallons every other day. Most of the milk is homogenized; some is skimmed. Cream is bottled here too. "Stay as long as

Not sure where the town is? Check the map on page 2.

you like. Go around the barn where the cows and calves are. We answer questions while we're working."

Adoptions and Tours

Animal Rescue League of Boston 10 Chandler Street (corner Arlington and Tremont), Boston 02116

Phone: 617/426–9170.

Branch shelters: In Dedham at 238 Pine Street, 617/326–0729, and in Salem at 378 Highlands Avenue, 508/744–7910.

Parking: Lot available.

Ⓣ: Arlington on the Green Line, then an 8-minute walk. Cross over turnpike via the bridge.

Open: Daily 10–4.

Adoption fees: $30.75 for cats, $41.25 for dogs, includes first shots, worming, and spaying and neutering. $5 for rabbits, gerbils, hamsters, birds. $10 deposit for how-to-care-for video.

Tours: 90 minutes. For groups, ages 6 and up, by appointment, fall through late spring, Monday through Friday, 10–5.

Many cub scout troops and school groups visit the clinic, which sees about 20,000 animals a year. The most popular part of the clinic is the adoption kennel—noisy, but educational.

Adoption

If you'd like to adopt, call in advance to see what's available. "We don't always have kittens and puppies."

Massachusetts Society for the Prevention of Cruelty to Animals American Human Education Society, 350 South Huntington Avenue, Boston 02130

Phone: 617/522–5055 (shelter); 522–7400 for tours.

Parking: Lot available. No charge.

Ⓣ: Copley on the Green Line; then Arborway bus.

Open: Tuesday–Saturday 11–4.

Tours: By appointment, weekdays, for 10 to 20 people, ages 8 and up. One-hour visit includes a slide presentation about MSPCA history, services, and programs followed by every child's favorite part—a tour through the adoption center.

Adoption

People come here both to give up and to adopt cats and dogs. If you'd like to adopt, call before you come to check availability, fees, and identification requirements.

Arts

Bargains

How to see performances less expensively, inexpensively, or free:

- **Shop Bostix** for half-price arrangements (page 50).
- **Subscribe to a series.**
- **Join a museum.**
- **Use your student ID.**
- **Attend matinees.**
- **Check WGBH** (Boston's public television) **membership benefits.**

Or be on the lookout for

- **Preview performances.**
- **Rush seats.** Practices vary. Watch the ads or call. The Boston Symphony Orchestra sells a ticket per person on the day of performance only, for Friday afternoon and Tuesday, Thursday, and Saturday evening concerts. Tickets go on sale at Symphony Hall's Massachusetts Avenue entrance Friday mornings at 9 and at 5 for evening performances. . . . Students with valid ID may purchase almost any available Boston Ballet ticket for $11.75 an hour before performance.
- **Ushering:** Resident theater companies may exchange free admission for ushering at a single performance or series. Minimum-age requirements vary, but some companies accept high-schoolers.
- **Library events.**
- **Storytelling and readings at bookstores.** See page 48.
- **Community symphony orchestra schedules** including an annual youth concert.
- **One-time performances** by professionals, often sponsored by local groups.

Marvelous cultural bargains are offered at area universities, schools, museums, arts and community centers, churches and synagogues. Check newspaper listings and/or call about mailings, which may be free or well worth the price of postage.

Presentations

PLAYS FOR CHILDREN

Fantastic, energetic, creative groups are based in the Boston area. Their performances may be issue-oriented, educational, bilingual, and/or participatory. Always, economic survival is a major factor. What's doing this week? See the local newspaper for listings.

Act /Tunes Youth Theatre, Inc. Emerson Umbrella Center for the Arts, 40 Stowe Street, Concord 01742
Phone: 508/371–1482.
Productions: Eight performances (two done during school time) of each production by children, presented for all ages in October, December,

March, June. Plus family entertainment by professional touring companies during school vacation weeks.

Admission: $6, $8, or $10. Special events $6, group rates $5. All seats reserved.

Handicapped access: Accessible.

The Wizard of Oz, Tom Sawyer, and *The Hobbit* are among the musicals presented during the last eighteen years by this group, a nonprofit corporation that hires professional designers and directors. The elaborate productions, separate from the classes offered, are given in a 435-seat theater with a graduated floor and proscenium stage.

The Emerson Umbrella Center, located in the old Concord High School building, houses studios for more than seventy artists, some of whom become involved in productions.

Arts in the Parks Newton Parks and Recreation Department, 70 Crescent Street, Newton 02166

Phone: 617/552–7130 (recorded schedule information after hours).

Year round, professional and semiprofessional performances—as well as educational programs—are offered for age 18 months and up. The roster includes folk concerts (picnicking encouraged for summer schedule), school vacation programs, and festivals. Some are held on the banks of the Charles River or in a park designed by Frederick Law Olmsted. Tickets are free or moderately priced.

Boston Ballet 19 Clarendon Street, Boston, MA 02116–6110

Phone: 617/695–6950.

This internationally acclaimed company, founded in 1963, moved into its Graham Gund–designed home in 1991. (See Tours, page 258.) Performances at the restored Wang Center for the Performing Arts span the history of ballet, from classics to world premieres of works by distinguished choreographers. Family series tickets and group rates are available. Special school matinees are scheduled for *The Nutcracker* in December.

Wang Center **backstage tours,** conducted immediately after a performance, are booked through the group sales office for groups of at least 10 ticket buyers (25 for *The Nutcracker* and for all group tours; 50 maximum, regardless of the number of tickets purchased by the group). Tours for major donors are booked through the Development Department.

Classes at the country's fourth largest ballet school are offered for preschoolers through adults. One branch is currently in Newton; north and south shore locations may be developed. Among other programs: summer workshops, instruction for inner city public schoolchildren, and evening lectures.

Boston Children's Theatre 93 Massachusetts Avenue, Boston 02115; performances at: The New England Hall, 225 Clarendon Street (at Boylston), Boston

Phone: 617/424–6634.

Performances: On Saturdays and Sundays during the school year, three or four weekends per show. Plus one weekday with special performance for school groups.

Admission: $5–$8.50. Series (four shows) subscriptions and group rates available.

Age appeal: Depends on the production.

Touring: The March production tours to schools. Summers, the Stagemobile moves to many area outdoor locations. See Calendar, pages 273–283, for May festival, Halloween and December specials.

Casts for the annual series of four plays are selected from auditions open to all (not limited to those who are enrolled in the Theatre School). Because the New England Hall theater is fairly wide and deep, young children may prefer the close seats in the center section.

Boston Symphony Orchestra Youth Concerts 301 Massachusetts Avenue (corner Huntington Avenue), Boston 02115

Phone: 617/638–9375, Youth Activities Office.

Ⓣ: Symphony on the Arborway/Green Line, or Orange Line Massachusetts Avenue stop and walk 1 block.

Performances: Two sets: one in fall and one in spring. Saturday family series at 10 and 11:50 a.m. On weekdays for school groups; teaching materials and workshops available.

Admission: $15 for two-concert series. Series tickets go on sale the spring preceding each season. (Sorry, no preschoolers admitted.) Phone (credit card) orders: 617/266–1200.

A tradition for generations of children, these are one-hour concerts designed for elementary school–aged children and their parents and chaperones. Pre- and postconcert 20- to 30-minute activities on a first-come, first-served basis include instrumental demonstrations that vary according to that day's program, tours of Symphony Hall, and performances by student musicians.

The Children's Workshop 1963 Massachusetts Avenue, Cambridge 02140

Phone: 617/354–1633.

Location: 2 blocks north of Porter Square subway stop.

Performances: Saturday mornings September–June, and on school vacation days.

Admission: $2 children. Under age 1 free. $3–$4 adults.

Age appeal: Depending on performer, 2–10.

When former teachers created this toy store, their innovative programs were welcomed. Now, in addition to workshops in everything from tap dancing to making your own gingerbread house to aerobics for parents and toddlers, there are regularly scheduled performances: intimate, informal, intentionally interactive 45-minute events with singers, storytellers, or magicians. The audience sits on carpeting or folding chairs.

Emerson Stage Emerson College Division of Performing Arts, 100 Beacon Street, Boston 02116

Phone: 617/578–8780 or (box office) 578–8785.

Guest professional actors sometimes join the graduate and undergraduate students for the annual major production at the Emerson Majestic Theatre

Theater Seating Plans

NORTHEASTERN UNIVERSITY / BLACKMAN AUDITORIUM

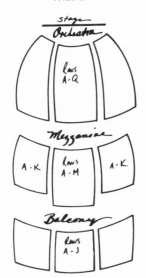

EMERSON MAJESTIC

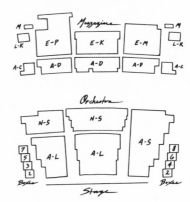

WILBUR

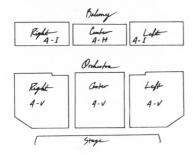

SANDERS

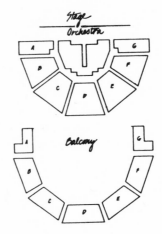

AMERICAN REPERTORY THEATRE / LOEB

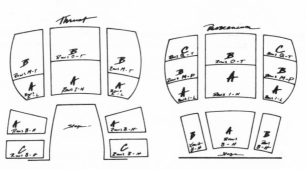

COLONIAL

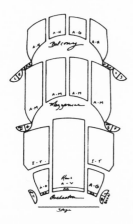

BERKLEE PERFORMANCE CENTER

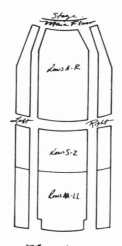

JORDAN HALL

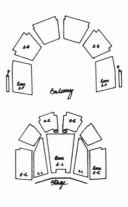

SYMPHONY HALL

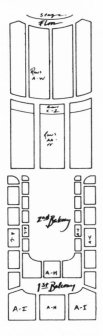

WANG CENTER

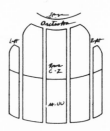

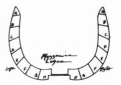

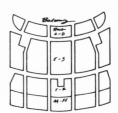

SHUBERT

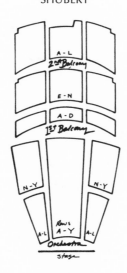

(handicapped accessible) at 219 Tremont Street (in Boston's theater district), which seats 850. Casts are multicultural. At least one performance of each production is signed. The age appeal varies from season to season. In addition to public performances, many are given during weekdays for school groups; $7 adults, $5 children.

During the school year an Emerson students' touring company travels to various sites. (Rates are based on a sliding scale.) In August high school students enrolled in the summer program give public performances in the school's studio theater, located at the foot of Beacon Hill at 69 Brimmer Street.

Folk Arts Center of New England Page 242.

Freelance Players 8 St. John's Street, Jamaica Plain 02130
Phone: 617/232–1175.

Four different companies perform original musicals. The scripts, forty to date, are published by and sold through the Freelance Press, Center Street, Dover, MA 02030. Three groups made up of 8- to 12-year-olds, tour to after-school programs, nursing homes, hospitals, and libraries with a one-hour fully costumed show. In December and in May, the teenage group does an elaborate production at the Park School in Brookline.

Huntington Theatre Company 264 Huntington Avenue, Boston 02115
Phone: 617/266–7900.

In an intimate 850-seat 1925 theater, classic and contemporary productions—five a year—are presented by New England's largest nonprofit resident professional theater company. (Annually, *A Christmas Carol* is scheduled in the Wilbur Theater.) The acclaimed company also provides educational materials and special programs for high school students. They welcome inquiries about backstage tours so you can see where the sets, props, and costumes are created. And every May there's a free open house with tours; programs; workshops in lighting, directing, and set design; and an opportunity to walk across the stage and see what the house looks like from the actor's point of view.

Discounts: Available day of performance. ID required for student rush seats. "Hot tix" on specific days, perhaps Tuesday and Wednesday for 8 p.m. performances. And discounted tickets are sold for the four preview performances of every production.

Longy School of Music One Follen Street, Cambridge 02138
Phone: 617/876–0956.
Performances: Family concerts include Familyfest, held in September. Several times a week concerts (many are free) are given by faculty, students, or visiting artists. Some programs are for and/or by children. No charge for place on the calendar mailing list.
Handicapped access: Accessible.

A beautiful century-old mansion houses the seventy-five-year-old music school. Offerings include courses; master classes; workshops in voice, jazz, chamber, American musical. Music and movement classes for ages 3–8 are extremely popular.

The intimate hall seats 270 and has a flat floor downstairs with raked seating in the L-shaped balcony.

Marco the Magi's "Le Grand David and his own Spectacular Magic Company" Cabot Street Cinema Theatre, 286 Cabot Street, Beverly 01915

Phone: 508/927–3677.

Location: 20 miles north of Boston.

Directions: Tobin/Mystic Bridge to Route 1 north, to Route 128 north, to exit 22E (Route 62). Follow Route 62 2½ miles to Cabot Street, turn right onto Cabot for 2 blocks to the Cabot Street Cinema Theatre. The Larcom Theatre is 4 blocks further south; opposite Beverly City Hall turn onto Wallis Street to number 14. From Salem, both theaters are just over the Salem–Beverly Bridge (Route 1A).

Performances:

At **Cabot Theatre,** from mid-September through July on Sundays at 3 p.m. One intermission, 2¼-hour show. First-come, first-served seating begins 45 minutes before the show. Even the waiting time is filled with showmanship—by jugglers and puppeteers in the lobby. At the **Larcom Theatre,** *An Anthology of Stage Magic,* 2 hours without an intermission, plays on selected Saturdays and holidays October through May. Doors open at 1 p.m. for 1:30 curtain. Reserved seating available.

Admission: $10–$15 for either theater. Advance tickets at Cabot Street box office, Monday–Saturday 9–9. Mail orders add $1 (to total order) handling charge, but call first to see what's available.

Age appeal: 5 all the way up.

Restaurants: Between the two theaters on Cabot Street is **Cabot Place,** with traditional New England and seafood fare popular with families before or after show. On Rantoul Street, near Beverly train depot, the contemporary **Union Grill**—not really family oriented—opened in 1988 to rave reviews and has since added another location just for takeout.

It's worth a special trip to see the longest-running resident stage magic troupe in American history. The captivating performances are given in two restored ornate theaters that were built for vaudeville—the Cabot in 1920 and the Larcom in 1912. You'll see disappearing and reappearing people and birds, trumpet players, tap dancers and barbershop singers, with yards of banners, scarves, ruffles, and brocaded costumes—all against gorgeous, endlessly changing backdrops created by the company itself. Constant surprises keep the interest of all ages right through to the cast's farewell in the lobby.

Another form of magic is the strong ensemble spirit and freshness of the company—thirty people, families and friends, who obviously love what they are doing. Performances, begun in 1977, are still led by originator Cesareo Pelaez (Marco the Magi), a silver-haired professor of psychology. He is also responsible for Marthalena's stage debut, which occurred when she crawled onto the stage from the wings. Marco reacted by making her part of the act! (Seth, the original child star, who began at age 4, is now in college.)

New England Conservatory 290 Huntington Avenue, Boston 02115; Jordan Hall, 30 Gainsborough Street, Boston 02115

Phone: 617/262–1120.

Ⓣ: Symphony on Arborway/Green Line or Massachusetts Avenue on Orange Line.

There's no charge for the monthly concert calendar, which lists all conservatory concerts and events (almost all are free) held September–June evenings in Jordan Hall. This auditorium is known for its wonderful acoustics and fabulous sight lines from more than 1,000 seats, all close to the stage. (Refurbishing plans for the summer of 1994 include restoration of gilt work, addition of air conditioning, and releveling of seats, which have settled on an angle over time.) There are faculty recitals and student ensembles (symphony, chorus, jazz band), and some guest artists perform. Two operas are also produced each year in the Emerson Majestic Theatre at 219 Tremont Street.

Puppet Showplace 32 Station Street, Brookline 02146

Phone: 617/731–6400.

Ⓣ: Brookline Village on the Riverside/Green Line, and you're there.

Performances: Year round. Weekends at 1 and 3. Most summer Thursdays at 11 and 1; other weekdays by appointment.

Admission: $5 per person. Prepaid reservations encouraged. Group rates available.

Age appeal: "All shows are created for people five years of age and older." Some evening performances are specifically for adults.

An intimate setting, brick walls, and effective lighting all contribute to this inviting theater, which holds 120 people. It's almost as much fun to watch the children as it is the forty-five-minute performances. Rotating puppeteers make their own sets and costumes.

This is the only permanent year-round puppet center in New England and headquarters for the Boston Area Guild of Puppetry. They publish a di-

"SIDEWALK SAM"

A major summer attraction for more than twenty-five years. Sometimes called the Picasso of the pavements. A joy for all ages—on Boston Common or City Hall Plaza, in Copley Square, or at Downtown Crossing, Faneuil Hall Markeplace, or South Station. Many masterpiece reproductions are among the thousand or more artworks Bob Guillemin has done on Boston's sidewalks. Each is completed in one day. Although the pastels fade in a few hours, those done in paint last all summer long.

An artist who has a both a bachelor's and a master's degree in fine arts, "Sidewalk Sam" has exhibited at the Museum of Fine Arts, at the Institute of Contemporary Art, and in Newbury Street galleries. For one Earth Day celebration he saw thousands of children chalk Storrow Drive with drawings of bumblebees and flowers—all part of his dream "to turn Boston into a giant open air art museum."

rectory of all puppeteers in the region, and they maintain a reference library open to the public. Displays of puppets are on loan from all over the United States and some foreign countries. And the theater can be rented.

What's around? A neighborhood with enough to fill an afternoon. Next door is Tuesday's Ice Cream Parlor. Around the corner is the Children's Book Shop. No Kidding has a great selection of toys. Bertucci's pizza, popular with families, is among the seventeen restaurants within walking distance indicated on a neighborhood map provided to showgoers.

Puppeteer Paul L'Ecuyer saw his first Hubert Hosmer production at age 3. Three decades later, Mr. Hosmer, an octogenarian, delights in telling about the map that Paul drew as a child "in case Dad couldn't find his way from nearby Lunenburg to the Toy Cupboard Theater."

Toy Cupboard Theatre and Museums 57 East George Hill Road, South Lancaster 01561

Phone: 508/365–9519.

Location: 57 miles northwest of Boston.

Directions: Route 2 to I–495 south to exit 27 for Route 62 west. Beyond Route 110, turn left on Route 70 south for 2 miles. Left onto George Hill Road at Atlantic Union College.

Performances: Puppet shows July and August, at 2 and 3:30 on Wednesday and Thursday and some Saturdays and Sundays. Admission: $1. Age appeal: 4–6.

Museums: Usually 2–5 p.m. on summer weekends and maybe other times too. Best to call ahead.

Picnicking: Allowed on the grounds. Simple, please.

★ Birthday parties are welcome.

A legend. Created by Herbert Hosmer over fifty years ago. Although he is still official museum tour guide—and, still, a collector of dollhouses, puppets, marionettes, and children's books—the shows are now given by professional puppeteer Paul L'Ecuyer and his partner, Jeffrey Koslik.

Step through one of the three archways of the two-hundred-year-old building, once a woodshed. Take your place on a pine bench in this 75-seat theater and see a children's classic. After each performance the audience is invited to take a closer look at the puppets. Punch and cookies are served, and lollipops and balloons are "on the house."

Watertown Children's Theatre P.O. Box 54, Watertown 02172

Phone: 617/926–ARTS.

Performances: November and March at Hosmer School, Mount Auburn Street, Watertown. Plus a signing tour at schools for the deaf and at service organizations.

Admission: $4–$7.

About 100 children, ages 5 to 15, participate in musicals such as *Annie, Oklahoma!, Bye Bye Birdie,* or *The Wizard of Oz* produced by this nonprofit organization. Also offered are workshops and classes in theater arts, acting, set design and construction, and singing. Children working in pairs do shadow signing, with one speaking and the other signing.

> Booking a touring company? The chemistry between audience and performer can vary from one location to another. It's an interesting phenomenon. Often the setting, orientation, and mood of the receiving group make a difference.

For the two major productions, there is some orchestral accompaniment. The school auditorium has a graduated floor.

WGBH (Channel 2) Educational Print and Outreach Department 125 Western Avenue, Boston 02134

Phone: 617/492–2777, extension 3848.

Staffers present school (all levels) and library sessions on subjects related to 'GBH programming, such as "Long Ago and Far Away" or "Nova." There is usually a screening, discussion, and/or featured books by a particular author or theme. Generally, this is a free community public service. A small charge is made to colleges and universities.

A new service: Workshops for parents and other adults who are interested in using programs with children at home or in classrooms.

The Outreach Department also produces the guides that accompany many PBS programs seen on WGBH.

Wheelock Family Theatre 200 The Riverway, Boston 02214

Phone: Box office 617/734–4760, 1–5:30 weekdays and on weekends during run of show. Office 617/734–5203, extension 147. TDD 617/731–4426.

Ⓣ: Fenway on the Riverside/Green Line, then 10-minute walk.

Performances: October–May. Three plays a year on Friday nights, Saturday afternoons and/or evenings, and Sunday afternoons.

Admission: $7.50 first four side rows and last four rows in back. $8 for rest. Group rates available. All reserved seating.

Age appeal: The family musical and the children's production are for all ages. A third production, usually a drama, is suggested for children who are at least 8 years old. For all productions, it is recommended that adults accompany children.

Handicapped access: Auditorium is accessible. Most performances interpreted in American Sign Language; some shows designated as audio-described for blind and visually impaired patrons.

On the campus of Wheelock College, this theater (founded in 1981 and getting quite a bit of media attention) has a nontraditional multigenerational, multicultural casting policy. Actors are a combination of professionals, non-professionals, community members, students, and children. The auditorium seats 650 and has a graduated floor. Most performances run about two hours, and refreshments are available during intermission.

The theater is a department of the college. Drama workshops for ages 6 through adult are offered on weekday and Saturday afternoons.

FRANKLIN ALIVE

He is dressed in a greatcoat, vest and britches, white hose, lace jabot, and buckle shoes. Bifocals (one of Ben Franklin's designs) and flowing white hair complete the picture—which has been known to stop Boston truck drivers; they can't believe their eyes. Bill Meikle, two-time Emmy award–winning actor, can be seen leading walking tours of Franklin's native Boston, "the world's second largest English-speaking city at the time of his birth"; at dinner theaters here and on Nantucket; in classrooms throughout the region; at conventions and family gatherings. Each appearance is one of a kind, with much interaction and dialogue that allows Dr. Franklin to muse about his childhood, politics, the work ethic, friends, food, inventions, the glass "armonica," family relationships—all sprinkled with humor, philosophy, and many anecdotes. Where might you meet him this week? Check with Franklin Alive, 182 Westminster Avenue, Arlington 02174, phone 617/648–0628.

Storytime

Author and illustrator appearances, and more:

Recorded Stories

Newton Library's Dial-a-Story: Phone 617/552–7148. For ages 3 and up, a 3- to 10-minute story, changed every 7–10 days.

Discovery Museum of Acton's Storyphone: Phone 508/264–4222. For preschoolers. Three-minute story, folk tale, or song, changed weekly.

Bookstore Programs

Bookstores that have programs include:

Charlesbank Bookshop has two free Saturday preschool programs a month. Authors, illustrators, or costumed characters appear from 1:30 to 2:30 at the main store, 660 Beacon Street in Boston's Kenmore Square, 617/236–7442. (For adults, weekday evening readings are held in a paneled reading room several times a month.) From 10:30 to 11:30 there are children's presentations in the Wellesley shop at 67 Central Street, 617/237–2837. Everything is announced in The Scoop, a newsletter available in stores or by mail (no charge).

The Children's Bookshop, 238 Washington Street, **Brookline,** 617/734–7323. (Ⓣ: Brookline Village on the Riverside/Green Line, then a 5-minute walk.) Considered a community institution, this bookstore, a pioneer in presenting author and illustrator appearances, holds spring and fall programs on weekends or weekdays. Picture books are usually featured in an intimate setting. Free. Call for a place on the mailing list.

Borders Book Shop, 85 Worcester Road (Route 9, near and on opposite side of Shoppers' World) in **Framingham,** 508/875–2321. Big two-storied store. Knowledgeable staff. Kids sit on carpeted floor in children's department for stories read by staffers for about 40 minutes every Tuesday at 10:30 a.m. Seasonal themes—including crafts sessions or professional storytellers—are the focus of 11 a.m. one-hour Saturday sessions for ages 3–7. Some school vacation programs also planned. And for adults: poetry readings second Tuesday of every month at 7 p.m., plus many fiction readings and, once a month, usually on Thursday evenings, cookbook demos in espresso bar. No charge for programs.

Waterstone's, 26 Exeter Street (at Newbury Street in **Boston**'s Back Bay) 617/859–7300, is the renowned British bookseller that in 1991 opened its first American store as Boston's largest bookstore. The former Exeter Street Theater building was originally a church. Sundays at 2:30 Miss Luna Moon tells stories, offers optional face painting, and gives out balloons. Geared for ages 3–10. Adult readings and discussions are among literary events held on weekday evenings. No charge for programs.

The Little Book Room, 561 Adams Street, **East Milton** Square, 617/696–0044, has a long-standing Tuesday morning story hour for ages 3–6. In addition, seasonal after-school and weekend series are held with authors, illustrators, and storytellers. No charge for programs.

Tatnuck Bookseller & Sons and Cafe offers "more than 5 miles of books" at 335 Chandler Street in **Worcester**; 800/262–6657 in Massachusetts, 800/642–6657 elsewhere, 508/756–7644 in Worcester. In this red brick building, a former factory with huge parking lot, there are story hours with crafts and healthy snacks on weekday mornings; kids' cooking classes; and, in the cafe, a children's menu, lunch, dinner, and Sunday brunch. Gallery concerts are held Friday and Saturday evenings. Free events include appearances by authors, illustrators, and poets. ★ A private banquet/meeting room is available. Open seven days a week and every night (Fridays and Saturdays until midnight) but Sunday, when they close at 5. Located one minute from the junction of Routes 9, 12, and 122; within an hour of Boston.

Longfellow's Bookstore, 410 Boston Post Road, **Sudbury** 01776, 508/443–5993. Spring and fall, professional storytellers give Sunday afternoon children's programs as well as adult programs on weekday evenings. This popular store, complete with fireplace, can seat 100.

WGBH Learningsmith, 199 Boylston Street, The Mall at **Chestnut Hill,** 617/965–4500. Play area for children and storytelling every Saturday morning at 11. The store of 10,000 items—and a play area for children—opened in October 1991 with a (highly successful) concept of learning categories: everything from instructional videos to language audiotapes.

Clearing-houses

Folk Arts Network P.O. Box 867, Cambridge 02238
Phone: 617/522–3407.

Concert series, family events, festivals, collaborative projects, conferences, lessons, and workshops are offered by this still-growing nonprofit organization, founded in 1982. Each edition of its bimonthly newspaper, *New En-*

Arts/Boston 100 Boylston Street, Suite 735, Boston 02116
Phone: 617/423–0372.

Best known for its half-price tickets, Arts/Boston is a nonprofit organization that makes live performances available to the public at low cost through two services:

- **Arts/Mail:** Advance tickets for music, theater, and dance—taking a chance on seat location—all at half price. Call or write for free annotated mailings that are far more than a list. In addition, the brochures offer discounted tickets for summer whale watches, trips to Tanglewood, and theater and opera trips to New York City and Europe.
- **Bostix:** The octagonally shaped ticket and information booth next to Faneuil Hall (Ⓣ: State Street on the Orange or Blue Line) is open Tuesday–Saturday 11–7, Sunday 11–4. Closed Mondays, Christmas, and New Year's Day. There's usually a line when the booth opens. Service charges range from $2 to $3.50 depending on face value. All sales are cash only. No credit cards.

   Half-price tickets: Availability is posted at the Bostix booth on the day of the performance. There's no way of knowing the list without going there. When the allotment sells out, that's it. Occasionally other tickets become available during the day. More tickets are available for Tuesday, Wednesday, and Thursday nights and for Sundays than for Friday and Saturday events. (BOSTIX seldom has tickets for a family show like *The Nutcracker*, which usually sells out on its own.)

   Arts/Reach: This program offers discounted tickets to human service organizations.

   Full-price tickets: Because BOSTIX has become a full-service Ticketmaster outlet, tickets to everything are now sold in advance here.

   Information: Printed materials—many are free—include maps, guides, and a walking tour in several languages.

gland *Folk Almanac*, lists more than 900 performances. Annotated lists in the comprehensive *Folk Directory* ($10) include 100 coffee houses (50 in the Greater Boston area), street and vaudeville performers, poetry and crafts organizations, storytellers and radio stations, puppeteers and producers, schools and camps.

Folksong Society of Greater Boston P.O. Box 492, Somerville 02143
Phone: 617/623–1806 (events line).

A very active organization that schedules concerts, workshops, singing parties, and family events—all centered in traditional folksinging.

League for the Advancement of New England Storytelling
P.O. Box 4183, Arlington 02174

Phone: 617/396–5363 (recording of events).

The ancient art of storytelling is alive and well. Modern-day storytellers, or revivalists, use published or original material from many cultures in programs that often incorporate drama, music, and mime. LANES, an organization of more than 300 members, publishes a newsletter and a directory. They have quarterly fun meetings in various locations. In addition to an annual March conference, they feature a fall festival (page 279).

New England Foundation for the Arts 26 Mount Auburn Street, Cambridge 02138

Phone: 617/492–2914.

This is a service organization for arts presenters. The roster of artists who perform or give workshops throughout New England is available to representatives of nonprofit groups. Applications for partial support grants are due three months before the scheduled performance.

The New England Theatre Conference Department of Theatre, Northeastern University, 360 Huntington Avenue, Boston 02115

Phone: 617/424–9275.

Information about children's theater groups is available from this nonprofit association of individuals and groups involved with various worlds of theater—children's, secondary school, college, university, community, and professional.

Young Audiences of Massachusetts One Kendall Square, Building 200, Cambridge 02139

Phone: 617/577–0570

Programs of fine music, theater, and dance are available through Young Audiences, a national nonprofit organization that booked more than 1,000 presentations last year. Audience participation is part of most presentations. Although concerts are usually at schools, arrangements can be made by other groups.

Day Trips

There's always more to see than time allows. Start early. . . . Some day-trippers are very energetic and go far afield. Others find that automobile confinement has its limitations. Survival suggestions (there's no magic formula): Pack snacks, books, or wrapped surprises for youngsters. Start a story and let others finish it. Count categories of things you see en route. (During a first-time canoe trip, such an activity countered one child's anxiety. See page 231. No report available about the impact on the parents.) Find signs that begin with every letter of the alphabet. Stop at a playground along the way. . . . Picnic lunches save time and money. . . . Prefer to let someone else do the planning? Go with a group. Trips are listed in newspaper calendars. . . . Leading a group? See the suggestions on page ix.

Concord

Location: 20 miles northwest of Boston.

Directions: Route 2 west. Or the Mass. Pike to Route 128 (I–95) north, to exit 46 (Route 2 west).

Train: 43-minute ride (with or without bicycle, page 222) on Fitchburg line from North Station (617/722–3200 or 800/392–6100); 10 minutes less from Porter Square, Cambridge (on Red Line). 1¼ miles to Old North Bridge. Minutes to Thoreau Lyceum; half mile to Boat House, page 228, and Concord Center; 1.1 miles to Walden Pond.

Restaurants: A traditional menu is served in old and newer dining rooms of **The Colonial Inn** (east end built in 1716), 58 Monument Square, 508/369–9200. **Walden Station,** a converted firehouse at 24 Walden Street (outside, look up and around at layers of historic church steeples), is a casual place with varied menu; 508/275–4700. Special for kids: chicken fingers, junior burgers, and pasta dishes.

A "must" stop

Old North Bridge Monument Street

Parking and admission: Free.

Talks: 20-minute presentations by National Park Service rangers near the bridge daily June–October, on weekends in spring and fall, and by request at other times.

Handicapped access: Limited. Assistance recommended.

This seems the perfect setting for an introduction to the history of this charming New England town. The bridge, the fourth reproduction at the scene of "the shot heard round the world," is beautiful any time of the day (especially at dusk) and all seasons of the year. It's a 10-minute walk, in part along the road the patriots marched in 1775, to the visitors' center on Liberty Street.

North Bridge Visitor Center 171 Liberty Street

Phone: 508/369–6993.

Directions: From Concord Center follow signs along Lowell Road to Liberty Street. Or walk from Old North Bridge.

The Buttrick Mansion (1911) serves as the **Minute Man National Park headquarters** with helpful rangers, much printed material, and a 12-min-

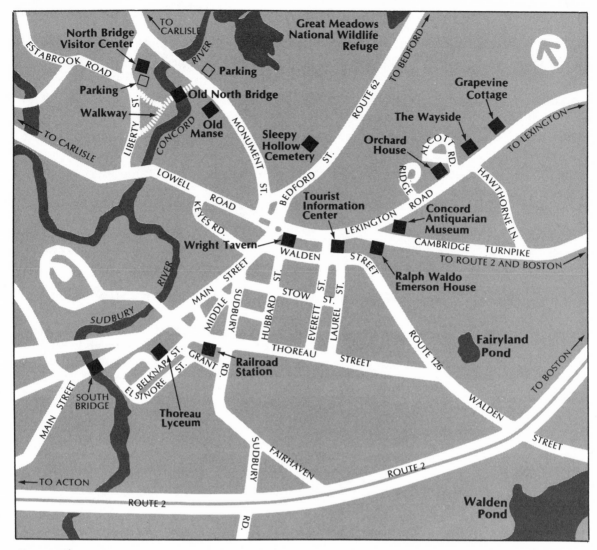

Concord

ute video that describes the events of April 19, 1775. The park is actually located in Lincoln, Lexington (page 66), and Concord.

If you're going into only one house

Orchard House 399 Lexington Road, P.O. Box 353, Concord 01742
Phone: 508/369–4118.

Open: April–October, Monday–Saturday 10–4:30, Sunday 1–4:30. November and March, Saturdays 10–4:30, Sundays 1–4:30.

Admission: $4 adults; $3.50 seniors, college students, and ages 13–18; $2.50 ages 6–12. Under 6 free. Group and family rates available. No charge for garden walk or a peek into the School of Philosophy.

Rave reviews come from all ages for the 40-minute tour of the home of Louisa May Alcott and her philosopher father Bronson. Because nothing is roped off, you feel like a guest, not just a tourist. Readers of *Little Women* will recognize the mood pillow and other items from the book. In addition, you become aware of Louisa's involvement in educational reform and

Commuters, picnickers, young children, and many others revere the postage stamp-sized **Coggin's Bakery** in the converted 150-year-old train (mail and freight) station at 68 Thoreau Street, 508/371–3040. It's open daily, until 4 Monday–Thursday, until 5 Fridays, 4 Saturday, noon Sunday. There's always something emerging from the ovens (in view)—maybe lemon blueberry muffins, chocolate chip cookies, a dozen kinds of croissants, cinnamon coffee cake, rum pecan or apple crunch pies, or Michael Coggin's mother's spanakopita (spinach pies). French bread is made here with imported French flour. Some people have breakfast or a sandwich at a cafe table in the waiting room with specially brewed coffee, hot chocolate, mochaccino (mocha coffee drink), juices, or iced drinks. The music is classical (opera on Saturdays). The commuter and freight train traffic adds to the scene.

women's rights. On the tour, Louisa shares center stage with her sister May, an accomplished artist who taught sculptor Daniel Chester French. Bronson Alcott's journal entries, including every change made in this house, illustrate his interest in architecture. Henry David Thoreau, his close friend, taught the Alcott girls to identify many plants. Today bee balm, lady fern, Jacob's ladder, Alcott spearmint, Emerson phlox, and jack-in-the-pulpit are among the labels in the wildflower garden.

Programs: Extensive. Summer lectures and "conversational series." Readings from letters, journals, and works of fiction. Sometimes, plays in Bronson's School of Philosophy. Games, hoop rolling, storytelling. Researchers welcome by appointment.

Near Orchard House

The Wayside Lexington Road

Phone: 508/369–6975 or 508/369–6993.

Open: April–October. Tours on the hour, Tuesday–Sunday. Closed Mondays except holidays.

Admission: $1 ages 17–61. Under 17 and 62 and over, free.

All three floors up to Nathaniel Hawthorne's study are covered in the 40-minute tour of the home, which is decorated as it was when Margaret Sidney, author of the *Five Little Peppers* books, lived here from 1883 to 1924. Many visitors ask why so many authors lived in Concord. "Ralph Waldo Emerson acted as a magnet. And the fact that three nineteenth-century authors lived at Wayside was a quirk of fate."

Next to the Old North Bridge

The Old Manse Monument Street

Phone: 508/369–3909.

Open: Mid-April through October, Monday and Wednesday–Saturday 10–4:30. Sundays and holidays 1–4:30.

Admission: $4 adults, $3.50 senior citizens, $2.50 ages 6–12.

Built in 1769–70 by Ralph Waldo Emerson's grandfather, the house remained in the Emerson family except for the three years it was rented to Nathaniel Hawthorne. During the 30-minute tour you'll see Hawthorne's writing on the windowpanes, and original wallpaper and furnishings dating back to 1769.

Out-of-towners see and many area residents miss

Sleepy Hollow Cemetery Bedford Street (off Monument)
Phone: 508/371–6265, weekdays 8:30–4:30.
Handicapped access: Some areas are very hilly.

The second entrance leads you to Authors' Ridge and the graves of Emerson, Thoreau, the Alcotts, Hawthorne, and Margaret Sidney. The setting is beautiful, and the tombstones make interesting reading.

Across from Concord Museum

Ralph Waldo Emerson House 28 Cambridge Turnpike (at Lexington Road)
Phone: 508/369–2236.
Open: Mid-April through October. Thursday–Saturday 10–4:30, Sunday and holidays, 2–4:30.
Admission: $3.50 adults, $2 ages 6–17.

During the half-hour tour you see everything—even Emerson's battered hat hanging on the wall of the carriage entrance.

Concord Museum 200 Lexington Road
Phone: 508/369–9609.
Open: Year round, Tuesday–Saturday 10–5, Sundays 1–5, and Monday holidays 10–5. Closed New Year's, Easter, Thanksgiving, and Christmas.
Admission: $5 adults, $4 senior citizens, $3 students, $2 age 15 and under. $12 family rate. $1 more per person for 45-minute tour offered several times a day.
Handicapped access: Full.

The Thoreau Room has the bed Henry David Thoreau slept in at Walden, and his flute and surveying instruments. And there's a replica of Emerson's study with its original furnishings. The museum, originally built in 1930, was doubled in size—to a total of twenty rooms—with a 1991 Graham Gund–designed addition that includes a skylit reception area, an orientation theater, and galleries. Four centuries of Concord's history are seen through both permanent and changing exhibits, among them antiques and Native American artifacts. During school vacations and in the summer, there are always child-oriented and family programs.

Not far from the railroad

Thoreau Lyceum 156 Belknap Street
Phone: 508/369–5912.
Open: March through December. Monday–Saturday 10–5, Sunday 2–5. Winters, usually open weekends and by appointment. Closed on holidays.
Admission: $2 adults, $1.50 students, $.50 grades K–8, free for preschoolers.

The original Concord grapevine, which still bears in September, is on the grounds of Grapevine Cottage, private property, at 491 Lexington Road.

Most visitors spend an hour at this learning center, "not a museum." A historian is happy to answer questions and talk about Mr. Thoreau "with people who know very little as well as with experts." In addition to the library and bookstore, there are displays—survey maps, letters, pictures, and other belongings of the Concord naturalist-writer-philosopher and his family. Behind the lyceum, headquarters for The Thoreau Society, Inc., 1,500 members worldwide, is a replica of Thoreau's Walden House at Walden Pond.

Down memory lane

West Concord Five & Ten 106 Commonwealth Avenue
Phone: 508/369–9011.

"A veritable clutter of items," postcards, a $1 toy aisle, jumper cables, toasters, stationery, among thousands above, below, and around you. This almost-famous store, discovered by the national media, is run by the founder's son, Maynard Forbes, a retired Army colonel. Sometimes specially priced treasures, maybe from the basement, are in the window with a "look what we've found" sign. Take Route 62 west, cross Route 2, ½ mile to West Concord business district. Beyond stop light, continue straight for 1 block over railroad tracks to three-storied building with big maroon awning.

Winand Chocolate Company 40 Beharrell Street (near the Five & Ten; turn left at post office)
Phone: 508/369–8588.
Open: 11–6, at least Thursday–Saturday.

T. Winand, trained in Paris as a chocolatier, uses chocolate that is low in sugar and high in cocoa content. Everyone who comes through the door gets a sample. From the store area you can see the process, but if you arrange ahead of time for a tour, you get a closer look—and some history. "Columbus discovered but didn't like chocolate; Cortez took it back to Spain from South America." Winand's has become well known for its truffle fillings and specialties such as a yule log filled with chocolate candies.

Edaville Railroad

NOSTALGIA WITH AN AMUSEMENT PARK TOUCH

Phone: 508/866–4526.
Location: Route 58, South Carver 02355, 40 miles south of Boston.
Directions: I–93 south to Route 3 south, to Route 44, to Route 58 south. Or I–93 south to Route 3 south, to Route 18 south, to Route 58 south. Or I–93 south to Route 128 north, to Route 24, to Route 25, to Route 58 north. Then follow signs.
Open: May weekends and holidays, noon–5. Summer, 10–5:30 daily. Labor Day through last October weekend, Monday–Friday 10–3 (diesel trains); weekends and holidays 10–5:30 (steam trains). First November Friday through first Sunday after New Year's, weekdays 4–9; weekends 2–9. Closed Thanksgiving and Christmas. Open New Year's Day.
Average stay: 3 hours. Bring bicycles for a 6-mile loop around the lake through cranberry bog country. Keep bearing right on the paved roads from the parking lot exit.
Admission (includes all rides and exhibits): $12.50 adults, $8.50 senior citizens, $7.50 children under 12. Under age 3, free.

Eating: Picnic tables provided. Snack bar. Barbecued chicken dinner in summer.

The real draw is the half-hour ride (5½ miles) through woods and cranberry bogs on the old-fashioned narrow-gauge steam train built in 1907 and still powered by its original machinery. A bonus for early-fall passengers: seeing cranberry harvesters wet-picking the bogs. In addition there are rides on the 1858 carousel built in Amsterdam, and rides on a horse-drawn trolley car, on a fire engine, and in a miniature model T.

Touch possibilities include a petting zoo, a stationary train engine (sit in the cab), and an old Bridgton and Saco car with its wooden interior and seats that go either way. The indoor museum (no touching here) has a couple of antique autos, horse-drawn fire equipment, toy trains, and all sorts of railroad memorabilia. At work in their shops: a basketmaker, a woodworker, and a quilter.

Many weekends there are special events—a Civil War reenactment; an antique auto show; a railroad flea market; and, the highlight for many, a cranberry festival held the last two weekends in September and the first weekend in October.

Fall River

Battleship Cove

WAR SHIPS, MUSEUMS, AND A CAROUSEL

Battleship Massachusetts Battleship Cove, Fall River 02721
Phone: 508/678–1100.

Directions: I–93 south to Route 128 north, to Route 24 south to Route 79 (exit 7) to Davol Street at sign for cove.

Parking: Free. During busy summer hours, to save searching for a space in the main parking area, try the boathouse parking lot (first lot you come to) and plan on walking about five minutes more.

Open: Year round, daily 9–5. Closed Thanksgiving, Christmas, and New Year's Day.

Average stay: 3 hours.

Admission (to all the ships): $8 adults, $4 ages 6–14; under 6 free. AAA members and senior citizens, 25 percent less. Group rates available.

★ Corporate and group functions.

Combination ideas: Whaling Museum in New Bedford, page 169, Horseneck State Beach, page 219, or a visit to one of the many factory outlets in the area (most are open Monday through Saturday; a brochure is available at the cove).

Tour the **USS *Lionfish*** first. It's a quick down-and-out walk through the submarine. Young children and people who don't like close spaces should stay on the main deck. The **USS *Joseph P. Kennedy, Jr.*** is a destroyer that saw service during the Korean and Vietnamese conflicts. Added in 1992: a full-scale model of a Patriot missile. Most of your time will be on the **USS *Massachusetts***, a World War II battleship with a main deck twice the size of a football field. It has knobs and wheels to turn, guns to aim, and turrets to climb. There's plenty of up and down and back and forth to see the forecastle, the stern, the wardroom (the air-conditioned snack bar's here), the open bridge, the conning tower, and the galleys where meals were prepared for more than 2,300 officers and men. Taped information and sound effects at each of the thirty-eight stations give an idea of what life on board was like.

Fall River Carousel Battleship Cove, 1 Central Street, Fall River 02720

Phone: 508/324–4300.

Rides: $.75 each or $5 for ten.

Open: Year round, daily. Summers, Monday–Saturday 10–9, Sunday 12–9. Other seasons, call for times.

School groups: Inquire about educational programs coordinated with the Fall River Heritage Park and the nearby Marine Museum.

★ Parties booked.

Climb the grand staircase (or take an elevator) to the second floor of this brand-new turreted Victorian pavilion set with the water as a backdrop. There it is—the glorious restored 1920 carousel that went round and round until 1986 at Lincoln Park in nearby North Dartmouth. (It is number 54 of 200 made by the Philadelphia Toboggan Company. Only a handful are intact today.) Before being reopened here in 1992, it was completely refurbished. Researchers found the original stencils. All the hand-carved horses—the huge outer row and the double row of jumpers as well as the two chariots—were hand painted once again. A restored band organ was installed in the pavilion, which has a peaked, beamed ceiling and a cupola. (Lots of windows open to a breeze in warm weather.) In a function room with glass doors (more breeze) are regularly scheduled free events for children such as a teddy-bear hospital clinic, clown day, or participatory crafts programs. Carts outside the building sell cotton candy, pretzels, hot dogs, and soft ice cream. You are welcome to picnic on the large front lawn.

Gloucester

Fascinating, fun, and different. No designated walking trail. Few fancy boutiques. Insights into the fishing industry and art world. Unique museums. Open space. Salt air.

Location: 35 miles north of Boston.

Directions: Tobin/Mystic Bridge to Route 1 north, to Route 128 north.

Train: 1-hour ride from North Station, 617/722–3200 or 800/392–6099.

Information: Cape Ann Chamber of Commerce, 33 Commercial Street, Gloucester 01930, 508/283–1601. Free parking area. Open May through early October, Monday–Friday 8–6, Saturday 10–6, Sunday 10–4. Rest of year, Monday–Friday 10–12. Information booth on the boulevard near drawbridge, open late June through Labor Day, Monday–Saturday 10–6, Sunday 10–4.

Restaurants: Many menus posted in Cape Ann Chamber office (see above). *In town:* **Halibut Point Restaurant & Pub,** 289 Main Street (two-way part of street), 508/281–1900. Casual. Good for families. Bar and tables in front; less-lively room in back. Grill in window. Everything from hot dogs to chowder, sandwiches, and seafood dinners. **Imperial Marina,** 17 Rogers Street, 508/281–6573, serves Chinese food. And at 17 Rear Rogers Street with a harbor view: **Rogers Street Grill,** 508/283–9656, with moderate prices for sandwiches, baked stuffed mushrooms, salads, entrees including broiled fish, chicken tarragon, and filet mignon. Before opening **Le Bistro** at 2 Main Street (508/281–8055) on lower level of Blackburn Tavern in 1989, Anna Lisa Tornberg cooked at the Bostonian Hotel's Seasons restaurant and at Biba in Boston. Here she serves imaginative dinners and her own bread, by a fireplace in the winter. Closed Mondays. The **White Rainbow** at 65 Main

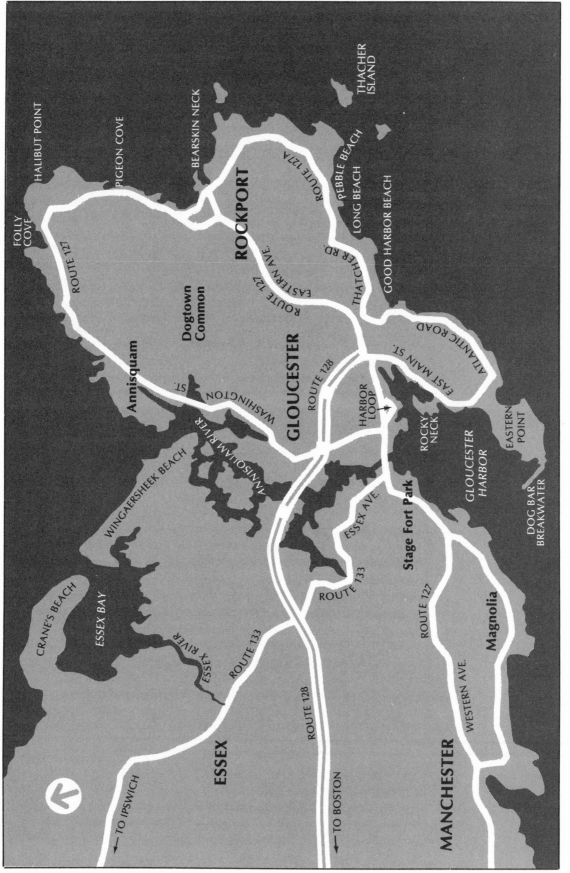

Cape Ann

Street, 508/283–1812, with candlelight and creative cuisine, is acknowledged as "most romantic." *On Rocky Neck:* **The Rudder,** 73 Rocky Neck Avenue, 508/283–7967, is open for lunch and dinner spring through fall, as it has been for 35 years. Mother (Evie) and two daughters (Susan and Paula) offer an experience in food (children's menu too) and evening entertainment (maybe sing-alongs or baton twirling). In a former fish-packing plant filled with memorabilia. Outside deck over water. No reservations; often a wait.

In Town

If you come from Routes 128 and 133, turn right for Stage Fort Park, left for the harbor and town.

Stage Fort Park (page 213), a defense fort during the Revolution and the War of 1812, is a wonderful picnicking place with lots of grass on a high hill overlooking the water. . . . The **Fisherman's Statue,** a memorial to those who have "gone down to the sea in ships," is along the boulevard near the drawbridge. . . . At the **Gloucester Marine Railways Corporation,** on the Harbor Loop, you may see boats (occasionally, a wooden one) being repaired, with rib cages exposed. . . . The hilltop blue-trimmed church with distinctive architecture is Our Lady of Good Voyage, 142 Prospect Street. To see the extensive collection of **ship models** in the welcoming sanctuary, ring the bell of the rectory. . . . Some parishioners (many from the Azores) may be working on their boats in port at the large **State Fish Pier** (where noncommercial fishermen drop a line) located off of Main Street where it intersects with Route 128. . . . About ten **whale watches** (page 253) a day leave from Gloucester. . . . East Gloucester and Eastern Point (see below) can be a destination in themselves.

One of a kind

The *Adventure* Gloucester Adventure Inc., P.O. Box 1307, Gloucester 01930

Phone: 508/281–8079.

Breakfast: 9–noon every Sunday, year round, in the ship's galley (accommodates 40) below. $4.50 per person. Menu varies. Could be juice, muffins, eggs and ham or French toast, coffee. Made on the original wood stove.

Tours: Year round, 45–60 minutes, Wednesday through Sunday, 9–4. Donations suggested. Fee charged when boat is docked in another port.

A beauty in full sail. Built in 1926 and now on the National Register of Historic Places, this 121-foot two-master, the nation's last active dory fishing schooner, was a Maine windjammer cruise boat in the 1960s–1980s. The tour includes a half-hour video, seen in the captain's quarters, about the boat's history and (ongoing) restoration. At press time the *Adventure* has plans to become what may be the country's only tall ship bed and breakfast (with double-bed staterooms, bunk cabins, showers, continental breakfast).

Membership—open to the public—includes ship store discounts, a quarterly newsletter, and eligibility for special events such as occasional free sails.

Along Route 127

Hammond Castle Museum 80 Hesperus Avenue, Gloucester 01930

Phone: 508/283–2081; recorded message 283–2080.

Directions: From Boston, Tobin/Mystic Bridge to Route 1 north, to Route 128 north, to exit 14 (Route 133 east), to Route 127 for about 1 mile to Hesperus on the left.

Open: Summer (self-guided tours) 10–5 daily; some evenings. Rest of year (45-minute guided tour) 10–5, closed Monday and Tuesday.

Admission: $5 adult, $4 senior citizen, $3 ages 6–12, under 6 free.

★ Corporate functions, dinners, weddings.

A drawbridge leads to the castle, but you enter through a small iron door into a 100-foot hall filled with art and religious exhibits. The highlight for many is the 8,600-pipe organ with parts from ancient churches. During most tours, thanks to a computer-activated mechanism, you hear the organ for a few minutes. Children, too, seem to be fascinated with the idea of being in a castle, one that has a plant-filled, glass-roofed courtyard and pool walled with the facades of fourteenth-century French village houses and shops. When inventor John Hays Hammond, Jr., designed and built the castle (1926–28), he used portions of houses and churches from abroad to resemble not one particular castle, but the structures of Europe in medieval times. What a setting—for everything from pops and classical organ concerts to medieval feasts, a murder mystery night, and weddings too.

Groups: Organ demonstrations arranged. School programs offered.

East Gloucester and Eastern Point

Boat from Boston to Rocky Neck: A.C. Cruise Lines, page 232.

Rocky Neck

The country's oldest existing art colony is a tiny community, chock full of artists' studios, small shops, and waterside restaurants. It is also a great place for a close-up view of a large ship in a cradle for repair.

Toward the tip of East Gloucester

Beauport Museum 75 Eastern Point Boulevard, Gloucester 01930

Phone: 508/283–0800.

Open: Weekdays May 15 through October 15, 10–4 (when last tour starts); Saturdays mid-September through mid-October, 1–4.

Admission: $5 adults, $4.50 seniors, $2.50 ages 6–12. Under 6 free. Group rates arranged.

"Why would anyone, especially an unmarried man, need five dining rooms?"

—A 10-YEAR-OLD VISITOR

Twenty-six rooms in an hour! It's a quick trip through what has been called the most fascinating house in America. Each of the rooms, including those moved here from pre-Revolutionary houses, was designed and decorated to represent a different period of American life. Henry Davis Sleeper, a Boston architect and interior decorator, originally built Beauport as his small summer house and entertained many well-known names here. He enlarged the house over the first three decades of this century. The gardens, including a sundial garden and one overlooking the harbor, have just been restored with perennials, annuals, and shrubs of the period—and welcome seating.

Beyond Beauport, more estates, and Niles Beach, is the must-see **Dog Bar Breakwater** and the now-automated **Eastern Point Light**—both built after the gale of 1898 with granite from Rockport quarries. Step over the small rocky beach to reach the half-mile-long breakwater. Fish for flounder, mackerel, and pollock. Collect colorful sea anemones for saltwater aquariums. Picnic. An extraordinary vantage point. Watch vessels, windsurfers, your footing—and the kids. Good cycling destination. Limited parking on summer weekends.

For a **scenic ride** from Beauport, turn right onto Farrington Avenue to Atlantic Road toward Rockport. Spectacular views of the varied coastline along Bass Rocks, Good Harbor Beach, sandy Long Beach, and—assuming the road has been restored from the Halloween storm of 1991—along Pebble Beach (named for its smooth stones, once used as ballast on Gloucester fishing vessels).

Hull

Location: 16 miles south of Boston.

Directions: See Nantasket Beach, page 217.

Boat: Memorial Day through Labor Day, Nantasket boat, page 234.

Restaurants: Nantasket Lobster Pound/Jake's Seafood Restaurant, Steamboat Wharf, 617/925–1024, April–Thanksgiving, recently remodeled with a canopied patio on the water. Fresh seafood—grilled, broiled, or fried. High chairs, booster seats, children's menus ($.95–$5.95). Even a coloring contest for kids. Takeout and retail fish market too. **LaDelat,** 181 Nantasket Avenue, 617/925–4587, serves Vietnamese food. **Healthy Indulgence Boardwalk Cafe,** 205 Nantasket Avenue, has salads in Syrian bread, and frozen yogurt. Not really child-oriented, at the south end of the beach, about a 10-minute walk from the Carousel, in an "unrestored" summer cottage area, is **Saparito's Florence Club Cafe,** 11 Rockland Circle (617/925–3023), a tiny place known for its Italian menu. Reserve a week ahead for weekends.

The Carousel under the Clock 105 Nantasket Avenue, Hull 02045
Phone: 617/925–0472.

Open: End of March through October (Halloween). Summer, 10–10; call for spring and fall schedules.

Admission: $1.25 per person or $6 for six rides.

★ Inquire about birthday party packages.

Nostalgia buffs, kids of all ages, and romantics too ride stationary horses, forty-two jumpers (those that go up and down), and two Roman chariots. The 1928 Wurlitzer band organ plays fox trots and band marches. Everyone smiles—and feels happy that this attraction remained in Hull when the amusements of Paragon Park were auctioned in 1985. (The horses had to be purchased piece by piece or in small lots. One is restored; others are "as was" with the paint layers added through the years.) Now the treasure runs in this perfect spot, between the bay and the ocean. When your five-minute ride is over, ask the operator for a peek inside the motor room so you can see the back of the band organ, the rolls of music, the bellows, gears, and shaft.

Right here: 3-mile-long Nantasket Beach, a miniature 18-hole golf course with waterfalls and replicas of historic landmarks, a penny arcade, and an art gallery. More to come; check on the latest with the Hull Cultural Alliance, P.O. Box 74, Hull 02045, 617/925–1077.

Much quieter, 3 1/2 miles down the road

Hull Lifesaving Museum 1117 Nantasket Avenue
Phone: 617/925–5433.

Open: Year round. Weekends, including Monday holidays, noon–5. July and August, Wednesday–Sunday, noon–5.

Admission: $2 adults, $1 ages 5–17.

Handicapped access: First floor accessible. Many activities for visually and hearing impaired.

Picnicking: On grounds of museum.

Average stay: One hour. Best for ages 5–13.

Facing the only nonautomated lighthouse in America, this 100-year-old station was home to lifesavers who would row out to rescue ships. Put on earphones to hear men talking about the storms of 1888. In the radio room, learn the Morse Code and operate telegraph keys. Make signal flags to take home. Try on period clothes. Band a lobster. Hear Edward Rowe Snow's stories of pirates, lighthouses, and shipwrecks. Climb up into the cupola (former observation tower) and look through binoculars to see two lighthouses. Depending on the weather, the hour, and the season, you might see that nonautomated light, Boston Light, turned on.

Groups or birthday parties: Make advance arrangements to participate in a breeches buoy drill on land—as rescuers did when they practiced for rescues.

Next to museum

Fort Revere Water Tower Fort Revere Park

Parking: Up on the hill in designated area.

Open: Summer weekends, 1–5. (No rest rooms.)

Admission: $1 adults, $.50 children.

Groups: Call 617/925–1577 for appointment.

Boston Harbor islands, Hingham Harbor to the south, and the North Shore too are all part of the spectacular 360-degree view you have from the observation platform here at the 1903 concrete water tower. It's about 100 steps up an interior circular staircase to reach the enclosed platform, which can hold about 30 people. Bring binoculars, telescopes, and your camera. An interpreter is available to answer questions and share historical information.

Lexington

Location: 12 miles northwest of Boston.

Directions: Route 2 west to exit 54B, Waltham Street. Follow signs to Lexington Center.

Ⓣ: Red Line to Alewife, then Ⓣ bus 62 (Bedford) or 76 (Hanscom Field) to Lexington Center.

Restaurants: In Lexington Center, Mandarin, Szechuan, and Polynesian food at **Yangtze River**, 25 Depot Square, 617/861–6030. **Bel Canto**, 1709 Massachusetts Avenue, 617/861–6556, serves great soups, salads, deep-dish pizza, baked pasta dishes, and beers and wines. Northern Italian food is featured at **Sweet Peppers** at 20 Waltham Street, 617/862–1880. And if you're headed toward Cambridge, about 15 minutes down Massachusetts Avenue, a little beyond the Arlington line on the left in Cambridge, is **Marino's,** 2465 Massachusetts Avenue, 617/868–5454. No reservations and quite a wait on Thursday, Friday, and Saturday nights. (Can you arrive before 6?) Homemade breads, homegrown herbs, acclaimed Italian cuisine.

For ice cream plus sandwiches, salads, and some fun: **Chadwick's Ice Cream Parlour,** 903 Waltham Street at Concord Avenue—a purple building, a noisy bustling place decorated with flocked wallpaper, a 1907

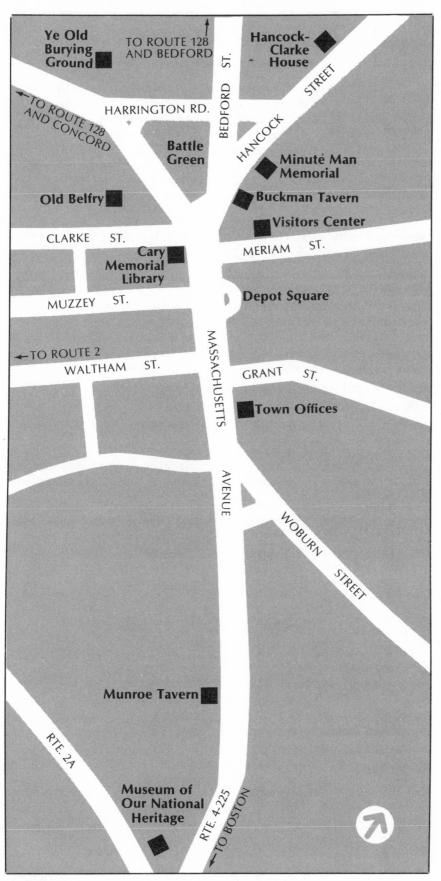

Lexington

nickelodeon that works, a printed barbershop clock that runs backward, a high-wheeler that's ridden now and then by owner John Adams (his real name!), and an 1878 Lamson Cash Railway System. ★ Chadwick's announces about a hundred birthdays each day (a free sundae for the celebrant) with bells and drums, hats, favors, candles and chorus. From Lexington Center, turn onto Waltham Street for 3 miles. From Boston, take the Waltham–Spring Street exit off Route 2 west, and bear right all the way. Question? Call 617/861–1166.

Picnicking: At Fiske Hill or Battle Road Visitor's Center, page 69.

Combination idea: Most day-trippers combine Lexington with Concord (page 55), just 5 miles along Route 2A.

The first stop

The Battle Green Lexington Center

The site of the first Battle of the Revolution is a triangular-shaped area bordered with trees, monuments, the prominent Minuteman Statue of Captain John Parker (a backdrop for many photographers), and a boulder inscribed with Parker's famous command.

*Across from
Minuteman Statue*

Visitor's Center 1875 Massachusetts Avenue

Phone: 617/862–1450.

Open: June–October 9–5 daily. April, May, November 10–4 daily. December–March, Monday–Friday 11–3, weekends 10–4.

What to see? A diorama of the Battle of Lexington. Shards and artifacts found in the 1960s, when the town's historical society unearthed the original foundation of the Hancock-Clarke House (below).

*Just beyond the Green
and the Unitarian
Church*

Ye Old Burying Ground Harrington Road

The graves of Captain Parker, Governor Eustis, Reverend John Hancock, and Reverend Jonas Clarke. The oldest stone is dated 1690. No permit necessary for **gravestone rubbing,** but please notify the Cemetery Commission at 617/861–2717.

Historic Houses

The Lexington Historical Society (P.O. Box 514, Lexington 02173, 617/862–1703) interprets these historic sites.

Open: Mid-April through October.

Admission: For one house, $2.50 adults ($5 for all three houses), $1 ages 6–16.

Buckman Tavern 1 Bedford Street

Open: Mid-April through October, Monday–Saturday 10–5, Sunday 1–5.

Handicapped access: First floor accessible.

Busiest because it's just across from the Green. This is where the Minutemen met on April 19, 1775. It takes about 30 minutes for the guided tour through the seven rooms, built in 1690.

A 10-minute walk (west) from the Green

Hancock-Clarke House 35 Hancock Street

Open: Mid-April through October, Monday–Saturday 10–5, Sunday 1–5.

Handicapped access: Two steps to get in, and two steps inside.

This is where John Hancock and Samuel Adams were sleeping when Paul Revere arrived the night of April 18, 1775. During the 30-minute tour, guides share anecdotes about the personal and political lives of famous residents. Furnishings in the eight rooms, built in 1698, include a rotisserie in the family room, a large chopping bowl Mrs. Clarke used to prepare food for her twelve children, and a trundle bed. In the 1960s the original site was excavated, and in 1974 the house was moved back to its first foundation, across the street.

1 mile toward Arlington from the Green

Munroe Tavern 1332 Massachusetts Avenue

Open: Mid-April through October, Friday and Saturday (and Monday if a holiday) 10–4:30; Sunday 1–4:30.

Handicapped access: A slight hill and two steps. Three of five furnished public rooms are accessible.

It's a 30-minute tour in the tavern, built in 1690 and used as a hospital on April 19, 1775. On the grounds are two small gardens, one with wildflowers, the other with eighteenth-century flowers. Inquire about children's activities scheduled through the season. Call 617/862–1703 to arrange weekday tours.

Minute Man National Historical Park

Headquarters: In North Bridge Visitor Center, page 55.

Directions: About 2 miles from Battle Green. Follow Massachusetts Avenue west. Just after Route 128, turn right on Wood Street, left on Old Massachusetts Avenue.

Admission: Free.

Fiske Hill is a popular picnic area in a wooded glen, but few follow the 1-mile marked loop trail across fields and woods to the foundation remains of the eighteenth-century Fiske farmhouse.

More picnic tables are about 2 blocks beyond Fiske Hill at the **Battle Road Visitor's Center,** 617/862–7753. In season (spring and fall weekends, 8:30–5, and daily in summer until 6) helpful staffers show a 22-minute film about the events leading up to the battles in Lexington and Concord. And rest rooms are available here.

Lowell

Location: 30 miles northwest of Boston.

Directions: I–93 north to 495 south to exit 44 (Lowell) for about 5 miles. Take Lowell Connector (exit 36) to Thorndike Street exit (5N) which becomes Dutton Street in about a mile. Follow national park signs.

Parking: Free in Market Mills Visitor Parking Lot. City garages, $.50 per hour.

Train: 45-minute ride from North Station (617/722–3200 or 800/392–6100); then a 15-minute walk.

Picnicking: Tables on Merrimack Street at the Boston & Marine Railroad Commemorative or next to Boott Mill on the lawn of Boarding House Park.

Restaurants: Many. Reasonably priced. The Market Mills complex has ethnic food booths. Within minutes' walk from Park Visitor Center: Greek cuisine at **Athenian Corner,** 207 Market Street, and the well-proven old-timer, **Olympia Restaurant** at 453 Market Street. **Naikon Thai** (huge weekday lunch buffet) is opposite City Hall, a building with lovely old stained-glass windows, at 368 Merrimack Street. Lebanese food is served at **Sundance Cafe & Restaurant,** 135 Central Street. **La Boniche French Country Restaurant** is at 110 Gorham Street. For Indian food—**Bombay Mahal Restaurant,** 4345 Middle Street.

Lowell National Historical Park Visitor Center Market Mills, 246 Market Street (corner of Dutton)

Phone: 508/970–5000 (V/TDD).

Open: Year round, 8:30–5. Closed Thanksgiving, Christmas, New Year's.

Tours: Year round, daily. Vary in length from one hour to a little over two hours. Call for current schedule. Reservations (accepted by phone) strongly recommended. Through music, exhibits, demonstrations, and some role players, you get a strong feel for the history of Lowell's people, the mills, and the canals. Summer tours include wonderful boat rides—maybe one at sunset—through the canal system (with operating gates) and rides aboard reproduction turn-of-the-century open-air trolleys.

Handicapped access: Fully accessible: Visitor Center; Boott Cotton Mills Museum; The Mogan Cultural Center restored boardinghouse with exhibits. Available: tactile pedestrian maps, braille and large-print literature, cassette tapes of park brochures, and printed narrations of audiovisual programs.

Fees: No charge for walking tours or for Visitor Center, Working People Exhibit (mill girls and immigrants) in boardinghouse, or Waterpower Exhibit (audiovisuals and models of lock chambers, waterwheels, turbines). Boat-and-trolley tour and Boott Cotton Mills Museum: each: $3 adults; $2 age 62 and older; $1 ages 6–16; free age 5 and under.

Reminder: Wear walking shoes and dress for the weather.

How to "do" Lowell: Start at the (air-conditioned) Visitor Center. If you haven't preregistered for at least one tour, sign up for one here. Check out the schedule of events. Take 20 minutes to see the award-winning multi-image presentation that explains how Lowell evolved into America's first industrial city, the first to mass-produce cotton cloth. Then set forth with a knowledgeable guide or with plenty of helpful printed information in hand. Remember to look up—to see a mill clock tower and, on some buildings, maybe even a vintage "Father John's Medicine" or "Ayers Sarsaparilla" sign. And if you arrive in town between 8 and 9 a.m., even on Sundays, you'll probably see Steve and/or George Tournas stretching phyllo dough—for Greek pastries—into 7-foot squares. They are at the Smyrna Lowell Confectionary Co., 503 Market Street, in the recently renovated tin-ceilinged store established by their grandfather in 1903.

Nontourists become tourists in Lowell. On foot, by boat, by trolley, and by (their own) bicycle, they explore the country's first planned industrial city, one that has seemingly endless brick mills lining more than 5 miles of canals. They come for unusual tours in a city that is an urban national park. They come from near and far to enjoy the New England Quilt Museum; festivals, family programs, crafts, and food demonstrations (all part of Lowell's cultural plan); Victorian architecture (mostly single-family homes); places

Jack Kerouac wrote about (the Worthen Bar on Worthen Street still has exposed belts that drive the fans); some cobblestoned and lanterned streets; and, as of 1993, the restored promenade along the intricate network of canals. Visitors find a multiethnic city where Moxie was produced, where a patent medicine industry thrived, where water technology is fascinating, where thousands of teachers and school groups from all over the country enroll in Tsongas Industrial History Center workshops.

Unforgettable: The **Boott Cotton Mills Museum,** a multimillion-dollar public/private restoration that opened in 1992. Enter via the same canal bridge used by mill workers for over 100 years. In a recreated 1910 weave room (a story in itself, considering that there were no looms left in the mill) you see, hear, and smell eighty-eight operating power looms. A few produce cotton cloth. There's plenty of clatter and vibration. Ear plugs are provided. Air filtration systems remove cotton fiber dust. A railing separates visitors from the moving leather belts. On the second floor huge, wonderful, and dramatic exhibits tell the story of the rise and decline of Lowell's textile industry.

On other floors in this five-storied mill: the Tsongas Industrial History Center (many hands-on opportunities for groups including the use of looms); the National Park Service Cultural Resources Center and its staff of archaeologists, conservators, scientists, and craftsmen; the New England Folklife Center, founder of the Lowell Folk Festival, complete with exhibits and a demonstration kitchen; and the Lowell Historical Society.

Lynn

Location: 9 miles north of Boston.

Directions: Callahan Tunnel and continue on Route 1A (the Lynnway).

Parking: Garage at Lynn Ⓣ station, 1½ blocks from visitor center. Reasonable rates.

Train: Rockport commuter line from North Station (617/722–3200 or 800/392–6099), 25 minutes to Central Square/Lynn station, minutes' walk to everything.

Eating: (Some day, a cafe in the visitors' center.) Across the street from visitor center is **Capitol Diner,** 617/595–9314. Open Monday–Friday 5 a.m.–6:30 p.m., Saturday 5–2, closed Sunday. "Air cooled." Father-and-son business owned by same family since 1928. After one visit, waitress Marie remembers your beverage order. Enter through small landscaped yard with a live "attack rooster" (so the sign reads) in the garden. Sit at red leather counter stools or at a table for two. Posted menu might announce, "New! Banana Nut Muffins." Hash and eggs, $3.20. Meat loaf dinner, $3.85. On the waterfront: Reasonably priced seafood at **Port Hole Restaurant,** 98 Lynnway, 617/595–7733, "where everyone in town celebrates events." **Christy's** on Lynnway for takeout. **La Petite Cafe,** an upscale deli at 224 Monroe Street, is open 6–4 weekdays; 617/598–5250. Or bring a lunch to eat on the waterfront.

Lynn Heritage State Park 154 Lynnway, Lynn 01902
Phone: 617/598–1974.

Admission: Free.

Handicapped access: Accessible.

Visitor Center: Open at least Sundays 1–5, Wednesday 9–4:30. Call (phone above) to check on hours and programming—perhaps a guided walk, "resident shoemaker," or performances.

A gem. Accessible by Ⓣ. Combines indoor and outdoor activities. Enlightening. Thought-provoking. Fascinating. Bravo. Go!

Even the landscaped entrance—with turn-of-the-century–style fountain—is well done and welcoming to this two-storied, large but intimate museum established in a recycled 1889 building. Plan on at least an hour and maybe two. First, step into the "10-footer," an early shoe shop. Smell the leather and hear a conversation between shoemaker and apprentice about work, dreams, politics. Then it's on to the fast-moving 8-minute introductory film through 300 years' history of "shoe city." Enter various settings where you stand; sit; push buttons; hear the music of the Hutchinson Family Singers, who spread the message of abolition, suffrage, and temperance throughout New England in the 1830s. A 5-minute presentation about the strike of 1860 uses dramatic lighting effects. Beyond seeing how the Industrial Revolution transformed shoemaking from home craft to factory production, you are reminded that Lynn was the home of Mary Baker Eddy, Marshmallow Fluff, Lydia Pinkham's vegetable compound for women's ills, an active theater district, and, just when the shoe industry failed, General Electric. Another hit, maybe a highlight: the Oral History Lunch Counter—this alone could take a half hour—with videos of a GE worker reading poems, a shoe factory worker, and other Lynn residents who share anecdotes about Nahant Beach or about ice cutting.

Outside, follow the 10-minute trail of painted yellow footprints by the Lynn Community College campus and via the Lynnway overpass to the landscaped **Waterfront Park.** More surprises: acres of grass, a large pavilion built over the water, summer concerts on Sundays and Wednesdays, swooping seagulls, a marina, views of Nahant, and paddleboats (page 230). When you walk the boardwalk (everyone does), be sure to see the huge mosaic, designed by Lilli Ann and Marvin Rosenberg, mounted on a condominium wall. Kids, too, will spend a long time commenting on the rich cultural heritage portrayed in the clay pieces made by 300 residents.

Combination idea: Saugus Ironworks, page 114, about 20 minutes away.

Marblehead

Location: 17 miles north of Boston.

Directions: Callahan Tunnel to Route 1A north, to Route 129 east.

Ⓣ: Haymarket on the Orange or Green Line; then 55-minute ride on Ⓣ bus 441 or 442 (617/722–3200).

Information: Yellow booth on Pleasant Street, spring and fall weekends and daily in July and August. Chamber of Commerce office, 62 Pleasant Street, 617/631–2868, 9–3 weekdays year round.

Restaurants: An incredible variety of possibilities in this small community. **The Barnacle,** 141 Front Street with harbor view, is known for its chowder. For lobster—**The Sail Loft** at 15 State Street. For takeout, **Good Taste** at 32 Atlantic or **Truffles,** 112 Washington Street. For fine dining and ambience, **Rosalie's** at 18 Sewall.

Picnicking: At Fort Sewall (lovely shade trees and benches) or at Redd Pond in town. Chandler Hovey Park (some shaded area) at the tip of Marblehead Neck by the lighthouse is a marvelous vantage point. (On the way to the park, stop to see the garden and English country cottage at Stowaway Sweets, the candy shop on the corner of Beach Street and Atlantic Avenue.)

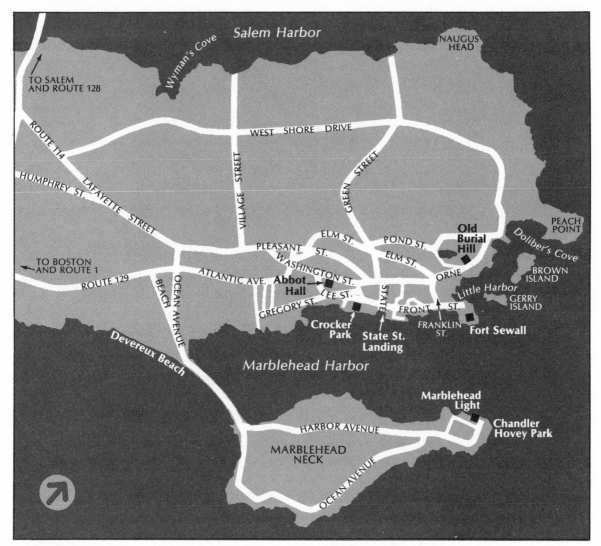

Marblehead

The entire town, pronounced Marble*head* by most natives, is 4.4 square miles in all. Even if you're caught on a one-way street, you're never very far off course. As a day-tripper you'll have plenty of company all summer long and on fall weekends. Fall weekdays are quieter. Walkers find charm everywhere as they amble along winding streets with hidden lanes, interesting doorways, and old-fashioned gardens. A walking tour described in the Chamber of Commerce brochure includes the 1768 **Jeremiah Lee Mansion** and the 1728 **Hooper Mansion** with its flower garden open (in season) to the public (tour fee charged). In **Old Town,** parallel, sort of, to Washington Street and the shopping center, are Front Street and the harbor.

State Street Landing is the best place for a close-up of harbor activity in what has been dubbed the "yachting capital of the world." For more of an overview, walk to **Crocker Park,** a block toward the Boston Yacht Club, or look from the harbor entrance at Fort Sewall (1724) at the end of Front

Street. Not too far from **Fort Sewall,** off Orne Street, is **Old Burial Hill,** with gravestones of Revolutionary War soldiers.

Bring the whole family into **Abbot Hall,** the spired building with a clock in the tower. It's open year round weekdays 8–5; also May 30 through October Saturdays 9–6 and Sundays 11–6. Most visitors come to view the original *Spirit of '76,* the painting given to Marblehead by General John Devereux, whose son was the model for the drummer boy. Open the chest on the wall to see the deed to the town, dated 1684.

If you are in town at dusk, you may be rewarded with silhouettes of hundreds, sometimes thousands, of masts and sails against the sunset.

Mystic Seaport Museum

Phone: 203/572–0711.

Location: 100 miles southwest of Boston at Mystic, Connecticut 06355–0990.

Directions: I–93 south to Route 128 north, to I–95 south, exit 90, to Connecticut Route 27 south.

Open: Year round, daily except Christmas. October through April 9–4. Late June through Labor Day 9–8. Other months 9–5,

Admission: Adults $14.50, ages 6–15 $8.75, under 6 free. (Get ticket validated for free admission the next day.) Group rates available. Fee includes parking and all exhibits except May–October steamboat rides ($3 adults, $2 children age 6–15, 5 and under free; 90-minute evening cruise $7.50, $6). Also available are wooden classic boat rides (sailboat $3.50 per person) or rentals (rowboats $7 half hour, $10.50 hour; sailboat $14 hour); a half-hour planetarium show (adults $1; ages 6–15, 50 cents); and horse-and-carriage rides.

Eating: Picnic on lawn or benches throughout Seaport. Fast-food galley on premises. Full-service restaurant next door.

Educational programs: Many, including tours, sail education, classes in maritime skills, overnight programs for youth and school groups, planetarium programs, teacher training institutes.

Programs: Extensive. Vary. Demonstrations throughout the year. Participation possibilities in skills and trades. Help make rope or a cask. Watch sail setting and furling. Chantey singing. Fish drying. In December, day and evening Christmas-in-the-1800s walking tours.

★ Some buildings—and a tent too—can be rented for private or corporate events.

Handicapped access: Wheelchairs and printed access guide available. Many buildings are accessible.

Reminder: Wear comfortable shoes, a sunhat, and bring a jacket.

Pets: Leashed pets allowed on grounds but not inside buildings or on board vessels.

Re-created with buildings and shops moved from other locations, this is a nineteenth-century village with more than 400 historic ships and boats. Speak to costumed interpreters who explain their activities in the doctor's office, the apothecary shop, the tavern, and the general store. Step along the old ropewalk to see how rope was made. Smell the oakum used for caulking in the chandlery. The fires are burning in the shipsmith shop, where cask hoops, harpoons or lances are made. Foods cooking in the

Buckingham House are made from recipes of the 1800s. Several buildings exhibit models, scrimshaw, and art. Weekdays, craftsmen in the boat shop are building small craft using old methods.

Limited time? The most popular attractions are the ships. Board the *Joseph Conrad,* a training ship built in 1882; the *L. A. Dunton,* one of the last great Gloucester fishing schooners, with its nests of dories once used with long trawl lines; and the restored *Charles W. Morgan,* the only American wooden whaler in existence.

Special for kids: Games on the green. And in the children's museum: crafts programs, nineteenth-century toys to play with, and nineteenth-century clothes to try on.

Newport, Rhode Island

Location: 80 miles southwest of Boston.

Directions: I–93 south to Route 128 north, to Route 24. Then follow Route 138 or Route 114 into Newport.

Information: Gateway Visitor Information Center, 800/326–6030 or 401/849–8098, is located at 23 America's Cup Avenue, at the transportation center where buses arrive from and leave for both the Boston and Providence airports. (Driving, follow signs to the Center.) A recommended stop, open 9–5 seven days a week (closed Christmas Day), this is the ultimate in information centers—a large, air-conditioned facility with a knowledgeable, helpful staff who will draw routes for you on a free detailed map. You'll also find plenty of information about events and attractions. And there's a 6-minute orientation video, comfortable chairs, and rest rooms.

Parking: Thirty minutes for free at the Gateway Center; $.50 for every half hour thereafter.

America's first resort has been rediscovered. Get an early start. Decide whether you want to be inside and/or out. Within a few square miles are about one hundred attractions (plus a hundred restaurants) including historic sites, mansions, public beaches (**First Beach** is known for its good surfing), the **International Tennis Hall of Fame, harbor tours,** the **Newport Art Museum,** and **Touro Synagogue**—America's oldest. More than eighty sculptured trees and shrubs in addition to gardens are at **Green Animals,** 7 miles south of Newport on Route 138.

For a taste of Newport in a day, consider:

The Wharf Area. Shops and restaurants in revitalized eighteenth- and nineteenth-century buildings against a backdrop of yachts, sailboats, and tall ships.

Ocean Drive. This 10-mile, two-lane drive (challenging for cyclists, especially on weekends) is well signed. If you start from Thames Street, you'll come to the site of the Newport Jazz and Folk Festival—Fort Adams State Park (Memorial Day through Labor Day, $1 parking for nonresidents)—which has a swimming and a picnic area, grills and a fishing pier, and the Museum of Yachting. Then you'll travel by estates, condominiums, rocky beach areas, and, always, ocean views. Near the end of the drive is Brenton Point State Park, with parking, an elevated grassy area good for picnicking and kite flying, rest rooms, and a stone fishing pier.

Mansions. All are sumptuous. Most offer one-hour guided tours. Some are open April–November. Some are open winter weekends. Some have special holiday decorations in December. The last tour begins at 5 in the

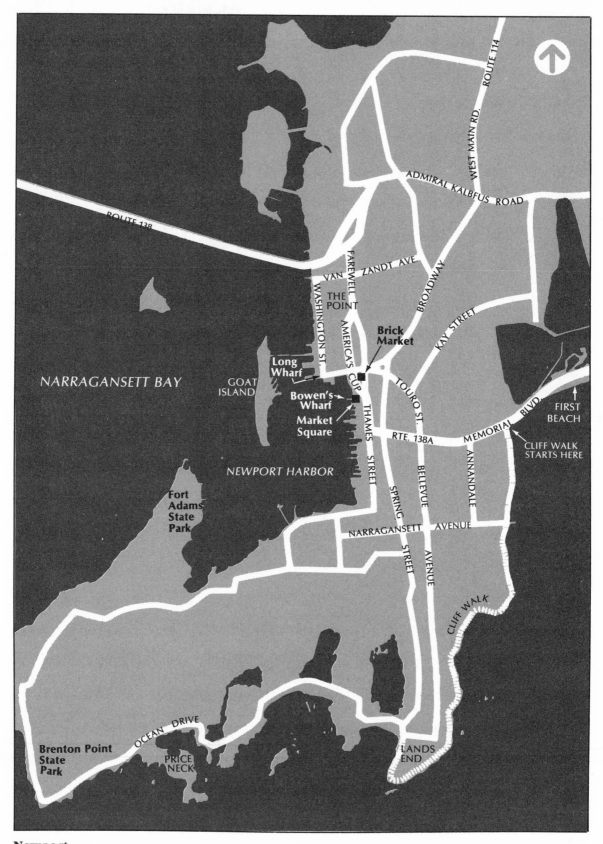

Newport

summer, at 4 in the winter. Belcourt Castle, open year round ($6.50 adults, $4 ages 13–18, $2 ages 6–12), is the one with a coronation coach hand-carved in 23-carat gold. At the Astors' Beechwood, open year round ($7.50 adults, $5.50 ages 6–12), you are guests, learning about history and customs from "guides" who dress and act as Mrs. Astor's servants and friends. Combination tickets are available for Preservation Society properties that include The Breakers ($6 adults, $3.50 ages 6–11), once the home of Cornelius Vanderbilt, and Marble House ($5 adults, $3 ages 6–11).

Not so opulent and a favorite for many of all ages: Hammersmith Farm on Ocean Drive. The last working farm in Newport is a twenty-eight-room shingled cottage surrounded by magnificent gardens. Site of Jacqueline Bouvier and John F. Kennedy's wedding reception, it was the Kennedy Summer White House in 1961–63. Open April through mid-November daily; last two weekends in March and November 10–5; extended summer hours; special Christmas hours. Adults $6, $3 for ages 6–12.

Cliff Walk. A free walkway developed by estate owners during Newport's Gilded Age. It starts on Memorial Boulevard near Newport Beach. The path, rough in spots, goes for almost 3 miles between dozens of mansions, including The Breakers, and an uninterrupted view of sailboats. Height (and drop) may make you uncomfortable with young children.

The Point. One of the oldest sections of Newport. Weave your way through the narrow streets where colonial homes have been restored.

Old Sturbridge Village

Phone: 508/347–3362; TDD 508/347–5383.

Location: One hour west of Boston on Route 20, at 1 Old Sturbridge Village Road, Sturbridge 01566

Directions: Mass. Pike to exit 9. Follow signs to Route 20 west.

Bus: Peter Pan (617/426–7838), 1 block from South Station.

Open: Year round. Closed Mondays November through April, and Christmas and New Year's days. May–October 9–5. November–April Tuesday–Sunday 10–4; many exhibits close 12:15–1 p.m. in winter (cafeteria open; entertainment in tavern).

Admission (also good for second consecutive open day): $14 adults, $7 ages 6–15. Under 6 free. Group rates available. (Package rates available for admission and lodging in adjacent motor lodge.)

Handicapped access: Most buildings are accessible; request access guide at Visitors' Center. Sign language interpreters available on third Saturday of every month.

Strollers: Sorry, cannot be accommodated in many buildings.

Programs (included in admission price): Check the handout for schedule of demonstrations or participatory activities—maybe sheep shearing, storytelling, straw braiding, or a chance to transform a tinned sheet into a cookie cutter.

Eating: Picnic area with a swing set and grills in a pine grove convenient to parking area. Light snacks, a cafeteria, and a buffet in the village's Bullard Tavern.

Workshops: Many. By preregistration. Hands-on possibilities and historical programs for children and adults. Topics include gardening, fashion, decorative arts, archaeology. The village's education department also develops workshops, study guides, and resource materials for specific age groups.

★ Weddings and meetings.

Reminder: Dress comfortably for outdoors. Wear comfortable shoes; paths are unpaved.

Rules: Leashed dogs allowed on grounds; hearing dogs (only) in buildings.

Plan to arrive early. There's more than a day of fascination for everyone at this outdoor living-history museum of early New England life. Forty buildings of the 1790–1840 period have been moved from all over New England and reconstructed on 200 rolling acres of meadow and woodland.

The costumed staff—including the miller, the basketmaker, the printer—enthusiastically explain what they're doing. For most children, the farmer is a favorite. He loves visitors—and animals (oxen, cows, and sheep). Each spring there are new young lambs and calves. More than 400 varieties of herbs flourish in the gardens. Year round, you can buy fresh warm cookies at the bakery. Folk art, textiles, glass, clocks, and lighting devices are among the extensive collections in galleries.

Rest on the village green. See the water-powered machinery saw logs into boards. Ride through the covered bridge and around the mill pond on a horse-drawn carryall. And if you're late for school, you'll hear about it from the teacher.

Plymouth

Location: 41 miles southeast of Boston.

Directions: I–93 south to Route 3 south, to exit 6 (Route 44) toward Plymouth. Turn right at the first lights to the center of town.

Bus: From Boston, Plymouth & Brockton bus from Greyhound or Peter Pan brings you to terminal 3 miles north of town center. Taxi $3–$5 to center, where you can board an all-day trolley ($3) that runs to Plimoth Plantation's Eel River site.

Information: Information booth (with rest rooms) is on Water Street across from the 1620 Restaurant. For advance information: Plymouth Visitor Information Service, P.O. Box ROCK, Plymouth 02361; phone 800/538–ROCK or 508/746–6668. For personalized assistance (and discount tickets to major attractions): Destination Plymouth, P.O. Box 4001, Plymouth 02361; phone 800/USA–1620 or 508/747–4161.

Restaurants: In town, the Lobster Hut features seafood, lobster rolls, coleslaw, french fries. Eat outside on picnic tables by boats and seagulls. Popular with the locals (you may have a wait), Isaac's on the Waterfront offers reasonable prices and a waterfront view from every table. Station One at 51 Main Street in a converted firehouse is known for its Sunday brunch as well as American and Cajun dishes—and its sidewalk cafe. Both entrees and vegetables are acclaimed at the Inn for All Seasons, a Victorian mansion with formal gardens, 3 miles from town, next to Plimoth Plantation's Eel River site.

Open: Most attractions are open spring through Thanksgiving.

Beyond the T-shirt and souvenir shops are attractions with and without admission fees that appeal to visitors from all over the world. There are **harbor tours, whale watching,** and **deep sea fishing trips** through Capt. John Boats, Town Wharf, phone 800/242–AHOY. Cape Cod Cruises, 800/242–2469, leave for **Provincetown** from State Pier. On land, a must (free and smaller than you imagined) is a view of **Plymouth Rock** from the portico on the waterfront. Across Leyden Street, the oldest street in the country, is **Brewster Gardens**, a small peaceful park. Posted in the park is a map leading to a short walking trail along Town Brook, over the wooden bridge, to Jenney Grist Mill, where you'll see a water-powered mill grinding corn, wheat, or rye, as the Pilgrims did more than three hundred years ago. Several **seventeenth- and eighteenth-century houses** (fee charged) are open to the public. Some feature fine antiques. Demonstrations such as weaving, candle dipping, and spinning are given in the Harlow Old Fort House. And the **Plymouth National Wax Museum** presents the Pilgrims' story with light, sound, and animation.

A major attraction

Plimoth Plantation P.O. Box 1620, Plymouth 02362

Phone: 508/746–1622.

Open: April through November. Mid-June through Labor Day, *Mayflower II,* 9–7; Pilgrim Village and Indian Homesite, 9:30–5:30. All exhibits 9–5 daily April through mid-June and Labor Day through November.

Admission: *Mayflower II* only: April and May, $5.50 adults, $3.75 ages 5–12; June–November $5.75 adults, $3.75 children.

    Mayflower II, Pilgrim Village, Hobbamock's (Wampanoag Indian) Homesite, and Crafts Center: $11 ages 5–12. No charge for under age 5. Adults $17, April and May; $18.50 June–November. Group rates available.

Directions: Route 3 south to exit 4, follow signs. About an hour from Boston or Providence, 20 minutes from Cape Cod Canal.

Programs: Monthly calendar of events includes workshops and free events (special demonstrations or children's games and songs). Also scheduled: classroom visits, field trips, courses, lectures, concerts, a high school–level dramatic presentation.

★ Corporate meetings, social events, weddings.

Handicapped access: Village paths are hilly and unpaved and can be rough.

Eating: In the village, at picnic pavilion (both roofed and open areas), or in visitor center's cafeteria, dining courtyard, or private function rooms. In fall, seventeenth-century dining by reservation. Thanksgiving week, buffet or Victorian dinner (several seatings). Reservations taken as early as January!

Average stay: 45 minutes on *Mayflower II;* 2½ hours in village and Indian homesite.

Foreign languages: Site map printed in Spanish, French, Japanese, German, Italian.

Rules: Sorry, no dogs allowed.

The dialect, the crops, the clothing, and, best of all, the conversation turns back the clock for visitors, who are encouraged to ask questions about seventeenth-century Plymouth. Perhaps you'll hear about Oceanus Hopkins, who was born on the *Mayflower* during its sixty-six-day crossing. Or see the two-man sawpit in operation. Up on some roof is the plantation's thatcher, trained by an Irishman who for many years practiced his native craft here. From time to time the programming includes "If I Were a Pilgrim," when children get to try on pilgrims' clothing. ("It's hot to wear in the summer!")

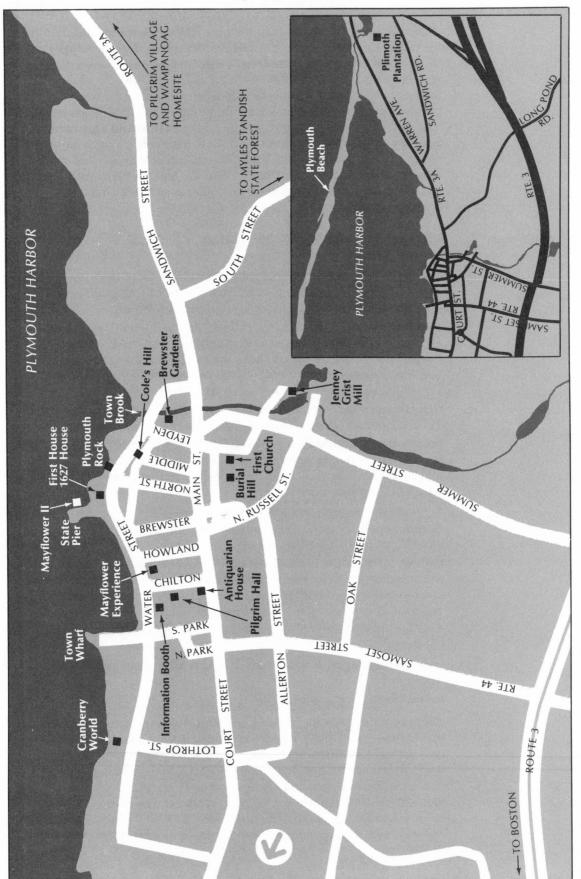

Plymouth

Cooking, gardening, some animals, and politics too are all part of this living history museum, a re-creation in two locations, 3 miles apart:

Waterfront Site: *Mayflower II* at State Pier in Plymouth harbor, adjacent to Plymouth Rock. An orientation exhibit helps to prompt lots of questions to the "crew" on this full-scale reproduction of the type of ship that brought the Pilgrims to the New World in 1620. It was a hard trip, and quarters for 102 passengers were mighty cramped.

Nearby: The J. Barnes Bake Shop, re-created by Plimoth Plantation, celebrates John Barnes, a seventeenth-century Plymouth bakehouse proprietor. Here you may purchase freshly made twentieth-century baked goods, including adaptations of seventeenth-century recipes such as cheate (whole wheat) bread and spice cake.

Eel River Site: Includes the 1627 Pilgrim Village and a walk along the river to **Hobbamock's (Wampanoag Indian) Homesite** with its large bark-covered two-fireplaced house. Native Americans and other staffers describe family life and demonstrate planting, food preparation, and tool making. In the **carriage house craft center:** demonstrations of seventeenth-century skills, focusing on replicas of baskets, fine furniture, maybe a boat—items that the colonists might have imported from England or elsewhere.

No charge and good

Cranberry World 225 Water Street, Plymouth 02360

Phone: 508/747–2350.

Location: Overlooking Plymouth Harbor, a 10-minute walk north of Plymouth Rock.

Open: May–November, 9:30–5 daily, including weekends and holidays.

Admission: Free. Advance reservations required for groups.

Average stay: 20–30 minutes.

Handicapped access: Accessible.

Well done. The air-conditioned visitor center—courtesy of Ocean Spray Cranberries, Inc., a grower cooperative—often sees repeat visitors, who learn something new every time. Wonderful displays explain the history, lore, and cultivation of cranberries from the 1600s through today. Guides (some are cranberry growers) are available to talk with you about the berry, which—a surprise to many—grows on a vine, not a bush. There are videos to see, taped interviews to hear, hand scoops to touch, baking aromas to smell (recipes available), and samples to taste. Indoors, there's a diorama of a cranberry wetland system that prompts an amazing variety of questions from young curious minds. The real thing? Demonstration bogs are outside.

Colonial Lantern Tour New World Tours, P.O. Box 3541, 25 Brewster Street, Plymouth 02361

Phone: 508/747–4161.

Open: 7:30–9 p.m., spring and fall weekends and daily June–August.

Fees: $7 adult, $5 ages 6–12, $20 family of four or more.

With candlelit punched-tin lantern in hand, see and hear about sites that have played a part in four centuries of Plymouth's history. You walk through the original plantation site (the town center), alleyways, and Brewster Gardens, and along the town brook. Wheelchairs and strollers can be accommodated.

Diane Finn, developer of these well-received tours, is a Plymouth teacher who wrote *The Secrets of Plymouth Rock,* a children's book illustrated by daughter Erin.

Portsmouth, New Hampshire

Location: 56 miles north of Boston.

Directions: Tobin/Mystic Bridge to Route 1 north to I–95 north to New Hampshire, exit 7.

Parking: Park once (at meter for two hours; in garage near Market Square if longer) and walk to just about everything.

Bus: Greyhound (617/423–5810) and C&J Trailways (617/426–7838 or 800/258–7111).

Information: Greater Portsmouth Chamber of Commerce at 500 Market Street, P.O. Box 239, Portsmouth 03802, 603/436–1118—plus, in season, a Market Square booth.

Restaurants: Dozens in town. The **Metro** on High Street is famous for its chowder. Inexpensive soups, salads, and light meals are available at **Stock Pot** at 53 Bow Street—with small deck overlooking the water. Penhallow Street has **Goldi's Deli** at number 106. At 51 Penhallow Street there's **Ceres Bakery** (closes at 5:30) with its almost-famous breads and pastries; some soups and salads too. A creative international menu is offered at **Karen's,** 105 Daniel Street. **Annabelle's Ice Cream** at 49 Ceres Street is considered a must by many; soups and sandwiches here too. Three book-lined dining rooms are in **The Library,** the mahogany-paneled former hotel at 401 State Street; imaginative dishes. The well-established **Warren's Lobster House** (big salad bar too) is still there, just over the bridge in Kittery.

Good eating, browsing (antiques and crafts), and a summer arts festival are some of the many reasons visitors come to this revitalized port town. Some come for walking tours, harbor cruises, historic sites, or a trip to Star Island (see page 237). With kids, for a sampler (a very full day), you might spend a couple of hours at Strawbery Banke, cross the street for a picnic lunch in the waterfront Prescott Park, walk up the hill to the Children's Museum, and then drive to Newcastle Beach for sand, a grassy park, and views of a lighthouse and the coastline.

Pleasure and working boats on the Piscataqua River form a picturesque backdrop for **Prescott Park's** expansive lawns, brick walkways, and beautiful flower gardens. The annual six-week summer Prescott Park Arts Festival includes art exhibits, afternoon children's presentations, and evening plays or concerts. (Free admission; donations welcomed. Bring your own chairs.)

Strawbery Banke Marcy and Hancock Streets (mailing address: P.O. Box 300, Portsmouth, NH 03802)

Open: May–October, 10–5 daily; plus last two April weekends, first two November weekends, and for Christmas Stroll evenings, first two December weekends.

Admission (good for two consecutive days): $9 adults, $8 seniors, $5 children under 17, $25 family. Under age 6, free. Group rates available.

Handicapped access: The restaurant and some of the homes are accessible.

Rules: Dogs allowed on leash on grounds only, not in houses.

Archaeological digs and oral history are part of the ongoing research at this museum in progress. Built in 1630 along a riverbank lined with wild strawberries, this urban community became important during the clipper ship era. Now forty-two buildings on a 10-acre area illustrate three centuries of history. You see a Revolutionary War tavern, a Victorian mansion, a 1940 store, a 1950s living room. Eight structures are furnished with period furniture and have guides. Others have exhibit rooms featuring architecture, house construction, tools, and social history. Some serve as shops for a wooden-boat builder, a leather worker, coopers, cabinetmakers, and potters. There are vegetable, herb, and flower gardens. Participatory possibilities in the Education Center include stenciling or nature printing.

Minutes' walk from Strawbery Banke

The Children's Museum of Portsmouth The South Meeting House, 280 Marcy Street

Phone: 603/436–3853.

Open: Tuesday–Saturday 10–5, Sunday 1–5. Also open Monday 10–5 during summer and school vacations.

Admission: $3.50 per person; $3 seniors. Free under age 1.

Average stay: 90 minutes.

Handicapped access: Fully accessible.

Children are encouraged to discover how things work and to use imagination in a converted (and air-conditioned) meeting house. Come prepared to accompany youngsters as they climb and touch and experience in this hands-on museum. Each self-guided exhibit is planned for a particular age level. Inquire about workshops and special events such as performances or participatory festivals.

Rockport

Map: See page 62.

Location: 44 miles north of Boston.

Directions: Tobin/Mystic Bridge to Route 1 north, to Route 128 north to exit 10 (Route 127 north).

Parking: July and August, $5 all day, in lot behind Upper Main Street information booth; free shuttle bus every 12 minutes or so.

Train: 70-minute ride from North Station (617/722–3200 or 800/392–6100) to Whistlestop Mall with supermarket (for picnic foods perhaps).

Information: Rockport Chamber of Commerce & Board of Trade, P.O. Box 67, 3 Main Street, Rockport 01966, 508/546–5997. Booth on Upper Main Street (Route 127) is open May–October, 1–5 daily.

Restaurants: Brackett's Ocean View, 508/546–2797, at 27 Main Street, overlooking the bay and open year round, serves everything from sandwiches to full dinners; good for families too. Open spring through fall: **The Greenery** (508/546–9593) at the entrance to Bearskin Neck features a salad bar, pita sandwiches, seafood, and their own baked goods. Farther out on Bearskin Neck is **My Place** (508/546–9667). Seafood, candlelight, and (often) sunsets from the porch. Reservations accepted after 12 the same day.

Combination idea: 10-minute drive to Gloucester, page 61.

The shoreline here gives the feeling of Maine. In the **center of town** are open spaces, galleries, artists at work along the harbor, the much-photographed and -painted and -reconstructed Motif Number 1, inviting lanes, and history. Main Street is full of contrasts: the tombstones in the Old Parish Burying Ground; saltwater taffy made in the window of Tuck's at number 15; Toad Hall Bookstore at number 51, in a granite building that was once a bank; clothing stores; and the home of the Rockport Art Association, site of the Rockport Chamber Music Festival. Most Bearskin Neck shops don't open until 12 on Sundays, making Sunday mornings, before the crowds arrive, a good time to walk the neck. Go all the way to the end for a great view of Headlands. For a harbor **view from the Headlands,** walk up Mount Pleasant Street from Dock Square, turn left on Norwood Avenue, left on Highland Avenue, through shrubbery to the Headlands.

Other ways to experience Rockport: For a waterside view, Rockport Schooner Co. (508/546–9876) offers a 90-minute **bay cruise** on a 56-foot **wooden schooner** that has been around the world since it was built in 1984. Departs from Tuna Wharf. $18 per person for sunset sails; day sails half price for under age 10. . . . Weather permitting, Sunday morning **free two-hour nature walks** (sorry, no dogs allowed) in the woods of Dogtown Common or along the coastline. Meet at Whistlestop Mall at 10. Call 508/546–5997 to check on schedule. . . . Take a one-hour **trolley tour** that has seventeen designated stops. The all-day on-and-off-as-you-please ticket includes restaurant discount coupons: $5 adults, $2 children under 12. Cape Ann Tours (508/546–5950) runs the trolleys from 10–6, allowing you to spend an hour at a beach or at spectacular **Halibut Point** (page 190), a primary destination for many North Shore day-trippers. . . . From Rockport Center, it's about a 10-minute drive along Route 127 to **Pigeon Cove.** At the (closed) tool company, turn right to see lobsters unloaded and

Thacher Island

Those historic twin granite lighthouses, a mile out to sea, are on an island that is a rare natural sanctuary. Every "good weather" summer weekend at 9 a.m. and 1 p.m., the Thacher Island 23-foot custom-built aluminum landing craft leaves Rockport's T-Wharf with a maximum of 15 passengers (first-come, first-served—no reservations accepted) for a 20-minute ride to the island. The last return trip leaves the island at 4 p.m. Sorry, no dogs allowed.

Photographers, artists, birdwatchers, scouts, and families with older children enjoy the trails, wildflowers, berries, birds, and the worth-the-climb 360-degree view from the North Tower lantern room.

Bring a hand-held cooler (there is no drinking water) and a sweater (it's about 20 degrees cooler than the shore).

It's as peaceful and as beautiful as you might imagine. There are no beaches. The shoreline is rocky and rough. There are two outhouses. There is plenty of poison ivy. No open fires are allowed.

Overnight arrangements: Reservations are necessary for camping and for the one apartment. For details call 508/546–2326 after April 1.

weighed. (No set schedule.) Almost across from the Pigeon Cove post office is a sign to the **Paper House** at 50 Pigeon Hill Street, 508/546–2629. It took twenty years to build this house, in which everything—lamps, chairs, grandfather clock, even the walls (215 thicknesses)—is made of paper. The fireplace mantel is rotogravure sections; the writing desk, newspaper reports of Lindbergh's flights. Mrs. Curtis welcomes visitors 10–5 daily in July and August, and often in the spring and fall. Average visit: 15 minutes. Admission: $1 adults, $.50 ages 6–14, free under age 6. . . . Continue along oceanside Route 127, pass the Old Farm Inn (1799) near the entrance to Halibut Point Reservation, and (6 miles from Bearskin Neck) take a right to **Annisquam,** a tranquil village with beautiful old large and small homes and a yacht club built out over the water. Here, spanning the cove, is a recently rebuilt wooden footbridge that you may feel you've discovered. Right here, in season, the Lobster Cove Market (open 7–7) sells everything from subs and lobster rolls to produce and beer. The waterside Land and Sea Restaurant serves inside and out on the deck until 3.

Salem

Ride the waves aboard a **harbor cruise** or **whale watch** trip (508/744–6311 or 800/696–6311) from Pickering Wharf or Salem Willows. . . . Use map in free brochure from information centers to follow painted red 1.7-mile-long **trail** by Salem's historic buildings and sites. Or limit your walk to quiet, elegant **Chestnut Street,** past magnificent houses once owned by sea captains. These include the city's best-kept secret: One Federal mansion, **Stephen Phillips Memorial Charitable Trust House,** 34 Chestnut Street, is open the Saturday before Memorial Day until mid-October. $1.50 adults, $.75 age 12 and under. Tour through two floors of treasures, including wood carvings, Oriental rugs, Chinese export porcelains—all collected by several generations of the Phillips family. The carriage house has seven restored antique carriages and two antique Pierce-Arrow automobiles. . . . Or get an overview of the city sitting on the trolley (see below). . . . Spend part of the day here, and then see "Le Grand David" in Beverly, page 43.

Location: 20 miles northeast of Boston.

Directions: Route 1A north right into town.

Parking: Weekends and holidays, free in municipal lots, on streets, and in Museum Place Garage (enter on Liberty Street), which is two doors from Essex Institute and opposite Peabody Museum. Weekdays, garage free first half hour, 50 cents each half hour thereafter, $4 maximum. Weekdays in Ⓣ parking lot next to bus and train station, $1 maximum.

Ⓣ and train: From Haymarket, Ⓣ bus 450 or 455. From North Station (617/722–3200 or 800/392–6099), half hour on Rockport train; 6-block walk to town center.

Information: Open year round and daily, information and rest rooms at Salem Maritime National Historic site on Derby Street, 508/744–4323, and at the National Park Service visitors' information center (follow signs leading into town), 508/741–3648, in the Salem Armory on Essex at New Liberty

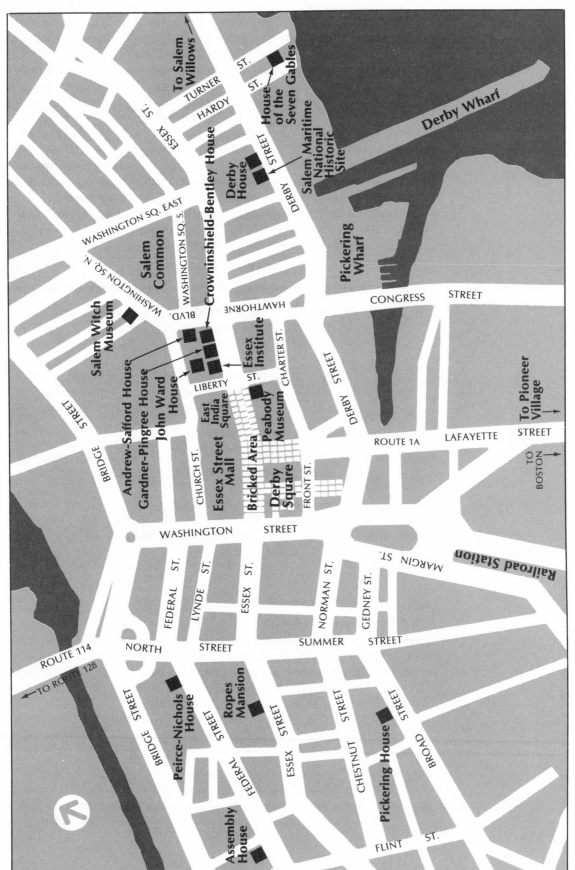

Salem

Street. The Chamber of Commerce, 32 Derby Square, between Pickering Wharf and Essex Street Mall, 508/744–0004, is open weekdays.

Picnicking: Salem Willows Park, page 215, and Winter Island Park, page 216.

Restaurants: Plenty including **Grand Turk Tavern**, 110 Derby Street, 508/745–7727, across from House of Seven Gables in a restored historic building with colonial atmosphere—tablecloths, fireplace, tin chandeliers. Menu with seafood, chicken, steak, pastas, moderate prices. Mexican specialties served 11:30–3 daily, 6–10 Monday–Saturday, at the bustling **In a Pig's Eye** (with bar), 148 Derby Street, 508/741–4436. **Caffe Graziani**, 133 Washington Street, 508/741–4282, open daily, serves homemade sandwiches, salads, pastas, soups. Traditional fare is at **Nathaniel's Restaurant** (508/744–4080 or 800/729–7829) in the Hotel Hawthorne, built in the 1920s and restored in 1987.

A GOOD WAY TO GET AROUND

Salem Trolley Corporation 59 Wharf Street

Phone: 508/744–5463.

Season: April–November.

Fee: All-day (10 a.m.–5 p.m.) pass includes discount tickets for some sites, stores, and restaurants. $8 adults, $3 ages 5–12, under 5 free, $7 senior citizens.

Boarding points: Visitor center and most attractions.

The one-hour narrated tour (could last all day if you get on and off at various sites) is on a trolley with both a driver and a guide, who are great resources for history and activities. (If you're researching the witch trials, they'll suggest the Essex Institute.) The continuous loop encompasses the area from Chestnut Street to Winter Island Park (gorgeous harbor view, park, beach, camping sites, electric and water hookups), where the lighthouse forms a great photographic backdrop.

Salem Maritime National Historic Site Derby Street

Phone: 508/744–4323.

Open: Year round daily, 8:30–5, in summer until 6.

Admission: Free.

Rest rooms: In the gray building at the end of the cobblestone driveway.

Demonstrations of shipbuilding skills and some hands-on activities are here at the site facing historic wharves (which may be closed off, depending on restoration work in progress). There's a 10-minute slide show about Massachusetts Bay's oldest seaport. Self-guided tours are available in the **Custom House,** which has an office once used by Nathaniel Hawthorne; in the **Bonded Warehouse** with its sample cargo; and in the **Scale House** with its weighing and measuring equipment. Rangers conduct 45-minute tours through the furnished merchant's **Derby House** (1762), and the seventeenth-century **Narbonne-Hale House** (architectural and archaeological focus).

Essex Institute 132 Essex Street, Salem 01970

Phone: 508/744–3390.

Open: Year round. May–November, Tuesday–Saturday 10–5, Sundays and holidays 12–5; also, June–October, Mondays 10–5, Thursday until 9 p.m. Daily house tours May–November. December–April, Tuesday–Sunday and holidays 12–5; house tours on weekends and holidays. Closed Thanksgiving, Christmas, New Year's Day.

Admission (guided tour of three houses and self-guided tour of galleries): $6 adults, $5 seniors, $3.50 ages 6–16. Free under age 6. Family rates available. Amex, MC, Visa.

★ Business meetings and social events.

This is a whole neighborhood: a city block with galleries, five historic houses, library, gardens and museum shop.

Visitors of all ages from all over the world come to see old dolls, toys, games, early uniforms, portraits, furniture, silver, and pottery. There is an audiovisual presentation. And you are allowed to use the heavy rubber mallet to strike the tall bell that was cast at the Paul Revere Company. The original Witch Trial documents are here. Guided house tours take you through three centuries of Salem's history. (Programs and tours are custom designed for specific age groups and interests.) Special exhibitions and programs are scheduled. In warm weather, the gardens—and an ice-cream parlor (with friendly staff) too—are enjoyed.

The Salem Witch Museum Washington Square
Phone: 508/744–1692.
Open: Year round, 10–5 daily, in summer until 7.
Admission: $4 adults, $2.50 ages 6–14, under 6 free. $3.50 senior citizens over 62. Group rates available.
Foreign languages: Translations available in French, German, Italian, Japanese, Spanish.
Handicapped access: Accessible.

Enter the stone Romanesque-style building across from the Common for an effective half-hour multisensory presentation (not a museum) about the witchcraft hysteria 300 years ago in Salem. In a darkened room with sound effects—even the wind doth blow—thirteen lighted life-sized stage settings explain some of the whys and wherefores of the witch trials, which led to the execution of twenty people.

House of the Seven Gables (1663) 54 Turner Street
Phone: 508/744–0991.
Parking: Free and plentiful.
Open: July and August, 9:30–5:30 daily. May, June, September–December, 10–4:30 daily. January–April, Monday–Saturday, 10–4:30, Sunday 12–4:30. Closed last two weeks of January, Thanksgiving, Christmas, New Year's Day.
Admission: For one-hour tour through the House of the Seven Gables and Nathaniel Hawthorne's Birthplace, $6.50 adults, $3 ages 6–12, $4 ages 13–17. Combination ticket with Pioneer Village (page 90): $9.50 adults, $5 ages 6–12, $6.50 ages 13–17. Group rates if prebooked for 10 or more. Proceeds support Settlement House.
Special programs and events: Spring lecture series. Educational programs for students. Summer evening presentations. Halloween week. December decor by twelve garden clubs.

The climb up the narrow, winding secret staircase is, for many, the most memorable part of this tour—which is not really geared for young children. An audiovisual presentation includes a very short version of the novel along with background information about the house, a neighborhood social work agency, one of the country's few original settlement houses still in operation.

Included is the low-ceilinged kitchen with beehive oven, the dining-room table set with blue and white Canton china, the attic with original beams, and the parlor with Hawthorne's desk and chair. Then you cross the compound to (furnished) Nathaniel Hawthorne's Birthplace where you get an idea of how he lived with his sea-captain dad (who went on long voyages), mom, and two siblings. Beyond the basic tour details, guides' expertise varies and may include information about Hawthorne, the Turners (who built the house), colonial lifestyles, and decorative arts.

Also on the grounds: a garden coffee shop, open May–October; small interior space, garden tables (some shaded). Eighteenth-century counting-house with office and push-button narrative that includes the origin of Venetian blinds. Lawns, chestnut trees, and nineteenth-century gardens. Sorry, no picnicking allowed.

Peabody Museum East India Square, Liberty and Essex Streets

Phone: 508/745–1876, 745–9500 (recorded message).

Parking: Garage across the mall, Liberty Street entrance.

Open: Year round, Monday–Saturday 10–5, Thursdays until 9. Sunday 12–5. Closed Thanksgiving, Christmas, New Year's Day. One-hour guided tours offered daily at 2.

Admission: $5 adults, $4 senior citizens and students with ID, $2.50 ages 6–16. $10 family rate. Group rates available.

Handicapped access: Elevator, rest rooms, telephone are accessible. Wheelchairs available.

Programs: Varied and extensive in the museum for all ages and in the classroom for students.

Strollers: Allowed.

★ Functions booked for organizations and corporations. No personal events.

If your children are museumgoers, this is worth a special trip. Step inside the reproduction saloon, and see the full-size cabin from *Cleopatra's Barge* (built in Salem in 1876). Enormous tusks on display are said to come from 150-year-old elephants. Here are ships' figureheads mounted along walls, ship models (in and out of bottles), nautical instruments, and bird and plants exhibits. Everything from flower holders to costumes to armor to ornate saddles is seen in the Chinese, Japanese, and Pacific Islands ethnological collections. Asian export arts—porcelain, gold, silver, paintings, furniture, and textiles—are in a spectacular wing built in 1988. The

Not sure where the town is? Check the map on page 2.

SALEM WITCH TRIALS TERCENTENARY MEMORIAL

Location: Between the Peabody Museum and the Essex Institute.

A place to reflect, to be reminded about injustice, tolerance, and understanding. You enter on stone engraved with excerpts from the pleas of innocence of accused persons. Some of their words are covered by a granite wall that has twenty cantilevered benches inscribed with the names of those who were executed. There's a view of the abutting Charter Street Burying Point, where John Hathorne, magistrate of the Witch Trials Court, is buried. And locust trees have been planted. Washington state–based multimedia artist Maggie Smith and architect James Cutler are responsible for the design, extraordinary in its simplicity, selected from a worldwide competition.

museum's collections of maritime history, ethnology, and natural history began in 1799, when the East India Marine Society was organized by a group of Salem captains and merchants.

Fine chocolate

Harbor Sweets 85 Leavitt Street, Salem 01970–5546
Phone: 508/745–7648.
Location: A 10-minute walk from Pickering Wharf to the end of Congress Street, then left onto Leavitt.

Visitors are fascinated with the history of this no-preservative specialty chocolate business, which started in Ben Strohecker's kitchen and basement. There on the wall of the small shop is a photograph of Ben's grandfather, the creator of a chocolate Easter rabbit, with a 6-foot version. Casual visitors are welcome to ask questions and to look into the production area, where you see the molds for custom pieces or for the nautically inspired Sweet Sloops and Sand Dollars. Informal 20-minute tours for groups (12 maximum) are scheduled year round during production hours. Yes, you are invited to taste.

A 5-minute drive from Salem center

Pioneer Village Forest River Park (Mailing address: c/o House of the Seven Gables Historic Site, 54 Turner Street, Salem, MA 01970)
Phone: 508/745–0525 (at Pioneer Village); 744–0991 (House of Seven Gables).
Open: Memorial Day weekend through October 31, Monday–Saturday 10–5, Sunday 12–5.
Directions: On Route 114/Lafayette Street, take West Street opposite Salem State College for .2 mile to park and village.
Admission: $4 adult, $3.50 senior citizens, $2.50 ages 6–12, $3.50 ages 13–17. Group rates available. Combination tickets with House of Seven Gables, see page 88.
Picnicking: Weekdays in the adjacent Forest River Park, page 215. (Park limited to residents only on summer weekends and holidays.)

"Do you really live here?" is the question young children most frequently ask the costumed guides who, during a one-hour tour, talk about the first settlement (1628) of the Massachusetts Bay Company and about the Salem (population 100) of 1630. The village, created in 1930 for a 300th anniversary pageant celebrating the arrival of John Winthrop, has been revitalized since closing for a few years in the mid-1980s. Among the twelve reproduction structures: two dugouts, an English wigwam (the English added thatching and chimneys to the style of the native Americans), thatched cottages (with straw- and cloth-filled mattresses), and the sparsely furnished two-story governor's house. Sometimes a blacksmith is working in the forge. Herbs and vegetables are growing in the period gardens. There are three sheep, two goats, and in the pond many ducks; cracked corn is sold, or bring your own feed.

Sandwich and the Canal Area

FOR A TASTE OF THE CAPE IN A DAY

"Tis a wonderful thing to sweeten the world which is in a jam and needs preserving."

—THORNTON W. BURGESS TO IDA PUTNAM

Location: 65 miles south of Boston.

Directions: I–93 south to Route 3 south, to the canal. Cross the Sagamore Bridge and take Route 6A east.

Restaurants: Simple Fare on Route 6A is just that—simple and reasonable. At **Captain Scott's** on Tupper Road next to the Sandwich Boat Basin, they serve everything from broiled seafood to steaks and chicken. Eat in the dining room or on covered deck. At **Horizons,** open April through October and located at Town Neck Beach, you overlook the beach, the canal entrance, and all of Cape Cod Bay. Sandwiches and fried food at lunch. Seafood dinners in the evening in main second-floor dining room. The **Daniel Webster Inn** (fine dining and lodging) has a fireplaced and paneled dining room, another with a brass chandelier, and a third that is a plant-filled conservatory overlooking gardens.

Sandwich, settled in 1637, is the oldest town on Cape Cod. Along Route 6A are several interesting stops. See the long pools filled with various sizes of brook, brown, and rainbow trout at the **state fish hatchery.** No charge. Open year round, 9–3:30 daily. . . . Near the cranberry bogs there's **Green Briar Nature Center and Jam Kitchen** at 6 Discovery Hill Road, 508/888–6870; nature center open spring through fall, Monday–Saturday 10–4 and Sunday 1–4, closed winter Sundays and Mondays. Donation appreciated. You are welcome to walk trails, none more than a mile long, in the Old Briar Patch that inspired Thornton Burgess when he was a boy. The 1903 kitchen, a working museum open mid-June through mid-December, prepares forty products, including relishes and cranberry items. Jams and jellies are made on stove burners lined up two by two. The specialty, a one-of-a-kind in the entire country, is a fruit topping that is solar cooked by the sun via a European method adapted by Burgess's friend Ida Putnam, who taught Martha Blake, who owned and operated the kitchen for several decades until 1979. Ms. Blake, now in her nineties, delights in volunteering in the kitchen every Wednesday. (Proceeds support the Thornton W. Burgess Society.) . . . **Titcomb's Bookshop** has expanded into a marvelous three-leveled barn built by the Titcombs' sons (a wrought-iron craftsman and a physicist) to look like the postcard picture of the original barn. Outside there's a steel statue of Ben Franklin. Inside there are "used, old used, collectible, rare, out-of-print books" along with new regional and children's books. Plenty of comfortable chairs too. (And, if you inquire, you might hear an enthusiastic report about Nancy Titcomb's daily morning beach walk.) . . . The **Wing Fort House** (1641), on Spring Hill Road (opposite Quaker Meetinghouse

The **Cape Cod Canal** area spans a 4-mile stretch between the Sagamore and Bourne bridges. For a close look, take Route 6 at the Sagamore Bridge and stop at the herring run, page 274.

Or use the level service roads (no cars allowed) that run on each side of the canal for walking, cycling, jogging, pushing a stroller, picnicking, and watching passing freighters, tankers, tugs, and barges. Crossing one of the bridges is an experience in itself—more frightening to many adults than to children.

Late June through August the U.S. Army Corps of Engineers runs **free** day and evening **guided walks, bike/hikes** (usually Saturday mornings) and **campfires** for families. For a schedule of programs, call 508/759–5991. Come with sturdy shoes, hats, and insect repellent.

Road), is furnished with Wing family antiques from different periods of its 300-year history. No hands-on possibilities, but the 30- to 60-minute visit does give a feel for the Cape lifestyle of years gone by. Open mid-June through September. Admission: $1 adults, $.25 under age 12.

Summer parking **in the center of Sandwich** is difficult. Find one place, stop into a local shop for a free walking tour brochure, explore and enjoy. Some attractions:

Underground spring: Next to Town Hall. Even lit for evening use! It's been flowing for hundreds of years. Bring a jug and fill up. Delicious and free. . . . From mid-June through early fall, Monday–Saturday 10–4:45, Sunday 1–4:45, the miller grinds organically grown corn into meal (sold in cloth bags) in the restored (1654) **Dexter's Grist Mill** on a pretty site with fieldstone wall and old English garden. The "historic and mechanical" tour lasts about 25 minutes. . . . **Hoxie House**, a restored saltbox, said to be the oldest (1637) on Cape Cod, is also open to the public. Tickets: for one place (the mill or the house), $1.50 adult, $.75 child; combination tickets for both places, $2.50 adult, $1 child.

Yesterday's Museum: Two floors of an old church filled with hundreds of beautifully costumed dolls in labeled glass cases, furnished Nuremberg kitchens, tiny shops, and miniature rooms. (That's a lot of looking! Plan to stay about an hour.) Special exhibits change and might include Lionel and American Flyer model trains or lead soldiers from World Wars I and II. Strollers allowed; exhibits geared to adults. Open mid-May through October, Monday–Saturday 10–4. Admission $3 adults, $2.50 seniors, $2 ages 11 and under. No charge for shop that sells antique and collectible dolls. Appraisal and repair service also offered.

The Thornton W. Burgess Museum: At 4 Water Street (508/888–4668) on Shawme Pond, a picture-book setting with swans and aggressive ducks that like to be fed. Inside the restored 1756 home, exhibits change from time to time. Children can look at original Burgess manuscripts and Harrison Cady's original illustrations. There are animal costumes to try on. More hands-on activities being developed. Donation appreciated.

Sandwich Glass Museum: Lovely shapes and colors, and rare pieces handsomely displayed in well-lit cases and windows. The beautiful collections are arranged in sequence of production, from 1825 to 1888. A scaled diorama of the Boston and Sandwich Glass Works depicts the stages of

"How does the corn become corn meal and what can you make with it?"
—MANY YOUNG VISITORS

glassmaking. Not a child's paradise, but school-aged children can learn on a treasure hunt, locating objects in the galleries. Open daily 9:30–4:30 April–October; Wednesday–Sunday 9:30–4 November–March. Admission is $3 adults, $.50 ages 6–12, under 6 free.

A mile down Grove Street from the glass museum

Heritage Plantation Grove and Pine Streets, Sandwich 02563–0566
Phone: 508/888–3300.

Open: Mid-May until Mid-October, 10–5 daily. (Sorry, no dogs allowed.)

Admission: $7 adults, $6 age 60 and older, $3.50 ages 6–18. Age 5 and under free. Group rates available.

Eating: Light breakfast, lunch, or snacks in cafe. Picnicking in the pine grove; No fires allowed.

Programs: Cultural events throughout the summer, and an extensive educational outreach program.

Allow a couple of hours to ride the open-air shuttle or walk (walking shoes recommended) through the meticulously maintained seventy-six acres, an indoor-outdoor museum of Americana and horticulture. Internationally recognized rhododendrons are in their glory in June. More than a thousand varieties of trees, shrubs, and flowers flourish here. Among the antique cars in the Round Barn is a Model T that you're allowed to sit in. (A photo opportunity!) Other beautifully displayed collections include Currier and Ives prints, cigar-store figures, weathervanes, trade signs, toys, and antique tools. Several buildings are air conditioned. The windmill that ground Orleans's grain for most of the nineteenth century provides a backdrop for photographs. A highlight for all ages: a ride on the 1912 restored carousel in its glass-walled rotunda.

For the "real" Cape, **walk a boardwalk** across marsh and creek to beach and dunes. When the generations-old boardwalk, site of many memories including weddings, was damaged by 1991 storms, townspeople "bought" new planks, received deeds, and had their own varied and sometimes cryptic messages inscribed. To see for yourself, from the only traffic light in Sandwich, turn left onto Jarvis Street to the end, then left on Factory Road to end. Turn right and wind around to the parking lot and boardwalk.

Wayside Inn Area

A SMALL OPEN AREA, A MIXTURE OF HISTORY AND ARCHITECTURE, ON WAYSIDE INN ROAD

Location: Sudbury, 20 miles west of Boston.

Directions: Follow Route 20 west, and you're there. Or take the Mass. Pike to Route 128 (I–95) north, to exit 49 (Route 20 west), for 11 miles.

Combination idea: Drive about 7 minutes to see Clydesdale horses, page 29.

Admission: For mill and schoolhouse, contributions accepted.

Tour: Brochure of self-guided walking tour of entire property available at the front door.

Even if the reproduction (1929) early American **gristmill** just off of Boston Post Road (Route 20) is closed, you'll have lots of company of all ages on the lawn (perfect for picnicking) and in the fields. In late spring, beside the path that leads from the mill along Hop Brook, there's often snow in the woods. Frequently the mill is used as a backdrop for wedding photographs. The miller/interpreter is on duty April through November, Wednesday–Sunday, usually 9–5. Most grinding—when the 2,000-pound millstone is turned by the waterwheel—takes place on weekend afternoons.

Also part of the Wayside Inn property, across the street from the mill:
★ The **Martha-Mary Chapel,** open by appointment and scene of hundreds of weddings every year. It was built from timber felled on the hill in the hurricane of 1938. . . . The **Red Schoolhouse,** attended by Mary and her little lamb, was built in Sterling, Massachusetts, in 1798, and was in actual use until 1952. Summers, from noon till 5, the schoolmistress/interpreter greets you.

If you're in the area at dusk, you may see the oil lamps being lit outside the **Wayside Inn** (508/443–8846). First licensed as a "house of public entertainment" for travelers in 1716, the inn, having known time and fire, is part original and part restored. It's open year round except Christmas. Dinner guests are welcome to look through the rooms, which are furnished with antique furnishings and Oriental rugs, but after 6 the light isn't good. On the grounds, to the right as you face the inn, is a quiet spot, a walled rose garden, complete with benches and a path leading to a bust of Longfellow.

Picnickers who are hankering for ice cream usually drive five minutes west to the (1790) Country Store complex. The parking area has lots of cone lickers but not too much atmosphere. The Country Store sells gift items, pickles from a barrel, and freshly made baked goods. Suspended from the ceiling are some antique tools and a plank from the Longfellow spreading chestnut tree. Nostalgia seekers enter the Olde Tyme Penny Candy shop to find glass jars filled with candy buttons, licorice whips, gum drops, miniature jelly beans, and lots more; a very few items do sell for one cent.

Historic Sites

Photo by Deborah Schenck

In Boston

Several historic sites in Boston that are not part of designated trails are in the Back Bay (page 126), and Beacon Hill (page 131).

Freedom Trail

Information: The National Park Service has visitor centers at 15 State Street (below) and in the Charlestown Navy Yard (page 108).

Parking: The best place is in Charlestown at the navy yard, page 107. Elsewhere, particularly in downtown Boston, parking demands time, luck, and often the expense of a garage.

Ⓣ: Most downtown sites are within short walking distance of one another, and near a Ⓣ stop. The water shuttle is the best way to get to the Charlestown sites by Ⓣ.

Open: Hours of inside sites vary from site to site. During the summer, most are open daily.

Admission: Most sites are free. Fees are charged at the Old South Meeting House, the Old State House, and the Paul Revere House.

The trail covers a 3-mile stretch—sixteen historic sites—in downtown Boston and Charlestown. Tourists, with eyes on maps and feet on red-brick or painted sidewalk lines, sometimes miss the blend of rooflines, the ghosts of painted signs on old buildings, and opportunities to people-watch.

The trail combines the resources of federal, state, city, and private organizations.

Freedom Trail sites are neither numbered nor sequential, so the trail can be picked up at any point. . . . It's possible to go in and out of the buildings and completely cover the trail in one exhausting day. But the city invites diversion, and it's okay to take detours! . . . Determined tourists find the most direct route for a complete tour begins at the State House or the Charlestown Navy Yard. Most visitors—with or without children—choose the navy yard, the sure way to see the USS *Constitution*. . . . Those with limited energy—or young children—may find the urban North End most fascinating, the harborside navy yard (with its Harborwalk) a day trip in itself.

IN THE CITY, THE RECOMMENDED FIRST STOP

Boston National Historical Park Visitor Center 15 State Street

Phone: 617/242–5642.

Directions: Across from the Old State House, 1 block from Faneuil Hall (away from the waterfront).

Ⓣ: State station on the Orange or Blue Line.

Open: Year round, 9–5 daily, until 6 in summer. Closed Thanksgiving, Christmas, and New Year's.

Educational programs: Call for current arrangements.

Helpful staff, free maps, plenty of printed information (some in French, Spanish, Italian, German, and Japanese), and welcome rest rooms. Check downstairs (in person only) for brochures on other sites in New England and on national parks all over the country. From here decide whether you'll walk to the State House (and conclude with a ride on the swan boats) or in

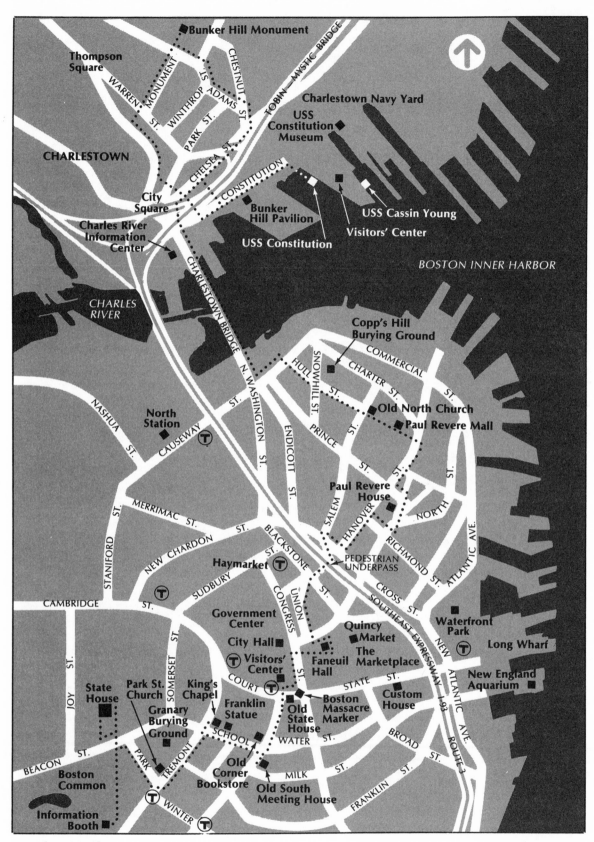

Freedom Trail

the opposite direction to more varied territory—by the Marketplace, through the North End, and on to the navy yard.

On historic Beacon Hill

State House Beacon Street at Park

Phone: 617/727–3676.

Open: Weekdays, except legal holidays, 9–5.

Handicapped access: Entrance on Bowdoin Street.

Average stay: Depending on interests, this could be a major stop—1½ to 2 hours.

Admission: Free.

Tours: Self-guided tour brochure at information desk. Free guided 45-minute tours (include history of building, Massachusetts' legislative process, and new reception area) are available year round, weekdays, except holidays, from 10 to 4. Available in Spanish, French, German, Italian, Portuguese, Chinese, Japanese, and Greek. Individuals are welcome to join a group. *Groups:* Please call ahead if more than 5 people. Schools should make at least 3 weeks' advance booking for spring. For appointments and information, call 617/727–3676 or write to the State House, Room 194, Boston 02133.

Open sessions: Meetings of the legislature and committee hearings are open to the public. For the schedule, call 617/727-2860 or check at the *information desk* at the top of the main steps in Doric Hall.

What was once John Hancock's pasture is now the site of a gold-domed building with impressive marble staircases and Bulfinch architectural details everywhere. The carved **Sacred Cod** still hangs in the House of Representatives, a reminder of one of the first major industries in the state. Topping the columned Doric Hall: a stained-glass skylight with the state seal.

You could spend some time in the house and senate; even when they're not in session, you can look at the roll board and think about procedures. In the Legislative Document Room, Room 428, are microfilms of newspapers dating back to the 1800s.

Across from Boston Common

Park Street Church Tremont and Park Streets

Phone: 617/523–3383.

Open: July and August, Tuesday–Saturday 9–12 and 12:30–3:30. Closed July 4.

Average stay: 10–15 minutes.

Admission: Free.

Handicapped access: Elevator available.

It's a two-flight climb to the sanctuary, whose spire and clock have been landmarks since 1810. When the town granary occupied the site, the sails for the USS *Constitution* were made here. Parishioners of 1829 heard William Lloyd Garrison give his first antislavery address. And two years later they heard the first public performance of "America." Sunday service in summer: 10:30. Other months: 9 and 10:45 a.m., 6 p.m.

Right next to the church

Granary Burying Ground Tremont Street

Ⓣ: Park Street.

Open: Daylight hours.

Once part of the Boston Common, this burial ground had several names before settling on "Granary"—after the granary that was on the site of the neighboring Park Street Church. More than 2,000 graves are here, including those of John Hancock, Paul Revere, Robert Treat Paine, and Samuel Adams. When the victims of the Boston Massacre were laid to rest here, 3,000 colonists came to honor them. Now, on some summer days, another 3,000 visitors come to this burial ground.

Across from the Parker House

King's Chapel 58 Tremont Street (corner of School)

Phone: 617/523–1749.

Ⓣ: Park Street.

Open: Year round, Tuesday–Saturday 10–4, with Tuesday recitals at 12:15, a church service Wednesdays at 12:15, and public readings Thursdays at 12:15. (Not open when used for church functions such as weddings or funerals.) Sunday services are at 11.

Admission: Free.

Handicapped access: Building is accessible; pews are a bit high for wheelchairs.

The solid gray Quincy granite exterior gives little hint of the striking beauty inside this living church. You are in a place with a history of "firsts"—King's Chapel was the first church of England in the Massachusetts Bay Colony, the first Unitarian church in America, the first church to use organ music. Its bell was made by Paul Revere; the governor's pew was used by George Washington. It is the oldest stone church in Boston. The 4-foot-thick walls were built in the 1750s around the original wooden structure, while the church was still in use. (Upon hearing that, some children say it was built in papier-mache style.) The steeple isn't pointed because the congregation ran out of money.

The first cemetery in town, the adjacent city-owned **Burying Ground** (not associated with the church), includes the graves of Governor Winthrop, Reverend John Cotten, and one gravestone written in French. Surprise: The large cryptlike structure near the church is a vent for the MBTA.

In back of King's Chapel, on the Old City Hall grounds

Benjamin Franklin Statue School Street

The statue dates back to 1856. The four bronze panels at its base show Franklin in several of his main areas of involvement—as a Founding Father, signing the Declaration of Independence; as a diplomat, signing a treaty

CITY CARPET

Every year, thousands of tourists and many Bostonians walk, hop, and skip on the hopscotch imbedded in the School Street sidewalk of Old City Hall. With brass letters, ceramic pieces, Venetian glass mosaic, even marbles, it tells the story of the Boston Latin School, America's first public school, built on this site in 1635. Designed and implemented by Lilli Ann Killen Rosenberg in 1983, this Freedom Trail surprise includes an alphabet, games of the period, and students' names—Samuel Adams, John Hancock, and Benjamin Franklin.

with France; as a printer; and as an inventor, experimenting with lightning and electricity.

Old Corner Bookstore Washington (formerly Cornhill) and School Streets
Phone: 617/523–6658.
Open: Monday–Saturday 9–6. Sundays 12–6.

Step into this literary landmark, which sells books about New England, travel guides, and worldwide maps. By design, the setting is a replica of what photographs suggested a nineteenth-century bookstore looked like. Oliver Wendell Holmes's desk is on display. This building has seen various uses—from apothecary shop and home (1718) to pizza parlor (1960)—and was, in the mid-nineteenth century, the country's leading bookselling and publishing house, Tichnor and Fields. (Sometimes, first editions are for sale here.) It was also the gathering place for literary figures like Holmes, Longfellow, Lowell, Whittier, and Hawthorne. Hear ye, architecture aficionados: Since becoming Globe Corner Bookstore in 1982, the shop has expanded by reversing the staircase so that "upstairs" is actually the second floor of the *adjoining* building.

"With those headphones, you feel like you're in the meeting. I almost raised my hand!"

—JOHN, WEST HARTFORD, CONN.

Old South Meeting House 310 Washington Street
Phone: 617/482–6439.
Directions: On the corner of Milk Street, 2 blocks north (toward Government Center) of Filene's and its renowned basement.
Ⓣ: State station on the Orange or Blue Line.
Open: April–October, 9:30–5 daily. November–March, 10–4 weekdays, 10–5 weekends. Closed Thanksgiving, December 24 and 25, and January 1.
Admission: $2.50 adults, $2 students and seniors, $1 children 6–18. Under 6 free.

This is a museum. When you step in, it looks like the meeting house it was. But you'll have to walk around the perimeter of the box pews to experience the low-placed exhibits. There are headphones that have a recorded seventeenth-century church service complete with child whispering to his mother. Another tape is of the famous Boston Tea Party, using the actual text. One exhibit explains what it was like when the British tore out the pews during the Revolution and established a riding academy here. You learn about the saving of Old South from the great fire of 1872 and, shortly thereafter, from demolition. Visiting school groups role play as Loyalists and Patriots.

Special events: Concert or lecture included in admission, October–April, Thursdays, 12:15. Dramatic presentations, April and October evenings. In summer, an old-fashioned town meeting in the park across the street.

Nearby: Between Old South Meeting House and Filene's Basement is Barnes & Noble's expanded store with a children's play area.

Across from the National Park Service visitor center

Old State House 206 Washington Street (actually in the middle of State Street)

Phone: 617/720–3290.

Ⓣ: On the Orange or Blue Line: State station—right under the Old State House.

Open: 9:30–5 daily. Closed Easter, Thanksgiving, Christmas, and New Year's.

Admission: $2 adults, $1.50 older adults and students, $.75 ages 6–18; under age 6 and all Massachusetts school children are free.

Average stay: 30 minutes.

Handicapped access: Partial.

Tours: Schedule group tours in advance.

After climbing the circular staircase to the second floor of this (now climate-controlled) museum, visitors can stand near the balcony where laws were proclaimed. It's a good vantage point for the site of the Boston Massacre. The building was once the seat of colonial government; it reopened in 1992 after undergoing a major preservation project. The history of the Old State House is seen in a video theater. There's a rocking horse, a Polly Sumner doll, a ship's figurehead, a USS *Constitution* model, and rotating exhibits that include firefighting in Boston, inns and taverns, and Boston during the Revolution. Outside are the gables, among the photographed architectural details in Boston, that still bear the lion and unicorn emblems of England.

Faneuil Hall Dock Square

Phone: 617/242–5642.

Ⓣ: State station on the Orange or Blue Line; Government Center on the Green or Blue Line.

Open: Year round, 9–5 daily except Thanksgiving, Christmas, and New Year's. **Armory** on the top (fourth) floor open weekdays 10–4.

Admission: Free.

Handicapped access: Accessible.

This is the real Faneuil Hall, the "Cradle of Liberty" that lends its name to the entire Marketplace. If you climb (or take the new elevator) to the second floor, you'll meet the lone interpreter/ranger, who gives 15-minute talks; and you will see the hall where eighteenth-century town meetings were held and where open meetings still take place today. In contrast to the active street scene outside, the atmosphere of the hall, especially in winter, encourages contemplative moments.

"Book" was, according to the family, Kenneth Gloss's first word. Kenneth, now father of two school-aged children, was born the year after his parents bought the **Brattle Book Shop**, the antiquarian book shop founded in 1825. Although he trained as a chemist, Kenneth, having spent many an hour with his father in The Search for old books, became a bookseller/lecturer/appraiser. Year round, he stocks thousands of $1 volumes in sidewalk stalls. Inside there are three floors with old postcards and magazines, general books, posters, children's books, and rare and expensive volumes. The Brattle Book Shop is at 9 West Street (between Boston Common Information Booth and Lafayette Place on Washington Street), 617/542–0210 or 800/447–9595.

The building, recently reopened with updated systems and climate control throughout, was built in 1742, burned in 1763, and enlarged in 1806. Atop it sits the grasshopper, forged in 1742 by Shem Drowne, maker of colonial weathervanes. To comply with the wishes of donor Peter Faneuil, the ground floor still has markets.

For more than two hundred years the top floor has been home to the Ancient and Honorable Artillery Company, chartered "as a nursery for soldiers and a school for officers" in 1638. In the freshly painted armory are displays of colonial uniforms and arms, polished artifacts, reframed paintings, and early flags with as many as fifteen stripes. ("Thank you for not touching.")

THE BILL OF RIGHTS WALKWAY

Thousands of brass letters, spelling out the Bill of Rights, are imbedded in the concrete in front of the Suffolk County Courthouse in Pemberton Square. From City Hall Plaza, cross Tremont Street and walk up the steps of Three Center Plaza to join many tourists who come to see and read. Artists: Lilli Ann and Marvin Rosenberg.

Facing Faneuil Hall

Quincy Market Dock Square

Ⓣ: State station on the Orange or Blue Line; Government Center on the Green or Blue Line.

Open: Year round, daily.

Beware. If you are a people-watcher and/or a shopper, you may never get very far beyond this Freedom Trail point. America's first real estate development of its kind has stalls that still sell—mostly in the ready-to-eat form—produce, cheese, poultry, meat, and much more (see page 134).

In the North End

Paul Revere House 19 North Square (between Richmond and Prince)

Phone: 617/523–2338.

Ⓣ: Haymarket on the Orange or Green Line, then a 10-minute walk.

Open: November through mid-April, 9:30–4:15 daily, except closed Mondays January–March. Mid-April through November, 9:30–5:15 daily. Closed Thanksgiving, Christmas, New Year's.

Average stay: 15–30 minutes. (Early afternoons, summer and fall, are particularly busy.)

Admission: $2 adults, $1.50 seniors and college students with ID, $.75 ages 5–17. Under age 5, active duty military, and other museum professionals with ID are free. Disabled visitors, half price. (Slightly higher fees on Christmas open house weekend.)

Special programs (included in admission fee): Saturday afternoons, May through October. Perhaps period music or demonstrations by a colonial tailor or a silversmith.

Foreign languages: Brochures available in English, Japanese, French, Spanish, Italian, and German.

Handicapped access: First floor is accessible by wheelchair; alternative interpretations of inaccessible areas are available. Tactile tours for the blind; large-print brochures for sight impaired.

Paul Revere was living here when he went on his famous express ride in April 1775. Built around 1680 and already ninety years old when purchased by Revere, this house is the oldest building in downtown Boston. Most of Revere's sixteen children (with two different wives) lived here at one time or another. The self-guided tour gives a feel for seventeenth- and eighteenth-century home life and for the events surrounding the life of Revere. In addition to the period rooms, there are changing exhibits that may include information about Revere's ride or early views of the Revere House, Revere silver, or some new information uncovered by ongoing research.

Next door, at 29 North Square, is the **Moses Pierce–Nathaniel Hichborn House** (1711), with tours (30–60 minutes) at 12:30 and 2:30 any day that the Paul Revere House is open. *Admission*: Same as Paul Revere House; or combination tickets available.

Following the Freedom Trail from here to the Old North Church, you first come to **Paul Revere Mall** on Hanover Street. It's a few steps down to the small park, where thirteen bronze tablets set in the walls tell the part played by the people of the North End in Boston's history from 1630 to 1918.

Steps at the far end of the mall lead to

Old North Church 193 Salem Street

Phone: 617/523–6676.

Directions: Parking is difficult. But if you are driving, take Causeway Street to Hull Street; go up over the hill and down to the church.

Walking from Hanover Street, find St. Stephen's Church (look for its white spire), cross the street, and walk through the mall to Old North.

Ⓣ: Haymarket on the Orange or Green Line, then a 10-minute walk.

Open: Year round, 9–5 daily. Sunday services at 9 (½ hour), 11 (1 hour), and 4 (½ hour).

Admission: Free.

Handicapped access: Accessible through the main entrance.

Staffers may point out the 1724 brass chandelier or the 1726 clock (the oldest working clock in a public building in the country), or the David Moore organ installed in 1992 in a 1759 Johnston organ case. Often there is some discussion about the role of the church in the Revolution—familiar details and new ones.

This gracious, well-maintained structure, Boston's oldest church, was built in 1723. Visitors can sit in the box pews marked with names of revolutionary parishioners, but the narrow steeple isn't open to the public. The old bells, still rung every Sunday at noon, were rung by Paul Revere when he was a fifteen-year-old member of the Bell Ringers' Guild, and later they signaled Cornwallis's surrender at Yorktown.

Replicas of the two lanterns that were displayed in the steeple on April 18, 1775, to signal the redcoats' leaving for Lexington and Concord are in the small museum next to the church.

A block away

Copp's Hill Burying Ground Snowhill and Charter Streets

Directions: From the front door of the Old North Church it's a 3-minute walk up Hull Street. (Directly across from the Hull Street gate is the narrowest house in Boston—only 9 feet 6 inches wide.)

Open: Daylight hours.

Located in an area with streets that were laid out in the seventeenth and early eighteenth centuries, the second oldest burial ground in Boston has thousands of grave markers, 150 of which were carved in the seventeenth century. Weather and time have worn away many of the names, but some gravestones illustrate changes in philosophical or theological concepts. And some show bullet marks from the muskets of the British, who used them as practice targets during the siege of Boston. The site offers a dramatic view of the harbor and "Old Ironsides." (Go through the cemetery to spend some time—maybe with a snack—on Copp's Hill Terrace, page 143.)

USS *Constitution* Page 108.

Bunker Hill Monument and Museum Page 111.

"Something different and interesting to do."

—TOURISTS FROM EVERYWHERE

Walking the Freedom Trail? The **Charles River Information Center** is on the way, near the Charlestown Bridge. Open year round, 9–3 weekdays, it is a place for learning about the river and watching the activity on it. Push a button and activate a 12-minute multimedia show that dramatically explains flood control and the water level in the Charles River Basin. (Visitors who do not live in New England are often surprised to learn that Boston Harbor tides—the difference between the high and low average—are 9½ feet.) The observation window overlooks three locks: two for pleasure boats and one for commercial vessels.

Directions, via an interesting route over the locks: From Boston, instead of crossing over the Charlestown Bridge, walk 1 block along Causeway Street toward the Boston Garden. Turn right on Beverly Street and walk into the parking lot of the dam. Continue across walks of locks (careful not to stand on movable gates) to Paul Revere Landing (possibly signed). Follow stairs to flag poles and visitors' entrance. Group tours offered; please see page 260.

**Just off the
Freedom Trail**

*Between
Government Center
and Massachusetts
General Hospital*

History comes to life

Harrison Gray Otis House 141 Cambridge Street, Boston 02114
Phone: 617/227–3956.

Open: Year round, Tuesday–Friday 12–5, Saturday 10–5.

Tours: On the hour; last tour at 4 p.m. $4 adults, $2 ages 12 and under.

You see two floors of high-style 1796–1820 Boston living during the 45-minute tour. The first of three homes designed for Otis, a Boston mayor, lawyer, and Congressman, this is the headquarters for the Society for the Preservation of New England Antiquities (SPNEA), the country's largest regional preservation organization.

"Unknown Hands," one of the SPNEA education department's acclaimed participatory programs, is conducted for school groups and others who have requested the opportunity to role-play. Players take the parts of 1810 Beacon Hill residents—artisans, servants, or merchants. They are guided through Otis's house by "house servants." They practice crafts and skills in a plaster workshop. And they explore "their own" Beacon Hill neighborhood and the daily lifestyles of 200 years ago. Among other SPNEA programs: **"Classic Times: Pompeii through Today,"** focusing on architecture.

Black Heritage Trail

Tours: 90-minute guided tours led by National Park Service, 617/742–5415. Or self-guided; brochure available at African Meeting House.

Plaques tell the stories of fourteen Beacon Hill churches, schools, and homes that belonged, from revolutionary times to the early twentieth century, to the community of free blacks.

The **African Meeting House** on Smith Court (off Joy Street, just up from Cambridge Street) is the oldest black church in New England. This is where William Lloyd Garrison founded the New England Anti-Slavery Society in 1832 and began the American abolitionist movement. Near the meetinghouse, also on Smith Court, are the **Abiel Smith School,** a landmark in the struggle for quality education for black children, and the **Smith Court Residences,** five houses typical of the homes occupied by black Bostonians throughout the nineteenth century.

There are three sites on Pinckney Street. The **George Middleton House** at numbers 5 and 7 is one of the oldest wooden structures on Beacon Hill. The **Phillips School** at the corner of Anderson was integrated in 1855. And the **John J. Smith House** at number 86, near West Cedar Street, was the home of a Massachusetts legislator.

At Mt. Vernon and Charles streets, the **Charles Street Meeting House,** recycled into a multiuse building, was originally built for a white congregation. Bought by a black congregation after the Civil War, it was the last black institution to leave the hill. The **Lewis Hayden House** at 66 Phillips Street (near Charles Street Circle) was the home of a leader of the abolitionist movement. At the other end of Phillips, toward Government Center, is **Coburn's Gaming House** at number 2.

On the Common, just across from the State House, is the **Robert Gould Shaw and 54th Regiment Memorial.** The bas-relief, by Augustus Saint-Gaudens, depicts the first black division from the North in the Civil War. Shaw, the leader, was white.

Charlestown Navy Yard

Location: Constitution Road, Charlestown.

Plan to spend varied hours and very little (or no) money here. Why rush just to cover an agenda? Those who come on a time-limited tour wish they could stay longer. Here, at the site of the largest preservation effort in the United States, much, in and out of the National Park, is open to the public— including the *Constitution,* Boston's number one historical attraction.

It's a big place. Warships were built here between 1800 and 1974. At the yard's peak, fifty thousand people worked here. Now there are museums, recreation areas, a grand waterfront walk, gardens, and housing.

Parking: (Reminder: Because the interchange of I–93 and Route 1 as well as the surface roads in Charlestown are under construction, there may be detours.) *Meters* on navy yard streets are in operation 9–6 weekdays only; free on weekends. Enter *garage* in yard by driving one gate past main Constitution and Shipyard Park gate. $6 all day or $1 for every half hour. On foot from garage to *Constitution:* Take Second Avenue between 9th and 5th streets, the completed granite walkway with shade trees, period benches, annual plantings, and Bishop's Crook lighting. *Or* take—

Free shuttle bus: Five-minute ride within the navy yard runs between the shuttle dock at Pier 4, the parking garage, and the Constitution; 10–6 weekends and holidays, and 6 a.m.–8 p.m. weekdays; not between 9:30 and 10:30 or between 3 and 4.

Ⓣ: Best by water, page 233. Ⓣ bus 93 from Haymarket (617/722–3200 for schedule.) Or by subway, Orange or Green Line to North Station, 15-minute walk along Freedom Trail across Charlestown Bridge.

Rest rooms: In National Park Visitor Center.

Dogs: Allowed on a leash; not unattended and not in buildings or on ships.

Eating: Plenty of benches in the navy yard, many by the water, for picnicking. The **Atrium Cafe** (there's no sign) in Building 149, opposite the parking garage, is best bet for nonpicnickers. Lovely atrium setting on first floor. Cafeteria style. Eat here or take out. Hot hors d'oeuvres, deli bar, light snacks, yogurt, salads. Weekdays 7–6 with half-hour breaks between meals; busy at lunch. Hours vary on Saturdays; closed Sundays. Snack food sold at **Shipyard Galley** (closed in winter) near *Constitution*. **Convenience Store** (617/242–6089) sells some groceries, ice cream bars, hot soups, $2.99 salad bar. **Blossoms** (617/242–1911), an upscale cafe at Second Avenue and 6th Street, serves imaginative soups, salads, burgers, hot specialties for lunch or takeout; dinners Friday and Saturday, closed Sunday. Enjoy a cool beverage and spectacular sunsets from the deck of **Marley's Landing Restaurant** (617/241–7755) on Pier 6.

"Doing" the Freedom Trail? In addition to "Old Ironsides" and the Bunker Hill monument, the two Charlestown Freedom Trail sites, there is much to see and do in the navy yard. With or without children, if you start here while you are fresh enough to savor the Charlestown waterfront, don't be surprised if this is as far as you get. . . . Logical add-ons: the North End, page 141, and Faneuil Hall, page 134. If you choose to park at the navy yard for the Freedom Trail, the best way to return to your car is via the water shuttle, page 234.

Boston National Historical Park: Charlestown Navy Yard

National Park Service Visitor Center

Phone: 617/242–5601.

Open: Year round, 9–5 daily except Thanksgiving, Christmas, and New Year's.

Handicapped access: Help is available.

Special programs: All free. Some offered in summer or on weekends only. July and August, **Navy yard tours** twice daily. **Commandant's house** was built in 1805 and changed over the years. Not antiques-filled. Tours, not really for children, May–October, 1st, 3rd, and 5th Sundays at 12:30, 1:30, and 2:30. **Navy Yard Museum** tour given year round in old paint shop that now has displays of processes developed here, such as the die-lock chain, last made here in 1973 just before the shipyard closed.

Plenty of information (including free maps) about the navy yard and other Freedom Trail sites. Also here: ship models in hallways, a ten-minute slide show on navy yard history, other videos on request.

    Naval fleets—about fifteen to twenty a year—**from around the world** dock here, spring through fall, and provide public viewing hours. Call 617/242–5601 to inquire about the country of origin, the type of ship, and visiting hours. No charge.

    Depending on the weather—not when it is cold and wet—free tours of the destroyer **USS *Cassin Young*** include the narrow passageways, the cramped crew's quarters, the eating area, and the pilot house.

On the Freedom Trail

USS *Constitution*

    Ordinarily, "Old Ironsides" is open to the public for 25–minute tours 9–3:50 every day of the year (little to no wait if you come early in the morning). Top deck is open daily 9:30–sunset. The 44-gun frigate, launched in 1797 and undefeated in twenty-four battles, is still a commissioned U.S. Navy ship. Visitors see hammock beds, the dentist/surgeon/barber "all-purpose" chair, and the galley where soups and stews were cooked for more than four hundred men. Crew members help young children on the steep stairways that connect the three decks. No charge.

    As this book goes to press, the ship is in dry dock—maybe until 1994—with various forms of tours, depending on the extensive restoration work in progress. (Meanwhile, a free video tour of the ship is shown in the nearby Constitution Museum.) You may be able to walk on the main deck. From a platform along the length of the ship, you can observe some of the work being done. And you can see the crane, the same one that has assisted in the maintenance of Old Ironsides for more than fifty years, that moves along the track around the dry dock. (In 1822, the *Constitution* was the first ship to enter the dry dock. The last overhaul was in 1975.)

Just Outside the National Park Gates

INCLUDING SHIPYARD PARK

Playground (Boston Parks and Recreation)

Fabulous. Go see, even if you don't have kids in tow. It's beyond the Constitution Museum and faces Pier 4. The "ship," imbedded in sand, with decks, steering wheel, slide, and opportunities to climb to your heart's content, is surrounded by brick walkways, benches, flower beds—and a wading pool with water flowing from architecturally designed oversized pipes and faucets.

USS Constitution Museum

Phone: 617/426–1812.

Open: Daily, spring and fall 9–5, winter 10–4, June–September 9–6. Closed Thanksgiving, Christmas, and New Year's.

Admission: $3 adults, $2 senior citizens and students with ID, $1.50 ages 6–16, age 5 and under free. Group rates available.

Handicapped access: Fully accessible.

While the USS *Constitution* is undergoing its sixth overhaul, the museum, located in a marvelous 1832 granite building, has exhibits (many participatory) that explain whys, wherefores, and skills involved in the repairs. Touch "hidden" old *Constitution* wood and compare with new. Get an update on the work and, from the second floor of the museum, a topside view of the ship. Learn about its place in history. On display are paintings, medals, and the first keyed bugle in America. A computerized exhibit allows you to take the part of a new crew member excited about going to sea. If you meet the model-builder-at-work, he'll probably tell you that it takes about 1,000 hours to make a model clipper ship. The artist-in-residence studies ships' logs and then works to portray a dramatic moment. And there are opportunities for visitors to hoist a sail, turn a ship's wheel, and swing in a sailor's hammock.

Boston Marine Society Building 32

Open: Monday–Friday 10–3 year round.

Admission: Free.

An amazing display of ship models—most are at children's eye level—is here in the oldest marine society in the world. Established in 1742, before Massachusetts was a state, the society has one main room with a steering wheel (sorry, not to be turned) from the *Jamestown,* which took provisions to the Irish during the famine of 1847. There's a compass that was lighted by oil, a navigator's case, a sawfish skeleton, and a model of an eighteenth-century Chinese junk. Marine researchers may be at work in the library, a room with a detailed model of an English warship of 1600.

HarborWalk

Not to be missed. Filled with delightful surprises and views at every turn. If you walk the full length of every pier, from just outside the National Park en-

"Awesome."

—SIXTH GRADERS

Along the Freedom Trail route, next to "Old Ironsides," at 55 Constitution Road, is the **Whites of Their Eyes**—a multimedia show that recreates the Battle of Bunker Hill and the events leading up to it. Lighted areas show authentically dressed mannequins; voices tell of their official roles and personal concerns. In the darkened theater, sounds come from seven channels, pictures flash, soldiers charge up on the screen, and the town burns down behind you. Open April–November. June–September 9:30–5, other months 9:30–4. It's $3 for adults, $2 senior citizens, $1.50 for children under age 16 (not recommended for toddlers). Phone: 617/241-7575.

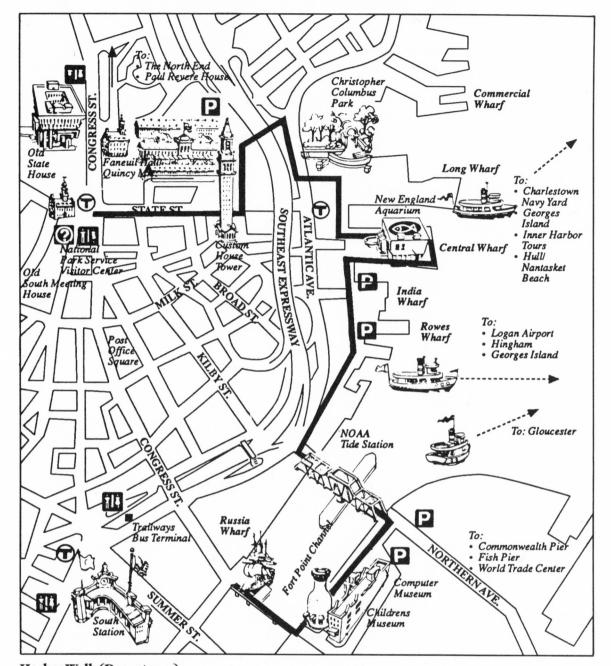

HarborWalk (Downtown)

trance to Pier 8 and 13th Street (award-winning affordable row houses by Bricklayers Union), you cover 1½ miles of continuous waterfront boardwalk.

The old and new are juxtaposed: the tall ship *Spirit of Massachusetts*, a sailing center, old painted numbers and signs, a dry dock surrounded by an inviting wooden walk, crane tracks, and everywhere, planters and benches. At Pier 5, in front of Flagship Wharf condominiums, there are steps (and a sign) to the public viewing deck that overlooks a marina to the left. Want shade? Behind Flagship Wharf (away from the water) the courtyard—with benches, trees, and a fountain—was created with the structural skeleton of Steam Engineering building No. 42. Go to the end of Constellation Wharf, Pier 7, for more benches and a great view of tugboats in East Boston. From here it's minutes to the parking garage on 13th and 4th streets or about 10 minutes to the water shuttle, trolley, or "Old Ironsides."

Bunker Hill

A 10-MINUTE WALK FROM THE NAVY YARD

Bunker Hill Monument and Museum Breed's Hill, Charlestown **Phone:** 617/241–5641.

Directions: If you're driving, the natural way to approach the monument is by Park, Commons, and Adams streets. More dramatic, and worth going a minute out of your way, is to go around Winthrop Square (past memorials to Charlestown men who fought at Bunker Hill), down Winthrop Street, right onto Warren Street, right onto Monument Avenue, a hill lined with gas lamps and historic brick residences.

Ⓣ: Bus 93 from Haymarket.

Open: Year round, 9–5 daily except Thanksgiving, Christmas, and New Year's. Last climb begins at 4:30.

Average stay: 15 minutes round trip, including 2–3 minutes at top for photos, view of harbor and city.

Admission: Free.

On the Freedom Trail

The granite for the monument came from Quincy, first from the quarries to the Neponset River by horse-drawn railroad cars, then by barge to Charlestown, Boston's oldest neighborhood (settled in 1625). The railroad—America's first commercial railway—was built for this contract. Yet the site is more remembered for the command "Don't fire until you see the whites of their eyes." As for the climb to the top of the monument, if it's the end of the day and/or it's hot, maybe you will think twice about ascending the 294 steps. Some youngsters appreciate adult accompaniment; some adults feel that once is fine, thank you. In the museum are good dioramas that illustrate the famous revolutionary battle.

Programs: 15-minute talks, spring through fall, hourly, 10–4. Firing demonstrations, mid-June until Labor Day, Thursday–Sunday.

In Nearby Communities

Very few historic homes report that they have as many visitors "as the original carpet can take." Actually, they are trying to achieve a delicate balance between preservation and education. At other than national historic sites, unless a special event is being held, you may be among the few in attendance. . . . Guides may change. Much depends on the mesh of personalities, a difficult aspect to guarantee in a book. . . . There are dozens of historic homes in the metropolitan area. Check with town halls or newspapers. The extent of restoration, furnishings, and research varies and often depends on funding. Many have participatory programs for schoolchildren and families. . . . Unless it's a designated children's day, historic house guides request (or require) that youngsters come with adults. . . . A small early house is a good introduction. If children enjoy it, take on an estate. . . . Parking at all of these sites is available in the neighborhood. . . . Many more historic sites are listed in Day Trips (pages 55–94).

One guide noted, "Some children are better behaved than adults on our house tour. And they ask lots of good questions: Why did they do that? Why did they do it that way? What is this used for?"

And from another: "Because our rooms are roped off, some children don't believe that anyone ever really lived here."

Brookline

Frederick Law Olmsted National Historic Site 99 Warren Street (corner of Dudley), Brookline 02146

Phone: 617/566–1689.

Directions: Route 9 west. Left onto Warren at the reservoir. (Note re-created front spruce gate of house.)

Ⓣ: Brookline Hills on the D (Riverside) Green Line; then a 15-minute walk.

Open: Year round for half-hour guided tours, Friday through Sunday 10–4. Group tours may be arranged at other times. Closed Thanksgiving, Christmas, and New Year's.

Admission: Free.

Programs: Vary throughout the year. Contact Boston Park Rangers, page 125, for Emerald Necklace walking tours.

America's first landscape architect lived here while he was designing Boston's park system. Visitors enter into the conservatory for a half-hour tour. You see an orientation video and samples of the collections, including lithographs, maps, photographs, and plans. For your self-guided tour of the grounds, which include a small planted sunken hollow and the south lawn edged with trees, a brochure describes Olmsted's design intent.

JFK's birthplace

John Fitzgerald Kennedy National Historic Site 83 Beals Street, Brookline 02146

Phone: 617/566–7937.

Parking: Some street parking. Or in Babcock Street municipal lot.

Ⓣ: 15-minute subway ride from downtown Boston to Coolidge Corner stop on C (Cleveland Circle/Beacon Street) Green Line, then a 15-minute walk.

Open: Year round, 10–4:30 daily except Thanksgiving, Christmas, and New Year's.

Admission: $1 ages 7–61. Free under 7 or over 61.

The thirty-fifth president of the United States lived here from his birth, May 29, 1917, until 1920. Rose Kennedy repurchased the house in 1966, supervised the restoration, and then gave the house, with many original furnishings, to the National Park Service. It's a 20-minute guided walk through the hall of the modest residence for a look at three rooms on the first floor and four (plus the bathroom with its original tile floor) on the second. Brochures direct you on a 45-minute walk to nearby places that played a part in the president's early days.

Cambridge

Longfellow National Historic Site (1759) 105 Brattle Street, Cambridge 02138

Phone: 617/876–4491.

Directions: .6 mile from Harvard Square along Brattle Street.

Open: Year round, 10–4:30 daily except Thanksgiving, Christmas, and New Year's.

Admission: $2 adults; under age 16 and over 62 free.

Special programs and events: Free poetry-writing workshops and kits (see below), garden concerts every other summer Sunday afternoon; poetry readings on alternate Sundays. Annual February 27th birthday celebration. Annual Christmas open house.

Longfellow lived and wrote here for forty-five years. During the half-hour tour you see many reminders of "The Children's Hour" and "The Village Blacksmith." Visitors also learn about the role of the house in American history.

Hint: *If you know you are coming with children,* call to make a reservation for a writing workshop. Visitors who do not make these necessary advance arrangements may request a take-home poetry-writing kit. This is all part of an award-winning Children's Hour Program conceived by Ranger Janice O'Connor, a Cambridge native who "wanted to make children's visits to the site more interesting." Teachers' kits that have been used with great success in grades 3–6 all over the country include slides (some students say that Longfellow looks like a scientist); a videotape about Longfellow; activities; a Longfellow "memory album" of photographs; and for each participant, an "I Am a Poet, Too" button. All free.

"I Am a Poet, Too."

A 10-minute walk from Longfellow site

Hooper-Lee-Nichols House 159 Brattle Street, Cambridge 02138

Phone: 617/547–4252.

Open: May–October, Tuesdays and Thursdays, 2–5, and tours on Sundays by appointment, 2–5. Year round, Monday–Friday for groups by special arrangement. Closed major holidays.

Admission: $2 adults; $1 under age 16 and senior citizens.

★ Small weddings and private parties.

It's a one-hour tour through this gracious Georgian mansion, converted in 1760 from a 1685 saltbox farmhouse. You will see old decor and construction revealed in an early restoration. The children's room include a mansard-roofed, furnished old Cambridge dollhouse.

Concord

See page 55.

Lexington

See page 66.

Lowell

See page 69.

Lynn

See page 71.

A little lost? Check the map on page 2.

ADAMS NATIONAL HISTORIC SITE

"The Old House" and Adams Presidential Birthplaces

Open: April 19 through November 10, 9–5 daily. Summer and Sundays are busiest. Reservations requested for groups of 8 or more.

Admission (Good for a week. Applies to "The Old House" and its library, carriage house, and grounds, plus the two birthplaces): $2 ages 16–62, under 16 free, over 62 free with National Park Golden Age passport available here.

Information: At visitor center in "The Old House," you can obtain information about other National Park sites and other historic sites in Quincy.

"The Old House" 135 Adams Street, Quincy 02169

Phone: 617/773–1177.

Directions: I–93 south to Furnace Brook Parkway exit. At the third set of lights, turn right on Adams Street for 1½ miles.

Ⓣ: Quincy Center on the Red Line (air conditioned); then a 10-minute walk.

Built in 1731 and enlarged several times, "The Old House" was the home from 1787 to 1927 of four generations of the Adams family. During the 45-minute site tour, rangers interpret the changing style and taste of the occupants to suit the level of visitors. Several tours are concurrent, so groups are small—usually ten people at most.

The surprise of the visit is the stone library building, filled from floor to ceiling, and balcony too, with books. In April the grounds are covered with thousands of daffodils. More than 2,000 plants bloom all summer long in the nineteenth-century formal garden. Displays in the nineteenth-century carriage house include a carriage, stalls, and tack room with saddles, and a nineteenth-century telephone.

The Adams Presidential Birthplaces John Adams, 133 Franklin Street (1681); John Quincy Adams, 141 Franklin Street (1662), Quincy 02169

Phone: 617/773–1770.

Directions: From "The Old House," 2 miles with twists and turns. Obtain map at "The Old House."

The two houses shared a well. That's why they were built just 75 feet apart. And no, the rangers explain, the houses have never been moved. During the half-hour tour of both furnished houses, the oldest presidential birthplaces in the country, you hear about colonial life and the influences on the Adams presidents of both their parents and the American Revolution.

Saugus Ironworks National Historic Site Central Street, Saugus 01906

Phone: 617/233–0050.

Directions: Tobin/Mystic Bridge to Route 1 north to Main Street (Saugus). Left on Central, and follow signs to the site.

Open: Year round, daily. April–October, 9–5, several guided tours daily. November–March, 9–4.

Average stay: 2 hours if you see everything including nature trail.

Admission: Free.

Picnicking: Allowed in designated areas throughout the park.

Summer programs: Weekend talks and demonstrations include cod salting, archaeological digs, charcoal making. Founders' Day, first Saturday after Labor Day, has many activities. Concerts are provided by the town on some Wednesday evenings. A highlight for visitors from all over the world.

Nature trail: ½ mile long, through woodland and by marsh. "A nice spot to enjoy the sounds of silence," commented an octogenarian.

It's best to visit the museum first for a slide-show orientation. There you can also see some of the artifacts that were found here in archaeological digs of the 1940s and '50s. From April until November, guided tours (about 45–60 minutes) include impressive demonstrations at the rolling and slitting mills with their working power waterwheels, huge wooden gears, bellows and giant forge hammer. And if you cross the river, you will have a chance to visit with the blacksmith. In winter, tours are self-guided and the mills are not in operation.

Stones from the original structure were used to rebuild the blast furnace, an (almost) 350-year-old forge where cast iron "sow" bars from the furnace were reheated and beaten into usable wrought iron. The original plant, built by John Winthrop in 1646, started America's iron industry and was in operation on the banks of the Saugus River for twenty years.

Waltham

Gore Place 52 Gore Street (Route 20); Waltham 02154

Phone: 617/894–2798.

Open: April 15 through November 15. Tuesday–Saturday 10–5, Sundays 2–5. Closed holidays.

Admission: $4 adults, $3 senior citizens and students with ID, $2 ages 5–12.

★ Corporate and private functions.

Strollers: Sorry, not allowed inside.

Picnicking: Allowed on the grounds.

All twenty-four rooms—filled with antique furnishings, textiles, paintings, and sculpture—are covered during the one-hour tour of this outstanding Federal period house. Younger people often comment on the flying staircase, which spirals up for three full flights. And there's a delightful nursery. On the acres of grounds: a restored herb garden; apple trees; a stable; and—the scene stealers—a small flock of historic breed sheep.

Looking Around

Look up! Tops of buildings often have original architecture. . . . Play the identification game before or after a trip. From photographs (there are several collections on Boston) see who can identify this doorway or that weathervane.

Viewpoints

In Boston

John Hancock Observatory John Hancock Tower, Copley Square (enter across from Trinity Church on St. James Avenue, right next to the Copley Plaza Hotel)

Phone: 617/247–1977.

Directions: Mass. Pike to Copley Square exit. Several nearby parking garages.

Ⓣ: Copley on the Green Line. Back Bay on the Orange Line.

Open: Year round, daily except Marathon Day (in April), Thanksgiving, Christmas, and when special events are booked here. Call to check. May–October, Monday–Saturday 9 a.m.–11 p.m., Sundays 10 a.m.–11 p.m. November–April, Monday–Saturday 9 a.m.–11 p.m., Sundays noon–11. Last tickets sold at 10:15 p.m.

Average stay: 30–40 minutes.

Admission: $2.25 adults, $1.75 students with IDs, $1.50 senior citizens and ages 5–15, free under 5.

Foreign languages: Brochures in Spanish, French, German, Italian, and Japanese.

Handicapped access: Accessible.

The best introduction to Boston

From the tallest tower in New England, you have a spectacular view and a sense of time and place. Sit on a grandstand seat by a windowed wall and listen to Boston historian Walter Muir Whitehill's fascinating taped narration. In addition, there is a 5-minute light and sound show that describes land changes here from the time of the Revolution. And telescopes ($.25) bring details of landmarks closer.

Next to Hynes Convention Center and Sheraton-Boston

The Skywalk Prudential Tower

Phone: 617/236–3318.

Directions: Mass. Pike to exit 22 (Copley Square).

Parking: (Underground) Prudential Center Garage; expensive.

Ⓣ: Copley or Auditorium on the Green Line.

Open: Monday–Saturday 10–10. Sunday 12–10.

Admission: $2.75 adults, $2.25 senior citizens, $1.75 ages 5–15, free under 5. Group rates (15 or more) available.

Handicapped access: Accessible.

At any hour, the 32-second elevator ride to the fiftieth floor may be the most memorable part of the visit for youngsters. To appreciate fully the panorama from all four sides of the building—and at its Copley Square competitor (above)—try to go when it's clear. From this vantage point, sunsets are particularly beautiful.

WHERE TO FROM THE OBSERVATORY OR SKYWALK?

From the reflecting pool at the **Christian Science Center,** walk through the passageway between the church's Colonnade building and the church, to the publishing society's bronze doors on Massachusetts Avenue. (ⓣ: Symphony, Hynes Convention Center/ICA, or Prudential on the Green Line.) Inside and free is the **Mapparium:**

As you cross the glass bridge through the glass globe (30 feet in diameter), pretend you're at the center of the earth. Notice the time zones, the blue-shaded ocean depths, and the relationships of land and water surfaces. The globe, in 608 individual sections, each a quarter inch thick, shows the world's political divisions in 1932. Its brilliant colors are heightened by several hundred electric lights. Speak, and everyone shall hear; the glass doesn't absorb sound. Open year round, Monday–Saturday, 9:30–4. Phone: 617/450–3790.

What else is here? They offer a free copy of the *Christian Science Monitor,* tours of the center (page 261), a reading room, and rest rooms that are often called the best in Boston.

West of Boston

Babson World Globe and Map Babson College, Babson Park, Forest Street, Wellesley 02157–0310

Phone: 617/235–1200.

Directions: Route 16 (Washington Street) west to Wellesley Hills Square. Turn left at Forest Street and continue to main gate of Babson College campus.

Parking and admission: Free.

Open: Globe is outside; always available. The map building is open year round, Monday–Friday 1–4 and by appointment. (Programs arranged for school groups.) Closed holidays.

The change from day to night and the progression of the four seasons are simulated as the 25-ton globe, mounted outdoors, revolves (most noticeably when it is sunny) on its 6-ton shaft. For a topside view of the recently restored globe, look out through the windows of the balcony of the nearby Coleman Map Building, which houses the largest relief model of the United States. When you look at that map, you see mountains, rivers, islands, and oceans as if you were 5,000 miles above the earth.

Nearby: A **duck pond** in a pretty setting at Wellesley Town Hall. From Babson drive to Washington Street and turn left. Watch on the right for the building that looks like a medieval castle. Bring bread to feed the ducks (up to 175 in winter, about 50 or 75 in summer). Also nearby, and worth a special trip, are the **Margaret C. Ferguson Greenhouses** (page 204), on the Wellesley College Campus.

Observatories

Boston University Astronomy Department Observatory
705 Commonwealth Avenue (adjacent to Marsh Chapel), Boston 02215
Phone: 617/353–2630 (every Wednesday's program confirmed after 5:30).

Ⓣ: BU East stop (at 705 Commonwealth) on the B (Boston College/Commonwealth) Green Line.

Open: Year round, clear Wednesday nights. October–March, 8–9 p.m. (Closed the Wednesday before Thanksgiving and Christmas.) April–September 8:30–9:30.

Admission: Free.

A very short orientation talk precedes observing opportunities that are on the roof or in an enclosed (unheated) area. (Dress for the outdoors.) Once a month, a 30-minute lecture is given. The taped telephone message keeps you up-to-date on plans for this week.

Harvard Smithsonian Center for Astrophysics 60 Garden
Street, Cambridge 02138

Phone: 617/495–7461.

Open nights for children ages 6–12 are scheduled in the fall and spring at 7 and 8:15. After a 30- to 45-minute lecture in astronomy, you can stargaze, weather permitting, as long as you wish with the staff-operated telescopes on the roof. (Free) tickets are essential. Call for arrangements.

For adults and young adults (minimum junior high school age), there is a free lecture every Thursday year round at 8 p.m., followed by a film or video and stargazing, weather permitting, on the roof. Dress warmly in the winter.

Wheaton College Observatory Science Center, Wheaton College,
East Main Street, Route 123, Norton 02766

Phone: 508/285–7722.

Free astronomy programs (a slide show) and stargazing on the roof (four 8-inch telescopes and two computerized 14-inch telescopes) every Thursday night that the college is in session. Call late in the afternoon to see if the weather is cooperating. Programs are held 7:30–8:30, 8–10 in the spring.

Getting Around

All these trolley companies have an all-day on-and-off arrangement as they tour through the neighborhoods and travel to sites (including the Charlestown Navy Yard), giving a narrative of Boston's history. If you just take the ride, the tour is about 90 minutes. *You may board at any of the 14 to 17 stops.*

Red Trolleys

Beantown Trolley and Brush Hill 435 High Street, Randolph 02368

March–December. $14 adults, $5 ages 5–12. Under 5 free. Phone: 617/236–2148, or 986–6100 groups.

Blue Trolleys

Boston Trolley Tours P.O. Box 267, Boston 02132

Year round. Handicapped accessible. $15 adults, $11 seniors and students, $5 ages 6–12. Under 6 free. Phone: 617/TROLLEY.

Green and Orange Trolleys

Old Town Trolley 329 West Second Street, Boston 02127

Narrated tours with sound effects. $14 adults, $10 seniors, $5 children 5–12, under 5 free. *Boston* tours year round. Phone: 617/269–7150.

Cambridge tours leave from in front of Out of Town News in Harvard Square, spring through fall. One narrated hour with several stops. $10 adults, $5 children 5–12, under 5 free.

Doubledecker Buses

The Gray Line 275 Tremont Street (at Tremont Hotel), Boston 02116

Boston tour is offered year round. Open top. $14 adults, $5 age 12 and under. Combination tickets with harbor cruise. Cambridge, Lexington, and Plymouth tours available. Air-conditioned coaches. Phone: 617/426–8805.

The Subway

PARK STREET MURAL

If you start at or pass through the Park Street Station, allow some time for the 110-foot, 12-ton mosaic by Lilli Ann Killen Rosenberg. It's on the north wall of the tracks (outbound) near the fare booth. The artist used old trolley parts, railroad spikes, seashells, stones, pieces of slate, marbles, and chips of colored and gold-leaf glass embedded in cast and carved concrete to depict Boston's growth from seaport to commercial complex. You'll notice tunnels and trolley tracks connecting different neighborhoods, and the dominating layers-of-earth theme that represents what was under the Common at the turn of the century. And the longer you look at the incredible detail, the more you see.

Sightseeing on the Ⓣ

Out-of-towners (particularly children) who have never been on a subway—or even a trolley—often feel that their first ride (not at rush hour, please) is an excursion in itself. Foreign visitors are surprised that most trains stop at every station.

A half-hour ride on the air-conditioned Red Line could start at Harvard Square (page 137). The train surfaces at Longfellow Bridge for a picture postcard scene of sailboats on the Charles, then goes back underground through Park Street Station and on to Quincy. Here, within walking distance, is the Adams National Historic Site (page 114).

The Riverside/Green Line (35 minutes from start to finish when all goes well) surfaces at Fenway, a familiar stop for Red Sox fans. Then the trolley travels by blossoms, foliage, or snow-laden bushes; a lake used for swimming and skating; and maybe deer (between Chestnut Hill and Newton Center).

Trains

Just Right

Amtrak

"All abo-o-ard!" That's the call—followed by a 5-minute ride from South Station to Back Bay on any one of four different Amtrak lines. The fare is $.85 adults; half fare ages 5–11; under age 5 free. Great for young children. A good way to get from the Children's Museum (page 151) to the swan boats (page 236).

Bonus: The revitalized South Station, the building with New England's only remaining hand-wound tower clock, is a good place to **eat with kids.** Lots of tables in big open light-filled concourse. (More upstairs, filled at lunch, on mezzanine where stock prices posted.) Vendors sell salads, fast foods, Italian foods, yogurt, coffee, chocolates, newspapers and magazines.

ONE-OF-A-KIND

All together. All near Aquarium, Quincy Market, and Filene's Basement.

The ultimate

The Chocolate Bar Cafe Fleuri, Meridien Hotel, 250 Franklin St.
Phone: 617/451–1900.
Available: Saturdays, September–May, 2:30–5:30.
Costs: $11.50 adults, $7.50 age 12 and under. ★ Birthday parties (all ages) of at least 8: no extra charge for a special cake and balloons.

The six-storied garden atrium smells like chocolate. The decorative sculptures are made of chocolate. The buffet is all you-know-what in the form of fondue, cakes, tortes, mousses, brownies, cookies, crepes, tarts, and dipped strawberries. ★ Reunions are booked here. Kids are welcome and feel comfortable in the relaxed Chocolate Bar atmosphere in this elegant hotel. Ask at the concierge's desk for directions to the two **N. C. Wyeth murals** commissioned in 1923.

In front of the hotel

Post Office Square Park bounded by Franklin, Pearl, Milk, and Congress streets
Parking: In garage beneath: all day $16 Monday–Friday, $5 weekends (617/423–1430).
Map of trees and area: At Franklin and Pearl streets.

Topping a seven-story parking garage is this magnificently landscaped space with trees on permanent loan from the Arnold Arboretum. It's a 1990s creation, 2.7 acres with a wildflower garden, a vine-covered arcade, grass for picnickers, and a bronze-and-glass fountain. And seating for 1,700, if you count the tables by the Milk Street Cafe (takeout too), the benches, and the granite walls that edge gardens. A delight.

Just inside bordering buildings

New England Telephone Headquarters Building 185
Franklin Street

No exterior sign announces the first-floor treasure, the reassembled attic **workshop of Alexander Graham Bell** complete with the world's first switchboards and replicas of the very first telephone. (If it's dark, ask security guard to light the display.) And there's a lot to see and think about as you look up and around the lobby at the circular **mural,** *Telephone Men and Women at Work.* All in a restored 1947 Art Deco building, open 8–5 daily.

John W. McCormack Post Office and Courthouse
Congress Street

At the **Philatelic Center,** stamp collectors purchase commemorative stamps, mint sets, and specialty items from the best selection available in the state. Open Monday–Friday, 9–1:30 and 2:45–4:30.

Hear train announcements. View the tracks. Free **special events** include summer Wednesday noontime concerts, museum presentations, model trains in December.

Nearby: It's a 10-minute walk across Atlantic Avenue to the lower-level **Whit's End** (617/426–9377) at 105A South Street, where Nancy Whittaker has a make-your-own-card area. For $1 per card, you have use of various ink colors and dozens of rubber stamps, including the Inkadinkadoo wonderwheel. (A hit with men and women: Boxer-short-stamping workshop, $12, includes instructions and materials.) In addition to the array of first-quality stamps for sale, there are bargain-priced factory seconds that you are welcome to test before buying.

Walking Tours

Boston By Foot 77 North Washington Street, Boston 02114
Phone: 617/367–2345.
Fees: $6 adults, $5 ages 6–12. Free for up to four with any library's BBF membership card.

Guides are knowledgeable volunteers, eager to share their enthusiasm for the city's history and architecture. The 90-minute personalized tours are held May through October, in all weather, just about every day of the week, usually at 10 and 2; also at 5:30 weekdays. Call for schedule of tours for Copley Square, the North End, Beacon Hill, the Downtown Skyline, or holiday tours such as "Beacon Hill with a BOO!" Reservations are not required.

"Knock three times and ask Captain Hook if he is there." Other activities and games are part of **Boston by Little Feet,** a 1-hour rain or shine tour focusing on the architecture and history of the downtown Freedom Trail area. Youngsters stopping to pace a plaza or examine a statue have come up with questions that stump guides. (Have you ever noticed the blocked opening near the Old South Meeting House clock?) For ages 6–12, accompanied by an adult, Saturdays at 10, Sundays at 2. $5 per person.

When Old City Hall was built, it was dubbed the French wedding cake. When New City Hall was built, people said it looked like an upside-down Lincoln Memorial; the back of a penny proves it.

Boston Park Rangers Boston Parks and Recreation Department, 1010 Massachusetts Avenue, Boston 02108
Phone: 617/522–2639 or 725–4505. TTY: 617/715–4006.
Fees: None. All free.
Programs: Year round, daily. All are available to groups by prearrangement.

In addition to patrolling, these multifaceted men and women lead a tour of historic burying grounds one day and a tour of art and architecture along Back Bay's Commonwealth Mall the next. Dressed in uniform with wide-brimmed hat, they teach fishing at Jamaica Pond or read *Make Way for Ducklings* near the swan boats. They also lead an all-day walk or bicycle ride of the whole Emerald Necklace from Boston Common to Franklin Park; cross-country skiing; botanical walks or stargazing in the Arnold Arboretum; birdwatching along the Muddy River; environmental education programs; and "Horse of Course," page 29.

Call for current programs or look for newspaper calendar listings.

Cambridge Page 139.

Historic Neighborhoods Foundation 2 Boylston Street, Boston 02116

Phone: 617/426–1885.

Fees: $5 per person. Advance reservations preferred at least a week in advance. Minimum of 6 required to guarantee a tour. Group rates available.

Walking tours, lectures, and teaching projects that focus on urban architecture and social and landscape history are year-round activities for this nonprofit educational group. Bilingual tours can be arranged. Ninety-minute walks through Beacon Hill (a sunset tour), the North End, the waterfront, and Chinatown are among the public tours scheduled May through August, some weekdays and Saturdays. The "Make Way for Ducklings" walk (through Beacon Hill and on Mrs. Mallard's route) is designed for ages 5 to 12. And the last Sunday in April (see Calendar, page 275), kids are invited to dress in costume for the Ducklings Day parade; $3 per person. $10 per family with advance registration.

National Park Service Page 97.

Exploring on Your Own

Back Bay

A SENSE OF ORDER—
Back Bay cross streets:
Arlington
Berkeley
Clarendon
Dartmouth
Exeter
Fairfield
Gloucester
Hereford

Location: See map, pages 4–5.

Parking: Boston Common Underground Garage.

Ⓣ: On Green Line, Arlington and Copley are near the Public Garden; Hynes Convention Center/ICA is at Massachusetts Avenue (Tower Records) and bordered by Boylston (Institute of Contemporary Art) and Newbury streets. On Orange Line, Back Bay station on Dartmouth Street is across from Copley Place.

Viewpoints: Please see page 119.

You don't have to be an architectural aficionado to appreciate the hundreds of details—chimneys, gables, balconies, bay windows—in this area. The elegant townhouses are built on tidal flats, filled through forty years' time. Number 32 Hereford has an iron balcony that was salvaged from the Tuileries during the Paris riots of 1871. Number 12 Fairfield, built in the late 1870s, has twenty different shapes of molded brick.

The promenade with benches and dog-walkers along wide **Commonwealth Avenue** is lined with trees that are lovingly cared for by the neighborhood association. The light-colored limestone at 287 Commonwealth, built in 1899, contrasts sharply with earlier homes nearby. ★ The *Boston Center for Adult Education* at number 5 has a magnificent ballroom with parquet floor, chandeliers, and mirrors; available for many kinds of functions. You are welcome "to look"—most weekdays before 5—whenever it is not in use.

Marlborough Street feels residential. At Berkeley and Marlborough is the First and Second Church in Boston. Very little of the old building is left from a devastating fire in 1968, but from Berkeley you can see the remaining wall with rose window frame, the porch, and the steeple and bell tower of the oldest church in the city.

Across the street at 53 Marlborough is the country's largest independent French cultural center, a handsome structure with parlor, library, gilded moldings, mahogany-paneled ballroom, and varying floor patterns. It was a private home until it became the *French Library* in 1961. (★ Nowadays it's

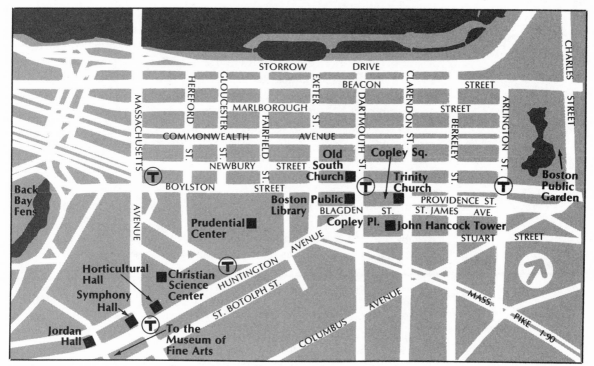

Back Bay

available for social and corporate functions, concerts, weddings, and meetings—and as a film location.) Your curiosity can be satisfied! Walk through the tall gates and enter, Tuesday–Saturday 9–5 (may be closed in August), and admire (no charge) the recent restoration done by skilled craftspeople. Members may borrow books and videocassettes. A newsletter lists scheduled events, including the annual July 14th Bastille Day Street Dance Festival.

On **Newbury Street** you need rooftops and stoops to give a sense of scale, because most of the homes have become art galleries or one- to three-level shops featuring designer clothes, antiques, crafts, and china from around the world. Outdoor cafes abound spring through fall. Summer blossoms thrive. At Berkeley Street, Louis of Boston occupies a building that was the first home of MIT and later of the Museum of Science (then known as the Museum of Natural History).

THE LANDMARK BEAR

Found! On the back, on the ribbon: "Daniel Long," the sculptor's signature. The full inscription reads:

A gift to the children of Boston from FAO Schwarz. His birthdate is unknown. Some say the teddy bear arrived at Plymouth Rock in 1620 carried carefully hidden by a young explorer. Other stories describe his origin as 1902 for President Theodore "Teddy" Roosevelt. Our children "know" he was born in Boston. For us, the teddy bear represents playfulness, a spirit of love, and the warmth of big hugs.

Steps away, on the corner of <u>B</u>erkeley and Boylston streets, the 12-by-8-foot, 6,000-pound bronze lovable-if-not-huggable FAO Schwarz teddy bear is very popular with photographers. Inside FAO Schwarz, where animated displays on two floors bring smiles to one and all, all year long, there are lots of touch and try possibilities. Rock on the bull, wind up toys, push buttons, and play computer games. Peek from the second floor at a glorious atrium in the center of 222 Berkeley Street.

Minutes' walk back on Newbury Street, past the wonderful, well-utilized playground on <u>C</u>larendon, come to <u>D</u>artmouth Street and the don't miss (walking west, you can't) Dubarry French Restaurant three-storied trompe l'oeil. For local artists Jack Kiligian and Joshua Winer, actors posed as many well-known Boston-based names, including Babe Ruth, Leonard Bernstein, Arthur Fiedler, John F. Kennedy, Crispus Attucks, John Harvard, and Abigail Adams. On the corner of <u>E</u>xeter Street, Waterstone's Booksellers, Britain's largest bookseller, opened its first American location in a former church (known for several decades as the Exeter Street Theatre) that still has stained-glass windows. At 229 Newbury is the small, theatrical, make-your-own-assortment candy store Sweet Enchantment, with a forest of wrapped goodies at everyone's eye level. Outside there's a scale with huge dial (it works). Across the street at The Blue Planet, number 228, more than one child has asked if they might bring a sleeping bag to spend the night by Jeff Hull's 14-foot-wide rain forest mural. Larry Murray opened this ecology store in 1991, following years as director of Arts/Boston (where he origi-nated Arts/Mail and helped create Bostix, page 50). His stock includes un-usual handcrafts, low-flow shower heads, ZOO DOO (organic fertilizer from zoo animal waste), and nature sounds or relaxing music on CDs that you can audition before you buy. A percentage of every sale is donated to more than a dozen national and six local environmental associations.

Copley Square is surrounded by buildings that could fill a day of look-ing. Beyond the Boston Public Library (page 129), **Copley Place** is home to upscale shops including Neiman Marcus, two hotels, several restaurants, and a three-storied waterfall (a good meeting place). Historic landmarks bordering Copley Square all give a sense of place: Trinity Church, page 265;

DUCKLINGS

A British-born urban planner, Suzanne deMonchaux, is interested in making cities a "hospitable place for children." In the early 1980s, when she moved here from Australia, she took her twin sons to the Boston Public Garden. Their familiarity with the classic children's book *Make Way for Ducklings* prompted them to ask, "Where are the ducks?" Subsequently Mrs. deMonchaux and sculptor Nancy Schön proposed the duck project, sanctioned by author Robert McCloskey, to the Friends of the Boston Public Garden.

Nancy Schön judged size and scale according to her first grand-child, not yet two years old. The now famous sculptures were in-stalled in the Public Garden in October 1987. When, in 1991, Mrs. Schön installed another set in a similar setting in Moscow, Russian chil-dren immediately rushed to sit on those ducks.

THE BOSTON PUBLIC LIBRARY

"Is that beautiful building a museum?" out-of-towners often ask. In part, yes—as many realize when they take the Boston Public Library tour, page 259.

The country's first major free municipal library has extraordinary collections, including rare books, prints, drawings, photographs, maps, musical scores, and databases. . . . In the microtext department you can view back editions of local, regional, national, and even international newspapers. (What was happening the day you were born?) . . . A computer speech synthesizer, closed-captioned and American Sign Language videos, TDDs and TV Decoders, a Kurzweil reading machine, a braille printer, and braille children's books are all part of the Access Center. . . . Wonderful changing exhibits are in the third-floor Wiggin Gallery. . . . The courtyard, resembling an Italian palazzo, is a hidden retreat, replete in summer with bubbling fountain, lilies, and blooming annuals. . . . The original duckling sculpture of "Quack" from the Boston Public Garden is scheduled to be a centerpiece in the children's room.

Currently the Charles Follen McKim–designed building along Dartmouth Street is undergoing a ten-year restoration project. When Phase One is completed by the end of 1993, you may, once again, enter through the Dartmouth Street bas-relief doors, the work of Daniel Chester French. They lead to a large hall where the names of famous Bostonians are set in the mosaic ceiling and where marble lions—with signs of "worn" backs, thanks to the tender touch of many hands—guard an impressive staircase. . . . In 1994 there will be a tea room and bookstore. . . . Extensive free programming continues for all ages and includes film showings, an authors' series, and presentations during school vacations. . . . Borrowing privileges are free to all state residents who present an ID with picture and an address. . . . Closed on Friday and Saturday nights and all day Sunday. Phone: 617/536–5400.

the New Old South Church; and the venerable, century-old **Copley Plaza Hotel** with its exquisite, ornate lobby complete with a Tea Court (high tea 3–5 p.m.). Buck-A-Book, hardly historic, sells bargain books across from Trinity Church at 553 Boylston Street. Between Berkeley and Clarendon, at 501 Boylston, are exhibits in the The New England Building lobby: Hoffbauer murals of colonial New England, and dioramas including "The Filling In of Back Bay 1858" and "The Boylston Street Fishweir" (un-covered during the 1913 excavation for the subway). The observatory in the mirror-covered John Hancock Tower, page 119, gives a good orientation to the Back Bay and all of Boston.

The **Boston Public Garden,** bounded by Arlington, Boylston, Beacon, and Charles Streets, offers colorful formal flower beds, rare old trees, statues, an oft-photographed bridge, and winding paved paths for strolling. But you'll have no peace with children if you don't head for the swan boats (open mid-April through fall, see page 236) and the duckling sculptures.

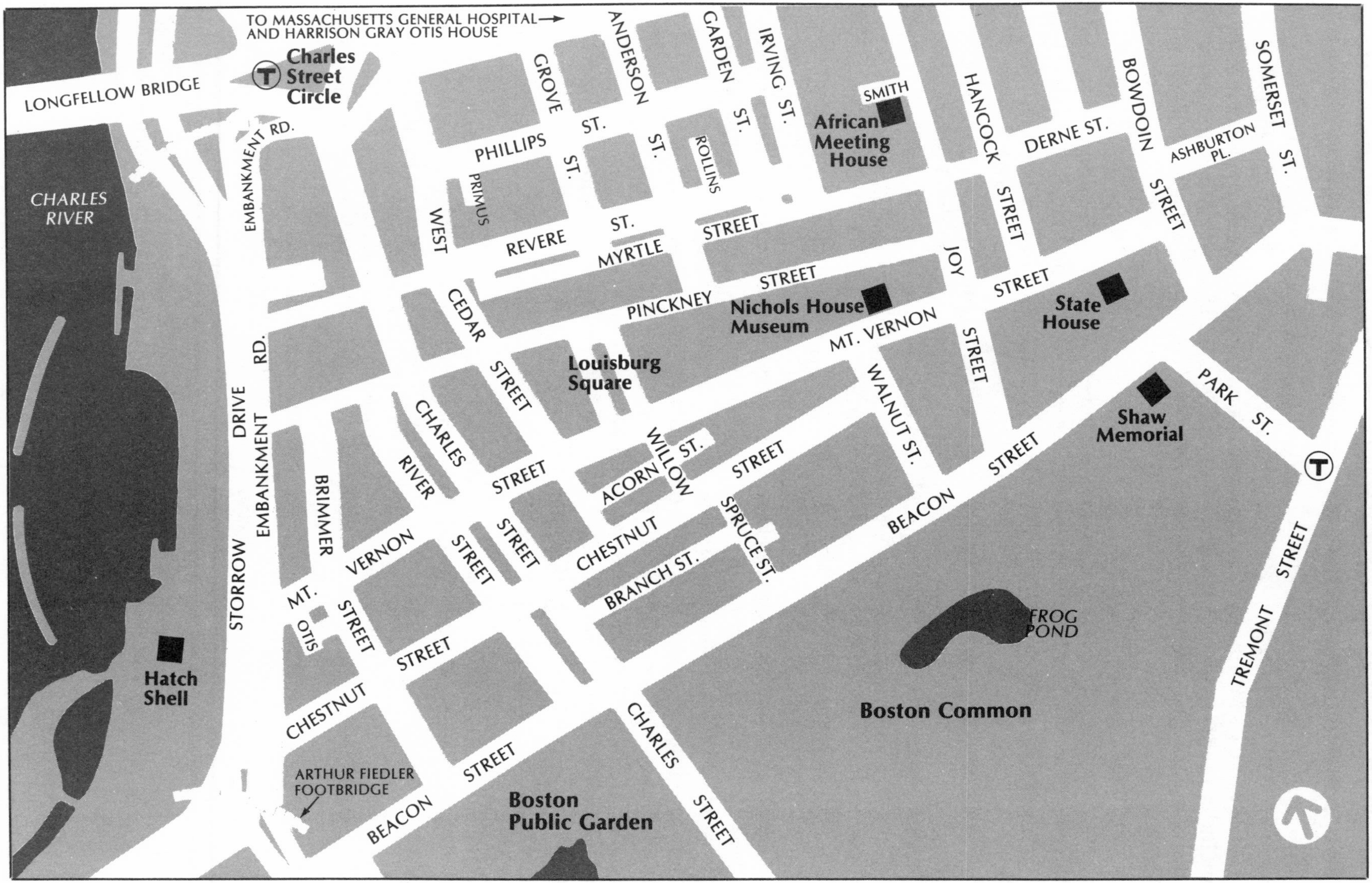

Beacon Hill

Map Labels:

SOMERSET ST.
ASHBURTON PL.
BOWDOIN STREET
DERNE ST.
HANCOCK STREET
PARK ST.
TREMONT STREET
State House
Shaw Memorial
FROG POND
Boston Common
BEACON STREET
JOY STREET
STREET
WALNUT ST.
MT. VERNON
SMITH
African Meeting House
Nichols House Museum
IRVING ST.
GARDEN ST.
ROLLINS
STREET
PINCKNEY STREET
WILLOW ST.
ACORN ST.
SPRUCE ST.
CHESTNUT ST.
BRANCH ST.
CHARLES STREET
ANDERSON ST.
GROVE ST.
MYRTLE ST.
REVERE ST.
Louisburg Square
PHILLIPS
PRIMUS
WEST
CEDAR STREET
CHARLES STREET
RIVER STREET
VERNON STREET
STREET
Boston Public Garden
MT.
OTIS
BRIMMER STREET
CHESTNUT STREET
BEACON
ARTHUR FIEDLER FOOTBRIDGE
TO MASSACHUSETTS GENERAL HOSPITAL→
AND HARRISON GRAY OTIS HOUSE
Charles Street Circle
LONGFELLOW BRIDGE
EMBANKMENT RD.
STORROW DRIVE
EMBANKMENT RD.
Hatch Shell
CHARLES RIVER

Beacon Hill

Two Beacon Street townhouses offer glimpses of varied Back Bay styles. The **Gibson House,** still relatively undiscovered, at 137 Beacon Street between Arlington and Berkeley streets, is a house filled with Victoriana— from the basement kitchen to the cat's bed in the upstairs music room. It takes almost an hour to see four floors of the home, built in 1860 and always lived in by the Gibson family. It's just as bachelor son Charles Hammond Gibson left it when he died in 1956. Tours at 1, 2, and 3, Wednesday–Sunday May through October, weekends November–April. Admission: $3. Groups, $4 per person.

The interior of **Fisher Junior College,** 118 Beacon Street, is very different, with a hanging marble stairway and a metal balustrade covered with 24-karat gold. Rugs are woven with the Greek design of the balustrade and walls. And the carved rosewood doors in the library have handwrought silver knobs. The school is open weekdays 9–4:30. And there's no charge to tour through the 1803 home.

Beacon Hill

Location: See map (facing).

Parking: Boston Common Underground Garage.

Restaurants: Along Charles Street there's a wide assortment. Among Thai restaurants is **The King & I** at 145 Charles, 617/227–3320. **Rebecca's** (valet parking at night) is at number 21, 617/742–9747. (Rebecca's Bakery is at the corner of Mt. Vernon.) Gelato is on the menu at the ever-so-casual **Il Dolce Momento,** 617/720–0477, located on the corner of Chestnut Street. **Romano's Bakery & Coffee Shop,** less hectic, popular at lunch and for relaxing with the newspaper, is at 89 Charles, 617/523–8704. The **Hungry i** at 71½ is for romantics (617/227–3524). With (or without) children, **Bel Canto** at 42 Charles (617/523–5575) offers the happy medium, with salads, deep-dish pizza, and calzone too. At the top of the hill, 2 blocks from the rear of the State House, in a not-so-elegant section—**Primo's Eating Place,** a simple place at 28 Myrtle Street, 617/742–5458, offers subs, pizza, Italian dinners.

Ⓣ: Park Street on the Red or Green Line.

A good starting point is the State House (page 99). Then wind your way to the Esplanade and the Community Boathouse on the river. (Storrow Drive pedestrian overpasses are at Beacon and Arlington, and at Charles Street Circle.)

CHEERS

The impact of one national television show has created a new kind of landmark, one that is as well known as the Freedom Trail. It's on Beacon Street near Charles Street, across from the Boston Public Garden's sculpted ducklings. To find the elegant townhouse with the pub setting used for the TV "Cheers" series, hundreds of thousands of souvenir shoppers per year look for the "Cheers" flag waving from the second story of the building with Hampshire House restaurant (upstairs) and Bull & Finch Pub (lower level). Talk about incongruity. You pass through a hall furnished with rococo-framed mirror, huge tapestry, and elaborate winding staircase to a shop with T-shirts and mugs for sale in a Georgian room with crystal sconces and chandeliers.

During the summer the entire scene is splashed with the color of flower boxes. As you wander up, down, and across the hill (which was at least 60 feet higher before its dirt became part of the Back Bay fill), you'll find antique gaslights, foot-scrapers at doorsteps, stables not converted to homes, interesting doorways, patterned brick sidewalks, underpasses and tunnels, and cobblestone driveways. Purple window panes—colored by the effect of sun on the original glass—are at 39–40 Beacon Street. And there are dramatic sunsets to be seen looking toward MIT from Pinckney and Joy streets, where the river is framed by buildings on each side of the hill.

Use the map to find **Acorn Street,** bordered by Willow and West Cedar (which runs off Chestnut near Charles). This narrow sloping street is one car wide and paved with river stones. Early residents were coachmen who served nearby families.

Follow Willow with its iron railings (used for support during icy weather and in the past as hitching posts) to Mt. Vernon for one of the entrances (Pinckney is the other) to **Louisburg Square** (pronounced *loo-iss-burg*).

Here simple doorways and three- and four-story bowfront brick homes frame a central park open only to proprietors of the square. While you're looking for number 4, where William Dean Howells, an editor of the *Atlantic Monthly,* lived, or number 10, once the home of Louisa May Alcott, the children may still be looking for a way into the iron-fenced oval park, with its statues of Aristides the Just (on the Mt. Vernon side) and Christopher Columbus (on the north side). Both were gifts of Joseph Iasigi, a Boston merchant; and both came as ballast in ships from Italy.

Mt. Vernon Street has several sizable old homes with elaborate iron fences. At the summit, number 55 (see below) is open to the public. Number 50, only 13 feet high, was once a stable for three horses. Some say it was planned so that the gentleman across the street could see his cattle grazing on the Common.

Joy Street brings you to the Museum of Afro American History (page 156), housed in two of the fourteen Black Heritage Trail buildings on the hill (page 106). At the end of Rollins Place, facing 24 Revere Street (near the top and unnumbered the last time we looked), is a housefront without a house. Those closed shutters hide a brick wall on a 40-foot cliff. (If you do walk in for a closer look, please keep the gate closed.) Farther down Revere Street are other picture-perfect cul-de-sacs—Goodwin Place, Sentry Hill Place, and Bellingham Place. Walkers with the energy to cross the hill for one more block find Primus Avenue, off Phillips near Charles. It has an iron grill-

JOHN HANCOCK WEATHER BEACON

First activated: Christmas Eve 1949.

> Steady blue, clear view;
> Flashing blue, clouds due;
> Steady red, rain ahead;
> Flashing red, snow instead.

In baseball season, flashing red indicates postponement of Red Sox games.

work entrance and an ascending path with a series of steps and interesting doors at each level.

Headed to the Esplanade on the river? To the footbridge over the lagoon and the sculpture of Arthur Fiedler? Connect with Chestnut Street. Discover interior design studios on cross streets, and mauve or black or bright yellow doorways of various widths.

Or, instead, walk to the Boston Public Garden and the swan boats via Charles Street (another filled-in area of Boston) known for its antiques shops, galleries, eateries, boutiques, and the Beacon Hill Thrift Shop too. Businesses and interiors change, but the architecture will remain as is. Beacon Hill was designated a National Historic Landmark in 1963.

Inside View

WITH LITTLE APPEAL
FOR CHILDREN

For an indoor "on high" (third-floor) view of Mt. Vernon Street—and a tour of the home of Rose Nichols, an early active member of the International League for Peace and Freedom, the Beacon Hill Reading Club, and the International Society of Pen Pals—visit the **Nichols House Museum** at 55 Mt. Vernon Street (between Joy and Walnut near rear of State House). The 40-minute tour of this 1804 Charles Bulfinch–designed residence is far from "standard." Return another time and you will likely hear the personable and knowledgeable guide tell different anecdotes about the family who lived in this antiques-filled, lovingly cared-for house for eighty years. Open afternoons 1–5. June through Labor Day, Tuesday–Saturday. March–May and September–November, Wednesday and Saturday. Winter Saturdays. Admission: $3 per person. Phone: 617/227–6993. ★ Small business or social functions.

Harrison Gray Otis House Page 106.

Chinatown

Location: See map, page 12.
Directions: Driving, take the Chinatown exit off the expressway (look for the pagoda). Walking from Downtown Crossing, follow Chauncy Street (in back of Jordan Marsh) to Harrison (and fabric shops).
Ⓣ: South Station on the Red Line.

The pagoda atop the Chinese Merchants Building is a landmark of Boston's small Chinatown, a community that was established well over a hundred years ago, a community that today is home to about 10,000 Chinese residents. Recently, as you can tell by the bakeries, restaurants, and markets, the area has become home to Vietnamese, Cambodians, and Thai as well.

A good meeting place is the 36-foot-high gateway, the business district's official entrance at Beach and Edinboro Streets. A gift from the government of Taiwan to commemorate America's bicentennial, it is topped with a green tile roof and flanked by four sizable marble lions. Although you'll find some gift, clothing, book, and video stores, and others selling jewelry or paintings, the predominant enterprises are food-oriented.

Opposite the gateway there's Hing Shing Pastry at number 67 Beach—and a short block away on your right is Ho Yuen Bakery. Both offer a wide assortment of labeled (in English and Chinese) goodies including mixed-nut pastries, black bean cakes, moon cakes, huge walnut and golden fish cookies, and meat-filled pastries.

Dim sum, with more than twenty items including steamed pastries filled with meats and vegetables, is available every day from 8:30 to 3 at **Imperial Teahouse** at 70 Beach Street, **China Pearl** at 9 Tyler Street, and **Golden Palace** at 14 Tyler Street. On the same Tyler Street Block, **China Grove** serves "Szechuan, Mandarin, Yangchow, and Taiwan cuisine," everything from noodles to whole fish, all garnished to artistic perfection. **Ocean Wealth's** tables have cloths; near the entrance (8 Tyler Street) are glass tanks filled with lobsters, crabs, and eels. (A couple of doors away, Aqua World Aquarium has a large tank with its own continuous live show in the window.) Tablecloths and Hong Kong cuisine are the order of the day 1 block over at the more spacious **New House of Toy** on Hudson Street.

From Beach and Harrison, continue to your right around the block for Cheng Kwong Seafood Market (below). Or take a detour, only because you're here, for fabrics such as silks, woolens, cottons, and lace—by crossing Harrison Street onto Chauncy Street for North End Fabrics, New England Textiles, and Winmil Fabrics.

The Cheng Kwong Seafood Market? With or without children, it's like taking a trip halfway around the world. Look for the sign on Essex Street (between Harrison and Edinboro) below the bright yellow Hoy Toy Noodle sign. Most of the fruits displayed on the sidewalk are familiar. Inside there are tanks with swimming fish at your children's eye level. In addition to buckets and counters filled with native and exotic fish (lift young children so that they can see the scaling process), there's an astonishing array of fresh greens, scallions, ginger, vegetables—all hand labeled in Chinese. The canned goods, however, are (colorfully) labeled in English too.

If, perchance, you want your choice of at least forty-six kinds of tea or noodles, and maybe some dishes and a rice cooker too, Mei Tun Supermarket on Lincoln Street at the Surface Road, next to the parking garage, has all of that in a well-lit, wide-aisled facility.

Faneuil Hall Marketplace

OFTEN CALLED QUINCY MARKET

Phone: 617/523–2980.

Directions: From the expressway south, take the Dock Square exit; going north, take the Atlantic Avenue exit.

Parking: Limited meter parking on nearby streets. Quincy Marketplace Garage.

Ⓣ: On Orange or Blue Line, State station; on Green or Blue Line, Government Center.

Walking: The cobblestones are hard on feet and strollers.

Open: Shops are open Monday through Saturday 10 to 9, Sundays noon to 6, until 7 in summer. Restaurants stay open later in the evening. The flower market, 617/742–3966, is open daily from early morn till 10, 11, or 12 at night.

Street entertainment: Free (hat is passed) and popular, April–October, 11–11. Check schedule at South Market Street information booth.

Rest rooms: They're there—and adequate. Look for signs or ask the guards. Or cross the street to McDonald's, which has large, handicapped-accessible second-floor rest rooms. And Boston City Hall has rest rooms too.

Bostix (tickets and performing arts information): Page 50.

A legend. A destination for 14 million people each year. The Marketplace, a cobblestoned, traffic-free shopping center, is an ongoing urban pageant, a dependable spot for people-watching and listening. Since its opening in 1976, it has been replicated in recycled structures all over the country.

Clipper ships and fishing boats no longer dock at the back doors of the copper-domed granite center building conceived by Boston's early nineteenth-century mayor, Josiah Quincy. But today, 160 years later, that building is still a market. Walk through (often crowded) aisles past dozens of stalls with freshly baked bread and arrays of chicken, meats, and seafood. Lots of little tables inside (often filled in winter) and benches outside for eating Greek salads, cookies, bagels, pizza, or yogurt cones. The two flanking brick buildings are filled with fine treasures and trinkets, jewelry, gifts, clothing, and home furnishings for sale.

There are plenty of restaurants with good food, hanging plants, and piano players. Here, too, is the original **Durgin Park** (617/227–2038), founded in 1827, with its Yankee cooking, family-style tables covered with red-checkered cloths, wooden floors, and tin ceilings. (Validated parking arrangements, $5 per day, at nearby garage.)

Yet more shops (most national chains): In newly built Marketplace Center, opened in 1985, on the route to the waterfront.

Participatory sculpture: Opposite Entrance 5 of the South Market sits the bronze interpretation of Boston Celtics coach and manager **Red Auerbach.** Join him (for a photograph) on the bench. Also sculpted by Lloyd Lillie: In Dock Square, north of the flower market, on the grassy area between

WHAT ABOUT THAT YELLOW AWNING?

It was June of 1991 when Vitali Valdez from the housekeeping department noticed that birds were nesting in a seventh-floor window box overlooking Fanueil Hall Marketplace. The place: the Bostonian Hotel. The variety, according to the Audubon Society: house finches. Until the four eggs were hatched, no one was booked into the suite-cum-nesting-balcony. Now the newly named House Finch Suite has a gold-plated nest, and its balcony has the Bostonian's only yellow awning.

STEAMING LANDMARKS

Across from the Government Center ⓣ station is the Steaming Kettle Coffee Shop with a landmark hanging high above its Court Street door: The 200-pound, gold leaf–covered copper kettle, which simmered over a century ago in front of the Oriental Tea Company in Scollay Square, still spouts steam.

In 1990 a steaming bean pot, 30 feet in diameter, was "piped to a box purchased from a spa manufacturer" and hung over the doorway of a new business. Bosworth's Boston Baked Beans is at 37 Union Street, a 1750s warehouse located between Marsh Lane and Marshall Street, and next to Union Oyster House, the country's oldest continuously running restaurant. If the aroma entices you into the pocket-sized emporium, created by the Stidsen family with Great-aunt Tootsie's recipes, you will see on the wall a portrait of Aunt Tootsie. She's flanked on the left by her Saturday-night bean pot (the model for the steaming pot) and on the right her nephew's bean pot. And what about the Bosworth name? Although contrived, it turns out to be that of early settlers. (Look for a plaque on the School Street entrance of the Parker House.)

McDonald's and City Hall, are two statues of mayor-governor-congressman **James Michael Curley.** One statue is standing, but most people sit on the bench to be photographed with the seated figure; others sit right on its knee (the shiny bronze attests to it).

Minutes from the Marketplace

Haymarket, just across from the North Market on Blackstone Street, behind the Bostonian Hotel, is open year round on Fridays and Saturdays, until about 8 in summer, 6 in winter. Vendors sell fruits and vegetables (at low prices) from inherited pushcart positions once occupied by horse-drawn wagons. The tradition includes displays and sales pitches. Go quickly! Whether it's development or regulation, the shrinking market always seems to be threatened with extinction.

Faneuil Hall (page 102), the real place with grasshopper weathervane, is a nearby **Freedom Trail** site. . . . Marshall Street is on the Blackstone Block, which still has a seventeenth-century street pattern. A short walk through a rather grubby tunnel brings you to the bustling North End (page 141). . . . The **waterfront,** page 144, is a 10-minute walk. . . . In the other direction is Boston City Hall and **Government Center,** just a couple of blocks away. During the summer free live entertainment is often scheduled at lunchtime and in the evening in City Hall Plaza, an area paved with two and a half million bricks. From here, it's a 5-minute walk to the **Harrison Gray Otis House,** page 106.

Harvard Square

JUST ACROSS THE RIVER IN CAMBRIDGE

Directions: Follow the signs on Memorial or Storrow Drive.

ⓣ (the best way): Harvard on the Red Line, 11 minutes from downtown Boston.

Parking: Limited on street. Several garages available.

Post office: Recently remodeled. Completely accessible. On the corner of Mount Auburn and Story streets.

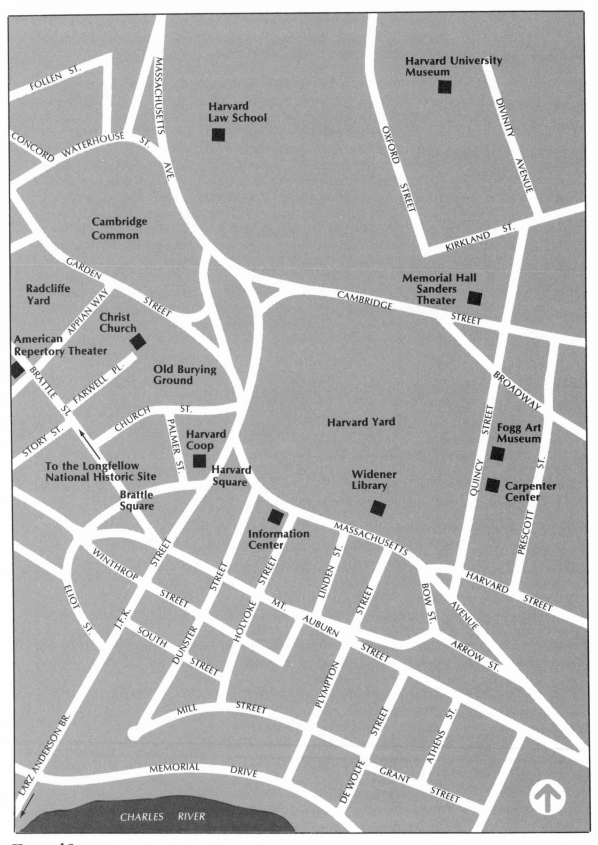

Harvard Square

Information: Cambridge Discovery (617/497–1630). Open Monday–Saturday 9–5 (9–6 June–September), Sunday 12–5. A valuable community resource with an information kiosk next to Out of Town News in the square. This is the place for directions; bus and subway schedules; summer walking tours of Harvard Square and Harvard University (fee charged); brochures (some free, some in foreign languages); information about entertainment, shopping, lodging, every restaurant in Cambridge, and the just-completed Cambridge African American Heritage Trail.

Also in the square, The **Harvard Information Center,** 617/495–1573, next to the Cambridge Trust Company in Holyoke Center at 1350 Massachusetts Avenue, is open year round 9–4:45 Monday–Saturday, plus June–August Sundays 1–4. Printed information about the university includes a self-guided walking tour in English, French, Spanish, Japanese, and German and a free copy of Harvard University Gazette (calendar lists performances and lectures).

Harvard University events line: 617/495–1718. Usually a long, varied list.
Tours: Students who lead the **Harvard University tours** are asked as many questions about themselves as about the university! One-hour tours leave year round from the information center. During the academic year they start at 10 and 2 Monday through Friday and at 2 on Saturday; June through August at 10, 11:15, 2, and 3:15 Monday–Saturday, at 1:30 and 3 on Sunday. Other tours of Harvard and of **Cambridge neighborhoods** are scheduled by organizations such as Cambridge Discovery (see above) and Boston By Foot, page 125.

Rest rooms: In the Harvard Coop—on the third floor of the bookstore and on the second floor of the main store.

Hidden treasure: It is just steps from Garden Street traffic, yet very quiet. Across from the Cambridge Common, next to Christ Church (the city's oldest), is a charming path by the Town Burying Ground, the resting place for many early settlers. If you continue along the path by the picket fences, this becomes an interesting route to Brattle Street, and the terrace (tables in summer) of the Blacksmith House Bakery and Cafe in the Cambridge Center for Adult Education. (Longfellow wrote "The Village Blacksmith" about Dexter Pratt, who owned that yellow house.)

For serious tourists: The musts include Harvard Yard ("the Yard"), the hidden treasure (above), and some museums, page 164.

Restaurants: Inexpensive and not fancy: **Bartley's Burger Cottage,** 1246 Massachusetts Avenue, 617/354–6559, closed Sundays. **Elsie's,** 71 Mount Auburn Street, 617/354–8362, known for huge sandwiches and salads. **Bertucci's,** 21 Brattle Street, 617/864–4748, for pizza, pasta, salads, calzones. **Wursthaus** at 4 John F. Kennedy Street, a real old-timer with wooden booths, serves German dishes, sandwiches, over 150 beers. **Grendel's Den,** 89 Winthrop, 617/491–1160, feels traditional and comfortable in upstairs dining room (varied menu with salad bar).

Harvard Square isn't a square at all. It's a wide area of historic and cultural resources with a shopping center that has, alas, been changed to the point of having many recognizable national names on the store fronts. Larger buildings have replaced most of the small shops. And still, more **bookstores** come. At last count there were twenty-five. Among those that offer dis-

counts are WordsWorth Books at 30 Brattle, also known for its authors series at Brattle Theater; and Barillari's at One Mifflin Place, known for its children's corner, espresso bar, and a small patio on the site of a tiny basement shop occupied decades ago by a tailor who encouraged my husband to marry me. Maps and travel books are featured at the Globe Corner Bookstore, 49 Palmer Street; foreign language books at Schoenhof's, 76A Mount Auburn Street; poetry books at Grolier Book Shop, 6 Plympton Street; stacks and overflowing aisles of used and out-of-print books at the Starr Book Co., 29 Plympton, in the whimsical triangular-shaped Harvard Lampoon Building.

Classic movies are shown in the renovated **Brattle Theater;** $3 for children under 12 and senior citizens. . . . Tucked in here and there are **cafes** such as the Algiers Coffee House on the lower level of the Brattle Theater. Scholars also frequent Pamplona (phoneless) at 12 Bow Street. . . . **Street performers** multiply in the evening. . . . **Out of Town News**—a can't-miss-it emporium in the Square—has hundreds of American and foreign newspapers and magazines. . . . That yellow frame house at the edge of **Harvard Yard** is now used by the alumni association, but it housed Harvard presidents for over a hundred years. Step inside the gate and walk through the yard, a quiet enclave of eighteenth-century red brick buildings on the campus of the country's oldest university. Go by Widener (the largest university library in the world), the statue of John Harvard, and the water pump for the best route to the glass flowers in the Botanical Museum (page 165). The Victorian building just beyond the yard is **Memorial Hall,** built as a Civil War memorial. Its wooden auditorium, Sanders Theater, makes an interesting setting for lectures and concerts.

To get to **Tory Row** with its lovely old **Brattle Street** homes, the Longfellow National Historic Site and Hooper-Lee-Nichols House (both open to the public, page 113), take Brattle Street from the square, passing Colonial Drug (hundreds of perfumes for sale); the Cambridge Center for Adult Education (a country estate in 1736); Church Street (great ten-year-old trompe l'oeil on Loew's Nickelodeon); and the home of the avant-garde American Repertory Theater.

Open space (minutes from the square): Away from the river—**Cambridge Common,** with an imaginative and handicapped-accessible fenced playground and a few picnic tables too. . . . Facing the river—the **John F. Kennedy Park,** on Memorial Drive at JFK Street, with a fountain, benches, famous JFK quotations etched in granite, plenty of grassy running and playing space. . . . **Along the Charles River** are views of domed Harvard dormitories, the Business School, the boathouse, sculls and small craft. The sidewalk is used for jogging, cycling, roller skating, and walking too.

Creek Lane 1631
Eliot Street

—SIGNPOSTS

North End

Directions: From the expressway south, take the Dock Square exit; going north, take the Atlantic Avenue exit. From the Marketplace, walk along Haymarket to Blackstone Street, to the cluttered pedestrian underpass.

Parking: It's just about impossible to park on North End streets. The Government Center and Marketplace garages are nearby.

Ⓣ: Haymarket on the Orange or Green Line; then walk through the underpass.

Festivals: Please see page 279.

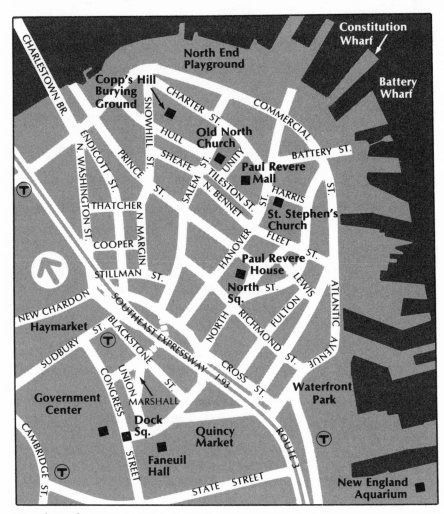

North End

The Italian-American section of Boston, separated from the rest of the city by a maze of highways, feels, some say, like Rome or Milan. Although the 1980s brought condominiums and some commercial changes to the narrow streets, there's still a Michelangelo Street, a sense of neighborhood and of history, and plenty of food.

You have to zig and zag to notice every last marinated olive, wheel of cheese, *cannolo,* and *ristorante.* Take the time to stop in, really to see, to listen, to taste, to smell, to gather cooking hints, to recall the days before supermarkets. People-watch from a cafe table.

For an Old World route, a sampler that takes you by one of everything including a few surprises, use the map above. Start on **Salem Street** (on Sunday, closed shops and not much fun) or **Hanover Street** near the expressway. On **Richmond Street** between Salem and Hanover is the public library known for its atrium, children's area, Italian book collection, and large, elaborate diorama of the ducal palace in Venice. Follow Richmond to reach **North Square** and the Paul Revere House, page 103. Come back to Hanover. Walk through the Paul Revere Mall to the Old North Church, page

104. (The restored bells ring about noon on Sunday, and on Saturday mornings during practice.) Then it's a three-minute walk up **Hull Street** and through Copp's Hill Burying Ground (page 105) to Charter Street and Copp's Hill Terrace, a historic lookout point (the British used it in 1776) with picnic tables and shade trees. Here, too, is the most incredible view of the water, the USS *Constitution,* Bunker Hill, and the Old Navy Yard. In the foreground; a recreational complex complete with children's playground and boccie court.

Food suggestions: Clustered along Hanover Street—marzipan and Florentines at **Modern Bakery**; cannoli across the street at **Mike's Pastry**; **Trio's** for fresh pasta, varieties by the dozen; several cafes, each with a different atmosphere. On Prince Street, one door in from Salem, **Parziale's Bakery** for breads of all sizes and shapes—and for Mrs. Parziale's comments/observations. **Polcari's**, another decades-old family business, is on the corner of Salem and Parmenter and offers bulk spices; black-eye beans and whole peas; Brazilian, French, or hazelnut coffee; and the neighborhood news. At 151 Richmond, pocket-sized **Salumeria Italiana** is known for its variety of cheeses, olive oils—and local shoppers. **Dairy Fresh Candies** at 57 Salem Street is a wonderland of stacked displays with sweets plain and fancy, boxed and bulk, domestic and imported. No tours at **Purity Cheese**, but from the front you can see cheese being made Tuesday–Friday mornings: 55 Endicott Street, corner of Cross near the expressway.

"When people ask, 'How do you make a pound of pasta at home?' we tell them about kneading the dough and sometimes we give them a demonstration. They can see the production of whatever we're making—maybe ravioli, ziti, or lasagna, maybe cheese, pumpkin, lobster, pesto, or tomato and basil. Our family is always coming up with something new. We make many different sauces, including ginger-vermouth, Newburg, bouillabaisse, sun-dried tomato. Everything is done fresh daily. No preservatives. Tourists are a joy! People from all over say they've never seen a place like this. Look at that wall—with postcards from Minnesota and Texas, from Hawaii, Paris, Japan, from the Bruins. We're here 9–6, Monday–Saturday, 9–1 on Sundays. Call me Louie."

Trio's (three decades old) is at 222 Hanover Street, 617/523–9636.

Restaurants (not expensive): **European** at 218 Hanover is large and good for groups. Big awning outside **Trattoria Il Panino,** 11 Parmenter, a popular small self-service place with long list of pastas plus sandwiches, salads, pizza, calzone. Pizza (only) at the original **Regina's,** 11½ Thacher Street. Around the corner, **Oasis,** 176 Endicott Street, features American cooking, tablecloths, funky (1930s) decor. Also near the Charlestown Bridge: **Massimino's,** 207 Endicott Street, for a full, wonderful, reasonably priced Italian meal. Almost-famous: For calamari (squid), **Daily Catch,** 323 Hanover Street—small, very informal, very popular.

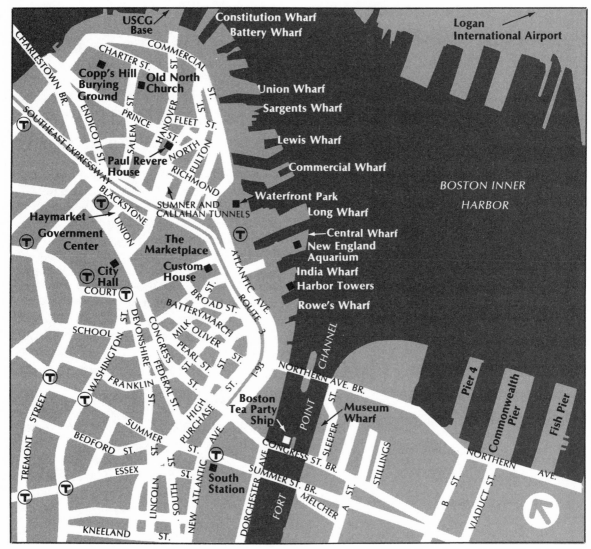

Waterfront

The Waterfront

DOWNTOWN BOSTON

Directions: Follow expressway signs to Atlantic Avenue and the waterfront.

Parking: Some meters on street. Garages (expensive) nearby.

Ⓣ: Aquarium on the Blue Line. South Station on the Red Line if you plan to start from the Tea Party Ship or the Children's Museum.

Picnicking: Many places with benches (see below) and harbor views.

Caution: As with wharves all over the world, along Boston's waterfront there is no fencing or barrier at the edge.

Rehabilitated. Renovated. Reconstructed. Recommended. And still being re-discovered by Bostonians. Here, in downtown Boston, is the original **HarborWalk,** which starts at the Old State House and goes along filled-in land, through Fanueil Hall Marketplace (good place for picnic food) and by the Custom House Tower, to the waterfront area that runs from Waterfront Park to the Boston Tea Party Ship Museum.

Christopher Columbus/Waterfront Park (see map), a promenade day and night, is a great open space—with some shade—for fun, relaxation, and festivals. More than one adult has rescued an overly courageous youngster from the crow's nest in the playground. Bring the Sunday paper to the Rose Fitzgerald Kennedy Garden, which is complete with tea roses, a fountain, and antique (in part) fencing. Walk to **Long Wharf,** Boston's oldest. Beyond the excursion-boat ticket booths (one sells $1 fares for a 10-minute "T" ride to the Navy Yard) and beyond the Chart House restaurant (located in a 1724 pilot house; closed for lunch, dinner entrees $14–$27, children's menu $2.50–$7) is a fantastic view from a 1-acre park with benches, telescopes, flagpoles, and planters. Here, set in granite, is a copy of the original compass rose, designed by an artisan whose shop was on Long Wharf.

Continue along the public walkway through the **Marriott Long Wharf Hotel**—with wall exhibit of area changes and an enormous ceiling mural over escalator—to the **New England Aquarium** and its sea walkway (often missed) that juts into the water. At this "stop" it's possible to spend 45 minutes without spending a dime. Attention-getting harbor seals cavort in the outside pool near the front entrance. Periodically, during feeding time, staff members talk about these rescued seals. Staying along the water, walk by the Boston Harbor Sailing Club, by the benches along East India Row, and around the Rowes Wharf complex that includes the ferry terminal (with rest rooms), departure point for some excursion boats and for other boats that go to the airport. Sit on the benches in the glass-enclosed octagonal rotunda. The Boston Harbor Hotel's outdoor **Rowes Wharf Cafe,** open in warm weather, is protected from winds by buildings. For a most unusual sight, walk under the Boston Harbor Hotel's majestic archway and look up to the top of the dome. Then, for an on-high view of Boston's skyline, enter number **30 Rowes Wharf** and take the express elevator to the Foster Rotunda on the ninth and tenth floors, open most weekdays (no charge) from 11 to 4.

More treats ahead: Outside, continue following the blue line across Northern Avenue and stop into the James Hook Lobster Co., where Al Hook welcomes visitors who ogle and ask questions about crabs and 10-pound lobsters kept in a saltwater pool. Kids can step on a scale that weighs up to 250 pounds. And you see hundreds of holding tanks used in the wholesale end of the business. Then it's over the new Northern Avenue Bridge (this replaced the landmark turntable bridge in 1992), past a few lobster boats, past Victoria Station (trainlike) restaurant, and on to the converted waterfront warehouse that houses the Children's Museum and the Computer Museum. There's more: You are minutes from the Congress Street Bridge and the Boston Tea Party ship, which is minutes from South Station, its food emporium (a little of everything), views of trains, and a Ⓣ stop.

Still more (someday): 43 continuous miles of the Massachusetts coastline will be accessible by foot. Meanwhile, several other finished segments, including the marvelous route at the Charlestown Navy Yard, page 109, are ready and waiting. Ocean views of sail and excursion boats, tugboats, freighters, and planes are also available from several other sites, including the Fish Pier; the World Trade Center's public walkway; Castle Island, page 185; and the Kennedy Library, page 155.

Museums

So many people converge on Boston's museums on weekends that museums in surrounding communities can be a pleasant change. . . . It helps to be aware of a child's attention span. . . . Special programs for children may be scheduled. Inquire about courses, demonstrations, special events for all ages, outreach programming, walking tours too. . . . Museum membership often includes free or reduced admission, a newsletter, special events, preferred enrollment for courses, and savings in the gift shop. . . . Outdoor museums— Mystic Seaport Museum, Old Sturbridge Village, Plimoth Plantation, Strawbery Banke—are included in Day Trips (pages 55–94). . . . Leading a group? Have you seen page ix?

Museums in general

Recorded information

EVENTS AND FEES

Blue Hills Trailside Museum: 617/333–0690.
Charles River Museum of Industry: 617/893–5410.
Children's Museum: 617/426–6500.
The Computer Museum: 617/423–6758.
DeCordova Museum and Sculpture Park: 617/259–8355.
Fruitlands Museum: 508/456–3924.
Isabella Stewart Gardner Museum: 617/734–1359.
Harvard University Natural History Museums: 617/495–1910.
John Woodman Higgins Armory: 508/853–6015.
Institute of Contemporary Art: 617/266–5151.
John F. Kennedy Library and Museum: 617/929–4567.
Museum of Afro American History: 617/742–1854.
Museum of Fine Arts: 617/267–9377.
Museum of Our National Heritage: 617/861–0729.
Museum of Science: 617/723–2500.
Museum of Transportation: 617/522–6140.
New England Aquarium: 617/973–5200.
Cardinal Spellman Philatelic Museum: 617/894–6735.
The Sports Museum of New England: 617/78–SPORT.
Worcester Art Museum: 508/799–4406.

Evening Hours

Schedules do change periodically. The following is a good outline, up to date at press time, but check for current arrangements.

Boston Tea Party Ship and Museum: Open March–December until dusk.
Children's Museum: Year round, open Fridays until 9.
The Computer Museum: Late June through Labor Day, open Fridays until 9.
Museum of Fine Arts: West Wing, Thursdays and Fridays until 9:45.
Museum of Science: June through September, open until 7 daily.
New England Aquarium: After Labor Day through June, open Thursdays until 8. July through Labor Day, Wednesdays and Thursdays until 8; Saturdays, Sundays, and holidays until 7.
The Sports Museum of New England: (Maybe) until 9:30 daily.

Closed Days

Holidays: Some museums are open. Check individual listings, or call the recorded-information numbers.

Mondays: Beware. Several are usually closed. Check!

Free or Reduced Admission

Several museums offer free or reduced admission in their museum benefits. Availability of free or reduced admission rates to nonmembers may vary according to funding, and from year to year. Here's the picture at press time:

Cardinal Spellman Philatelic Museum: Always free.

Children's Museum: $1 Fridays, 5–9 p.m.

The Computer Museum: Half price, Saturdays, 10–noon.

Isabella Stewart Gardner Museum: Free on Wednesdays to students with valid ID.

Harvard Museums of Natural History: Free Saturdays, 10–noon.

Institute of Contemporary Art: Free Thursdays, 5–8 p.m.

Museum of Fine Arts: Free Wednesdays, 4–9:45 p.m.

Museum of Our National Heritage: Always free to individuals; also free to school groups that book ahead of time.

Museum of Science: Exhibit halls are free, Wednesdays 1–5.

New England Aquarium: Varies. Call 617/973–5200.

> **Hint:** Check to see if your local library has a **museum membership card to loan.** If so, you may be able to reserve it ahead of time, with pickup and return required within 24 hours. Such memberships are often a gift to the library or a purchase by the library's Friends group.

In Boston

Boston Tea Party Ship and Museum Congress Street Bridge (off Atlantic Avenue on the way to Museum Wharf), Boston 02210

Phone: 617/338–1773.

Directions, parking, and Ⓣ: See Children's Museum, next page.

Open: March–December, 9–dusk. Closed Thanksgiving.

Average stay: 40 minutes.

Admission: $6 adults. $4 senior citizens, students, military. $4.80 AAA members, $3 ages 5–15, free under 5. Group rates available.

Handicapped access: Steps. Difficult access.

Step aboard this small ship, a privately owned replica of a Tea Party ship, and inspect the rigging, galley, and reconstructed captain's cabin. Museum exhibits show the economic and political conditions of prerevolutionary Boston. One audiovisual program tells the story of the Tea Party; another, of the 1973 voyage of this brig, *Beaver II.*

Visitors react in interesting ways. Tired scouts reported they had seen enough ships and videos by the time they arrived here. Danish tourists are intrigued with the fact that the two-masted brig was built in Denmark. Children enjoy throwing tea (bundles attached to a rope for retrieval) into the harbor. Some parents think the attraction is overpriced. Everyone welcomes the hot or iced tea served to guests. Summer tourists feel that the 20-minute reenactments (given about every 45 minutes) help to bring history alive. An additional major exhibit is planned.

Children's Museum Museum Wharf, 300 Congress Street, Boston 02210
Phone: 617/426–6500. Recorded message: 617/426–8855.
Educator line: 617/426–6500, extension 231, or (nationally) 800/370–5487 Eastern time.
Directions: Look for Museum Wharf milk-bottle logo signs. *From the north*: Expressway, Route 93, south to High and Congress Street exit. First left onto Congress Street. Cross bridge to museum. *From the south*: Expressway, Route 93, north to the Downtown/Mass. Pike/Chinatown exit. At end of ramp, turn right onto Kneeland Street toward South Station. At next light, turn left onto Atlantic Avenue. Go through 2 lights. Turn right onto Congress Street, over bridge to museum. *From the west*: Mass. Pike to end. Stay in right-hand lane for South Station/Chinatown/Kneeland Street exit. Straight ahead on Atlantic Avenue through 3 lights. Right on Congress Street, over bridge.
Parking: Nearby lots, about $4 or $5. Across from museum or 3 blocks down on Congress Street.
Ⓣ: South Station on the Red Line or commuter rail. Walk 1 block north along Atlantic Avenue. Turn right on Congress Street. Cross bridge to museum.
Open: Tuesday–Sunday 10–5 (Mondays too in summer); Fridays until 9. Closed Mondays except Boston school vacations and holidays. Closed Thanksgiving, Christmas, and New Year's.
Average stay: 3 hours.
Admission: $7 adults, $6 seniors and ages 2–15. $2 1-year-olds. Under age 1 free. $1 for everyone Fridays 5–9 p.m. *Friday night performances*: $1. Juggler, storyteller, musician, theater.
Groups: Please make advance arrangements.
Restaurants: Right here—McDonald's. Lightships on the water has everything from sandwiches to steaks, $2.95 children's menu. Victoria Station's moderately priced menu includes a salad bar; outside tables in good weather. Picnic tables under a tent (no building) are at Venus Seafood in the

COMING ATTRACTION

A big wave, a 45-foot-tall wave-shaped building with a floating urban education center and a public waterfront park, is expected in 1995. This spectacular waterfront wing (added onto the wool warehouse turned museum) will provide space for exhibits, art, an indoor/outdoor cafe, "a toddler terrace" for gardening and water play, a bridge for harbor views, and an aquatic laboratory. Once the project is completed, both the Children's Museum and the Computer Museum will share a dynamic, skylit entrance. The 1930s giant wooden milk bottle/lunch stand, moved here from Taunton in 1980, will remain on Museum Wharf.

Rough at the Northern Avenue Bridge; seafood, barbecued chicken, hot dogs, p.j. sandwiches too. Milk-bottle stand sells snacks, spring–fall.

Picnicking: Benches on the wharf.

Museum shop. Free admission. Great stock of everything including books. Kids' shop offers items from $.05 to $5.

Recycle shop: Free admission. Many industrial by-products. Good resource for craft and project materials. Inexpensive.

Programs and workshops: Many. Single or series. For kids, parents, teachers. Some programs interpreted in American Sign Language.

Volunteers: "From age 12 to all the way up."

★ Birthday parties: Yes! Three different plans. And many other special functions booked too.

Strollers: Allowed. Backpacks loaned free. (Changing tables in rest rooms too.)

What's where? Takeaway maps available. Touch screens too.

Handicapped access: Full. A TTY or audio enhance phone is available by request. Limited parking on a first-come, first-served basis.

The original touch-look-ask museum, a model for many such institutions throughout the country, is really a people museum. You'll still find computers, new how-do-they-work exhibits, a science playground with bubbles and exhibits such as "tops" and "salad-dressing physics." Kids are everywhere, exploring, discovering, and learning. For assistance or information, volunteers and staffers are everywhere. Preschoolers like Playspace, which also happens to be a good place for parents to meet and talk. The two-storied climbing sculpture is ever popular. Older children, ages 10–15, have a special activity space. And college students love this place.

A full-scale interior bridge leads to an environment where children learn about racism and cultural diversity. There are opportunities to learn words and expressions in several languages, to hear lullabies or play songs, to visit in a Native American wigwam or in a turn-of-the-century Japanese house where everyone removes shoes. Frequently, ethnic festivals are scheduled here. Those who "never want to leave" might look into Overnights, a sleepover program for youth groups and families, held on specific dates during the year.

The Computer Museum 300 Congress Street, Boston 02210

Phone: 617/426–2800 (live), 423–6758 (computer message).

Location: At Museum Wharf, near South Station; look for the big white milk bottle.

Directions, parking, and ⓣ: See Children's Museum, page 151.

Open: Late June through Labor Day 10–6 daily, Fridays until 9. Rest of year Tuesday–Sunday 10–5. Closed Mondays, except Boston school holidays.

Average stay: 2½ to 3 hours.

Admission: $6 adults, $5 students and seniors. Free for children under age 5. Half-price admission Saturdays 10–noon. Group rates available.

Museum hours and prices change. Call for today's information.

Tours: Orientation offered to visitors.

Programs: Many, including tours for school groups, contests, robot-building and teachers' workshops, and Mysterious Parts Searches of the Walk-Through Computer.

★ Special events booked: "Just about everything. Held in a function room or entire museum with your name on a giant screen of walk-through computer. Or combined with outside tent. Call us. It will work."

Handicapped access: Full.

The range of appeal spreads from beginner to expert, with some of the newest exhibits designed for children as young as 5. The world's sole computers-only museum began at Digital Equipment Corporation with founder Kenneth Olsen's collection of early giant-sized computers and robots. Now, throughout the converted wool warehouse, there are about a hundred hands-on exhibits. You can create computer animation, simulate flight, compose music, paint a map by talking to the computer, test machines that sense the environment, play games, learn about desktop publishing, experiment with voice synthesizers. One exhibit is a "cutting edge" computer-generated environment. Another is a walk-through two-storied working computer model, fifty times the size of a desktop computer, with 6-foot-tall floppy disks, a 25-foot operational keyboard, and a giant spinning disk drive that retrieves data. For a social and historical perspective, another exhibit traces the evolution of computers, starting with the electronic giants of the 1940s. There are films (back to the 1930s), music, pictures, videotapes (including the 1952 presidential election), and interactive computer stations. Thirty-minute shows, such as "The Great Train Rubbery," are presented in the computer animation theater every half hour.

Isabella Stewart Gardner Museum 2 Palace Road, Boston 02115

Phone: 617/566–1401 or (concert schedule) 734–1359.

Directions: From Copley Square, follow Huntington Avenue past the Museum of Fine Arts, to Museum Road on the right. Left on the Fenway for 1 block to the Gardner (look for the red roof and wrought-iron fence) on the left.

Parking: On neighboring streets.

Ⓣ: Ruggles/Museum on the Arborway/Green Line; then a 3-short-block walk.

Open: Tuesday–Sunday 11–5.

Average stay: 2 hours.

Admission: $6 adults, $3 seniors and students. Free, under age 12; special needs groups (please make advance reservations). Students with valid ID admitted free on Wednesdays.

Cafe: Open Tuesday–Friday 11:30–3, weekends 11:30–4. In warm weather, outside terrace open for dining. Bistro-style menu. Full meal or elegant desserts and tea. (Ice-cream cart is in outdoor garden in summer.)

Concerts: September–May, Saturdays and Sundays at 1:30. (Combination fee includes museum admission.)

Tours: At least Thursdays at 2:30. Other courtyard talks and programs for children and adults are scheduled.

Strollers: Allowed with rubber wheels.

Handicapped access: Two wheelchairs available on a first-come, first-served basis. (Elevators available.)

★ Corporate functions.

Thirty unusual display areas show Isabella Stewart Gardner's eclectic, extraordinary collection of paintings (many Dutch Baroque and Italian Renaissance), sculpture, tapestries, stained glass, furniture, tiles, doorways, gargoyles, and more. (In 1990 the museum made headlines when 13 of its 2,000 art works were taken in what is called the world's largest art theft.) Every room is decorated in a different style, none true to any one era.

Many visitors, including world travelers, return to the Italianate palacelike building just to sit around the central courtyard with its magnificent seasonal displays of flowers. It's particularly peaceful here on weekdays. The nasturtiums, trailing from third floor to ground, are usually in bloom from late March through April. Recently, all 1,400 glass roof panes were replaced as a first step toward a full museum climate control system.

"Children are encouraged! Some go on a treasure hunt to find the animals in the paintings—or to see if they can locate Isabelle, our live cat (Mrs. Gardner always had one), who likes the outdoor garden."

Institute of Contemporary Art 955 Boylston Street, Boston 02115

Phone: 617/266–5152, 266–5151 (recorded message).

Location: On the corner of Hereford Street, across from the Hynes Convention Center.

Ⓣ**:** Hynes Convention Center/ICA stop on Green Line, Boylston Street exit, 1-block walk.

Open: Wednesday–Sunday 11–5, Thursday–Saturday 11–8. Closed Monday and Tuesday.

Admission: $4 adults, $3 students with valid ID, $1.50 seniors and children under 16, $1 UMass/Boston and MIT students with valid ID. Free Thursdays 5–8 p.m.

Groups: Guided tours arranged in English and Spanish for 10–25 people.

Handicapped access: Assistance required. Please call in advance.

Although the exterior is unchanged, the recycled police station now has two and a half floors of gallery space. Rotating exhibits represent the vanguard of national and local art scenes. In addition, films and lectures are scheduled regularly.

"On a clear day, my father used to joke, you can almost see the coast of Ireland."

—CAROLINE KENNEDY

John F. Kennedy Library and Museum Columbia Point, Boston 02125

Phone: 617/929–4567. TTD: 617/929–4574.

Location: 4 miles southwest of Boston. On University of Massachusetts campus.

Directions: Route 3 south (Southeast Expressway/I–93) to JFK exit 15. Follow signs.

Parking: Free and plentiful. (Expressway is particularly busy during rush hours.)

Ⓣ: Red Line to JFK/UMass station; free shuttle bus runs every 20 minutes to library, 9–5 daily.

Boat: Please see page 235.

Average stay: 90 minutes.

Admission: $5 adult; $3 senior citizen (age 62 and above) and students with valid ID; $1 ages 6–15. Under 6 free. No charge but reservations required for October–April Saturday morning performances by storytellers, musicians, artists, and puppeteers. (Children should be accompanied by adults.)

Cafe: In lobby level, 10:30–3:30 daily.

Picnicking: Tables provided along the walkway by water.

★ Almost every kind of special event except private social occasions.

Handicapped access: Full. Wheelchairs available.

Most visitors never go into the library area, the busiest research facility of the eight presidential libraries. What they come to see are the public exhibits, starting with a superb introductory film (it seems shorter than its 30 minutes). In 1994 there will be new exhibits designed to address a generation that doesn't have memories of the Kennedy administration. Until then, a special traveling White House exhibit, a model of all the rooms, will be featured. Extensive ongoing programming includes the introductory film, lectures, public forums, seminars, conferences, and curriculum development.

Since the library opened in 1979, its landscaped grounds have only become more beautiful—with maturing shade trees, weeping willow, honey locust trees, and dune grass. There are manicured lawns, picnic tables, vistas—and, now, a public landing with boat service to downtown Boston.

JFK's birthplace: In Brookline. Open to the public. See page 112.

Nearby: Equidistant from the ferry landing and across the JFK Library parking lot, the **Massachusetts Archives** (617/727–2816), filled with documents and some records dating back to colonial days, are used by people researching in all kinds of history, including ancestors, treaties, town roads, election returns. The **Commonwealth Museum** (617/727–9268) has a slide show that illustrates how geography has influenced the history of three towns. Another exhibit tells the story of Quabbin Reservoir. Annually, one major exhibit travels throughout the state. Those who are studying Massachusetts or local history make a special point of coming here. Casual visitors spend about an hour. Both facilities are at 220 Morrissey Boulevard, Boston 02125.

Museum of Afro American History 46 Joy Street, Boston 02114

Phone: 617/742–1854 or 723–8863.

Directions: 1 block up from Cambridge Street, on Beacon Hill.

Open: 10–4 daily.

Ⓣ: Park Street station on Green or Red Line, then walk across Common to Joy Street; about a 10-minute walk.

Admission: $3 to gallery (includes guided tour of African Meeting House). No charge for guided tour of Black Heritage Trail, page 106.

The Abiel Smith School (page 106), part of the Black Heritage Trail, now houses the administrative offices and gift shop of the museum. A connecting courtyard brings you to the galleries located in the African Meeting House, chief artifact of the museum. Changing exhibits focus on African Americans throughout the world.

Depending on your interests, the tour of the African Meeting House lasts 30 to 75 minutes. It covers 187 years of history and is given from both architectural and historical points of view. Built by African Americans in 1806, the building was a synagogue from 1898 to 1972. Although much of the interior has been restored to its 1850 appearance, 85 percent is original construction. The exterior brick looks as it did in 1806.

Museum of Fine Arts   465 Huntington Avenue, Boston 02115–5597

Phone: 617/267–9300; 267–9377 recorded information (everything you want to know). TTY/TTD 617/267–9703, Monday–Wednesday 10–4.

Directions: 1 mile west of Copley Square on Huntington Avenue (see map, pages 4–5), between Northeastern University and Wentworth Institute. Eastbound on Mass. Pike, take exit 22; follow Prudential Center signs for Huntington Avenue. *Entrance is on Museum Road.*

Parking: Garage and parking lot on Museum Road across from West Wing entrance. $1.50 per half hour; $15 maximum. Metered street parking (watch the time) sometimes available.

Ⓣ: Ruggles/Museum stop on E (Arborway) Green Line.

Open: *Entire museum:* Tuesday 10–4:45; Wednesday 10–9:45; Thursday–Sunday 10–4:45. *West Wing* (selected exhibitions, auditorium, Museum Shop, and restaurants): Thursday and Friday 5–9:45. *Entrances to special exhibitions galleries close one-half hour before Museum closing; all galleries close 10 minutes before Museum closing.* Closed Mondays, New Year's, July 4, Labor Day, Thanksgiving, December 24 and 25.

Musical Instruments Collection: Year round, Tuesday–Friday 2–4; weekends 1–4:45. *Japanese Garden:* Open June through October. May be viewed from windows in North Gallery on Fenway side. *Museum Shop:* Tuesday and Saturday 10–4:30; Wednesday–Friday 10–9:30; Sunday noon–4:30.

Handicapped access: Free FM assistive listening devices for use in Remis Auditorium (reserve via TTY/TDD or with extension 302). Museum is wheelchair accessible.

Dining (all in West Wing): *Cafeteria* (quick, may be best for kids) on bottom floor: Tuesday, Saturday, Sunday 10–4; Wednesday–Friday 10–8. *Fine Arts Restaurant:* Tuesday–Sunday 11:30–2:30; Wednesday–Friday 5:30–8:30 (cocktails served). *Galleria Cafe:* Tuesday, Saturday, Sunday 10–4, Wednesday–Friday 10–9:30.

Admission: $7 adults ($6 when only West Wing is open); $6 senior citizens and full-time college students with ID; $3.50 ages 6–17. On Thursday and Friday evenings, adult fees reduced by $1, youth by $.50. Free to all Wednesdays after 4 p.m. *No admission charged for free programs or for visitors using only museum shop, restaurants, library, auditorium* (seats 380) *or seminar room* (seats 80). Free coat checking.

Programs: Talks, lectures (with opportunities to examine original objects), films (tickets for single films sold only one hour in advance), performances. Some for senior citizens, children, visitors with special needs (all ages), intergenerational groups—and "for people who didn't know they could feel comfortable in the museum." *Free programs require ticket* issued at auditorium an hour or less before event. *Summer concerts* are in the courtyard at 7:30 (bring blanket, chair, or sit on the grass); picnic or purchase meal here.

★ Special events for corporations and organizations (not private parties, fund raisers, or political events).

For children and families: *Activity booklets* available at information desk. *Free gallery and workshop programs* during school year for ages 6–12, usually Wednesday–Friday 3:30–4:45. *Family Place* is a drop-in program of self-paced activities for children 4 and up. Meets first Sunday of every month, 11–4, in lower rotunda; free with museum admission and no preregistration required.

All kinds of answers and help: The Information Center has a data bank of the collections and all art on display. What to see or do? Staff will offer suggestions, mark exhibit area on a takeaway map, maybe tell you about what not to miss along the way.

Foreign languages: Material available in Chinese, Japanese, Spanish, French, German.

Allow time. Plan—perhaps with help from the Information Center. This great cultural resource is much more than a setting for permanent and traveling exhibitions. Special events and educational programs are frequently planned. (Hints are included in the items above.) The celebrated West Wing, designed by I. M. Pei for major international exhibitions, is an exhibition in itself with its use of natural light and open space. Among almost 200 galleries: the finest Old Kingdom sculpture outside Cairo, the result of a forty-year expedition, with mummies, altars, and hieroglyphics. An extensive collection of Impressionist art. A restored Asian wing. A contemporary collection. Greek and Roman galleries. Paul Revere's work in the American silverware collection. The Decorative Arts Wing, with elaborate and simple period rooms representing four centuries. The Nubian Gallery with ancient African art. A Tapestry Gallery. A recently reopened Textile Gallery. And in the Musical Instruments Room—a 32-glass harmonica, the kind invented by Benjamin Franklin.

Museum of Science Science Park, Boston 02114–1099

Phone: 617/723–2500. TTY: 617/227–3235.

Directions: On the river at the end of Storrow Drive (see map, pages 4–5). *From north:* Routes 93 or 1 south to Storrow Drive/North Station exit. Right onto a ramp. At end follow CAMBRIDGE/SOMERVILLE signs. Go under a bridge with MUSEUM OF SCIENCE 200 YARDS sign. Turn right. *From south:* Southeast Expressway (Routes 93 or 3 north) to Storrow Drive/Cambridge exit 26. *From west:* Inbound on Storrow Drive. Bear left at rotary.

Parking: In garage attached to museum. $2 per hour, $10 maximum. For handicapped, free spaces at front door.

Ⓣ: Science Park on Lechmere/Green Line; some steps, then a 5-minute walk over overpass to museum.

Open: Hours are 9–5, except open until 7 June–September. Open daily June–December. Closed Mondays January–May. Air conditioned.

Average stay: 3 hours; much longer if Omni Theater and Planetarium included. Each show is 45–60 minutes.

Admission: *For each venue* (exhibit halls, Omni Theater, Planetarium, Laser Show): $6.50 adults; $4.50 seniors (65 and over), and ages 4–14. Under 4 free. (Tickets are for a specific time.) *For exhibit halls only:* $5 students with a valid ID. Museum exhibit halls are *free* Wednesday 1–5, from after Labor Day through May except school vacations and holidays. Group rates available with advance arrangements. *Combination tickets:* Two attractions for $10.50, three for $14.50. Less for age 14 and under, senior citizens, and students with ID. *MasterCard and Visa accepted at least one day in advance only;* $1 per person for each credit card ticket purchase for nonmembers.

Museum store: No museum admission required.

Restaurants: First-floor cafe (in the free/meeting-place area of museum) with light snacks and beverages; open 10–8:45. Friendly's Fast Service on second floor, open daily until a half hour before museum closes. Sixth-floor cafeteria where everyone wants a window seat, 8:30–3.

Lyman Library: Film loops, periodicals, books, and a children's corner. Everyone can browse; members and those currently enrolled in courses can borrow.

Hayden Planetarium: Children under 5 must be accompanied by an adult. Sorry, no groups of children under 5 for this 45-minute lecture-demonstration with its realistic depiction of skies—past, present, and future. Scheduled several times a day and at 7:30 Friday nights.

Laser shows: Thursday–Sunday.

Omni Theater: Tickets tend to sell out early. Larger-than-life images. You will feel in motion while watching the film. Special sound system for hearing impaired and infrared system with headsets for visually impaired. Spanish translation for most films. Most shows include a local favorite, a tour of New England.

Volunteers: Ages 14 up.

★ Corporate and organizational events (no private functions).

Questions: Members of the education department, library staffers, and guides are wonderful—and imaginative. They may have an immediate answer, a bibliography, or at least a lead.

Strollers: Allowed, and a help. (Also, changing rooms available.)

Handicapped access: Floors accessible by elevator. Several wheelchairs available. Special needs programs arranged. Braille materials and audio tours at the admissions desk.

ON THE GROUNDS AND FREE!

Picnic on the benches at the pavilion overlooking the river. . . . Look at the labeled rock garden in front of the museum. . . . Sit on the banks of the Charles and watch the boats going through the locks, to and from the harbor. (River excursions leave from the museum. See page 235.)

Before you go: Call for information about any special exhibits and for descriptions and times of shows. If possible, make advance reservations (by credit card only) for shows. All phone orders must be called in at least 1 day in advance; 3–4 days are recommended for weekends, holidays, and school vacations. (Today's and tonight's tickets are available in person only.)

Upon arrival, what to do first?

Buy show tickets. Some times may be sold out.

Check the flyer for today's programs. Demonstrations are geared for different age and interest levels and cover a wide range of subjects. Young children especially like the live animals; they usually don't appreciate the noise and 15-foot-long lightning bolts in the Theater of Electricity's 20-minute demonstrations.

Ask for help if there seems too much to choose from. Knowledgeable volunteers in the lobby know how to ask the right questions to help you plan your visit. If you wish a specific focus, such as natural history or space sciences, there are self-guided tours that could take about two hours.

Some of the permanent exhibits: Special Effects Stage, where visitors can walk on the moon or fly over Boston, thanks to audiovisual technology. One of the nation's largest free computer centers (no time limit) for families. Live Animal Stage, where museum demonstrators present animals such as owls, snakes, ducks, and porcupines. The Observatory, with dozens of "minds-on" activities. Find out what's at the end of a rainbow. Learn about time-lapse photography. Hear ultrasonic sounds usually heard only by bats or dolphins. Children's Discovery Space is made for kids to explore (grown-ups enjoy it too); it's a place that is still open while undergoing a major overhaul that will result in an all-new environment in 1995.

Three blocks from Faneuil Hall Marketplace

New England Aquarium Central Wharf, Boston 02110–3309
Phone: 617/973–5200.

Directions (barring detours caused by Central Artery–Third Harbor Tunnel project): On Southeast Expressway, Route 3 north, take Atlantic Avenue exit. Route 3 south, Callahan Tunnel exit. Follow fish logo signs.

Parking: Discounts at several garages with validated ticket. $3–$3.50 after 5 and on weekends at Rowes Wharf Garage, 617/439–0328; and at International Place Garage, 617/330–5243.

Ⓣ: Aquarium station on Blue Line.

Open: (Admission booth closes half hour before main building closes.) Once your hand is stamped, you can leave the building and return that day. From day after Labor Day through June 30, Monday–Wednesday and Friday 9–5; Thursday 9–8; Saturday, Sunday, holidays 9–6. July through Labor Day (*come early to avoid midday crowds*), Monday, Tuesday, Friday 9–6; Wednesday and Thursday 9–8; Saturday, Sunday, holidays 9–7. Closed Christmas Day and Thanksgiving Day. Open at noon on New Year's Day.

***Discovery*:** 20-minute sea lion presentation aboard the *Discovery*. First-come first-served seating; if you are on a schedule, plan to join the line when you hear the announcement. First show at 10 a.m. weekdays, at 10:30 weekends. Show at 6:30 evenings, when aquarium is open. If you arrive too late for a presentation, you get *Discovery* ticket for next day only.

Average stay: 2½–3 hours. To plan your visit, check the day's schedule of presentations when you enter.

Admission (includes sea lion and film presentations): $7.50 age 12 and over, $6.50 senior citizens with valid ID, $3.50 ages 3–11. Under 3 free. $1 less, 4–7:30 on Thursdays and summer Wednesdays. *Free times?* Check recorded message, 617/973–5200. *Boat trip* (see below): $8 adults, $6 ages 12–18, $5 under age 12. Combination with aquarium admission: $10 adults, $8.50 ages 12–18, $8 under age 12.

Programs: Many are held here. Others are in the field, sometimes to nearby islands. For adults; kids; parents and child; and community, school, and special needs groups.

★ Special events booked; all kinds except children's birthday parties and political events.

Boat trip: Daily summer "Science At Sea" trips open to the public. Naturalists on board. Just enjoy the scene. Or participate. (See page 233.)

Whale watches (on Aquarium's boat): Please see page 253.

Handicapped access: Fully accessible except for very top of aquarium's central tank. Some people report that the ramps are steep if you are pushing.

"The sea isn't the only thing that lives in the ocean."
"A tide pool is like a little swimming pool for animals."
"Sea urchins look like little porcupines."
—AQUARIUM VISITORS, AGE 5

Look, wonder, and learn from the visual feast—colorful fish and plant life of all sizes and shapes. There are more than seventy gallery tanks with a seemingly endless variety of inhabitants. And a saltwater tray complete with jackass penguins. A walkway spirals around the huge glass tank filled with hundreds of fish, even sharks, swimming through the tunnels and caves of the realistic-looking Caribbean coral reef in about 187,000 gallons of filtered, heated Boston Harbor seawater. Scuba divers enter to feed several times a day.

Close-up views become hands-on when you dip your hands into the tide pool exhibit that re-creates the New England shore. Toddlers watch the activity through a low long window. Or they climb up on the rocks and peer over the top. Staffers encourage all ages to hold a starfish or a periwinkle. Other exhibits utilize computer games. And throughout the day, there are special programs.

Reminder: The Aquarium is a major attraction. It is air conditioned. More than a million people a year come here. Half the visitors are adults without children. It's rather dark inside. And not very quiet. Pace yourself.

OUTSIDE AND FREE!

Near the aquarium entrance are **harbor seals** in an outdoor pool. Year round, at least three times a day, there are fascinating **talks** (the next time is posted) given by staffers who feed the cavorting seals. There's a question-and-answer time too. . . . Right here is the don't-miss (even ten minutes in one direction or the other is a treat) **HarborWalk,** page 109, the blue sidewalk line that includes a walkway beyond the Aquarium for a panoramic view of harbor, bridge, and airport.

In Cambridge

Harvard University Art Museums Cambridge 02138

Fogg Art Museum 32 Quincy Street (at Broadway, next to Harvard Yard)

Busch-Reisinger Museum in Werner Otto Hall (enter through Fogg Art Museum)

Arthur M. Sackler Museum 485 Broadway Street (across street from Fogg)

Phone: 617/495–9400; 495–4544 special tours and group reservations.

Location: One block east of Harvard MBTA stop. For a map stop at the Harvard Square information centers (page 139).

Directions: All are within a 10-minute walk of Harvard Square (page 137). Maps are available in the square at the information center in Holyoke Center and at the Cambridge Discovery booth.

Parking: Very difficult near the museums.

Ⓣ: Harvard stop on the Red Line.

Open: Tuesday–Sunday 10–5. Closed Mondays and major holidays.

Admission (covers all three museums): $4 per person. $2.50 senior citizens (over 65) and non-Harvard students. Under 18 free. Free Saturday mornings 10–noon.

Handicapped access: Enter Fogg through back door on Broadway. All galleries accessible by elevator; please call 617/495–4350 for arrangements. Front ramp entrance to Sackler; elevator to all floors.

A highlight for many adults. The most extensive art collection owned by any university in the world. With orientation and follow-up, the **Fogg** could be a fascinating place for youngsters. (Check the current program schedule.) The Italian Renaissance courtyard is surrounded by Romanesque and Gothic sculpture in the corridor and by galleries on two floors that duplicate, in materials and proportion, a sixteenth-century villa. Art of Europe and North America in all media from the Middle Ages to the present includes masterpieces by Giotto, Poussin, Rembrandt, Monet, Renoir, Van Gogh, Picasso, Rothko; master drawings and prints; and twentieth-century photographs. In a stunning recent addition to the museum are decorative arts including clocks, tables, chests, the university president's chair (used in every Harvard commencement), and rotating exhibits. Major pieces by Beckmann, Klee, Nolde, and Kandinsky are part of the German Expressionist collection in the **Busch-Reisinger.** The **Sackler,** built in 1986, is known for its ancient Chinese jades and Islamic and Indian art.

Harvard University Museums of Cultural and Natural History 26 Oxford Street (one side of the building)

Four museums under one roof; two entrances

Phone: 617/495–3045.

Peabody Museum of Archaeology and Ethnology 11 Divinity Avenue (the opposite side of the building)

Phone: 617/495–2248.

For all four museums: Recorded message: 617/495–1910. Groups, guided tours, special programs: 617/495–2341.

Children's programs: 617/495–2341. Many during school vacations; many are free. Some series of classes offered.

Admission to all four museums (payable at either entrance): $3 adults, $2 students and senior citizens, $1 ages 5–15. Free (except groups) Saturdays 9–11.

Peabody Museum Shop: Located on the first floor. Wide selection of ethnic arts from around the world. Open Monday–Saturday 10–4:30, Sunday 1–4:30.

Handicapped access: Elevators available (if possible, call in advance, especially on weekends).

These four museums are sometimes called Cambridge's best-kept secret. The entrance on Oxford Street brings you to three. The **Botanical Museum** houses the most popular exhibit: A climb to the third floor is rewarded by the famous Ware Collection—more than eight hundred species of hand-blown glass flowers that seem real in every detail. (The few cases of flowers outside the main exhibit may be enough for young children.) The creators, Leopold Blaschka and his son, developed the process and shared it with no one. Their sole customers, the Ware family, gave the collection to Harvard, which uses it as an important teaching tool. . . . The **Mineralogical Museum** houses a collection—used for teaching and research too—of more than fifty thousand specimens from all over the world. The third-floor exhibits include a large sampling of minerals and gemstones (one display shows the stages between rough and polished) and a meteorite exhibit with several sizable examples. . . . In the **Museum of Comparative Zoology** (Agassiz Museum), you are constantly looking up, down, and around. There are dinosaurs, rhinoceroses, elephants, and a 42-foot fossil kronosaurus (sea serpent) discovered in Australia in 1932. The largest turtle carapace ever found—6 feet by 8 feet, weighing 200 pounds—is here too. From a balcony there's a close-up of whale skeletons.

The **Peabody Museum** can be reached from the third floor of the Oxford Street entrance or by walking around the outside of the building to the entrance at 11 Divinity Avenue. At the front desk pick up a map to find your way to four floors of wonderful galleries. The Hall of the North American Indian (reopened in 1990 after being closed for ten years) focuses on the last five centuries of interaction between Native Americans and intruding populations. There's a Maya exhibit and ethnological material from the Pacific Islands. From the extensive collections changes are made in some galleries from year to year.

The Sports Museum of New England CambridgeSide Galleria, One CambridgeSide Place, Cambridge 02141

Phone: 617/78–SPORT.

Parking: $.99 for 90 minutes. After that, during day, $1 each half hour up to 5 hours, $20 maximum; $3 maximum in evening.

Ⓣ: Lechmere Station on Green Line, walk ½ block on First Street.

Open: Until the late 1992 grand opening: Monday–Saturday 10–9:30, Sunday noon–6. Call for new hours.

Admission: Free in preview gallery. After late 1992 opening, probably $5 adults, $3 children.

A teaser of what's to come. It may be the first of its kind in a shopping mall. The preview gallery hints at the exhibits and programs that will be in place in the full museum, which began in 1977 on Soldiers Field in Brighton. There's a big screen and many smaller videos—with some of the museum's 1,000 hours of sports footage. A 1915 World Championship Red Sox photo, baseball spikes circa 1895, Bruins' uniforms, 1955 Tony DeMarco boxing gloves, Head of the Charles regatta memorabilia, college sports, hockey, figure skating, the Boston Marathon, physically challenged athletes, life-size hand-carved wooden statues of Larry Bird, Bobby Orr, and Carl Yastrzemski —they are all here. The full museum will have equipment to try on, hoops and sticks to play with, educational programs, special events, and celebrity appearances. And a place to sit and enjoy those videos.

North of Boston

SEE "DAY TRIPS" TOO

Addison Gallery of American Art Phillips Academy, Main Street (Route 28), Andover 01810

Phone: 508/749–4015.

Location: 23 miles from Boston.

Directions: I–93 north to exit 15 (Route 125 north), to Route 28 north.

Open: September–July, Tuesday–Saturday 10–5, Sunday 1–5. Closed New Year's, Memorial Day, Labor Day, Thanksgiving, and Christmas.

Admission: Free.

Handicapped access: Elevator available by arrangement.

Special exhibits and a gallery of American art from colonial times to today. The permanent collection includes paintings, sculpture, graphic arts, furniture, glass, textiles, silver, and models—built to uniform scale—of famous American sailing ships.

The **R. S. Peabody Foundation for Archaeology** at the academy, on the corner of Phillips and Main, is open weekdays (except major holidays) 8:30 –4:15. The archaeological exhibits focus on New England and nearby Canada; the anthropological exhibits outline the physical and cultural evolution of man over a period of two million years. There's also a study on the comparative evolution of three cities—Boston, Mexico City, and Baghdad. Phone: 508/749–4491.

> **Nearby:** The Phillips Academy Bird Sanctuary at the end of Chapel Avenue, off Main Street. A 2-mile walk on wide, winding gravel paths among azaleas, rhododendrons, laurel, and ponds. Look for wild ducks and geese. Sorry, no picnicking and no dogs allowed.

Hammond Castle Museum Page 63.

Merrimack Valley Textile Museum 800 Massachusetts Avenue, North Andover 01845

Phone: 508/686–0191.

Location: 29 miles from Boston.

Directions: I–93 north to I–495 north, to exit 43 (Massachusetts Avenue, North Andover). East on Massachusetts Avenue for 1½ miles. The museum is on the left, a half mile beyond the second traffic light.

Open: Tuesday–Friday 9–5, weekends 1–5. Closed holidays.

Average stay: 45 minutes.

Admission: Free.

Tours: With impressive demonstrations of machinery, Tuesday through Friday at 10:30, 1, and 3; Sundays at 1:30 and 3.

School groups: Special programs arranged for grade 5 and up.

Handicapped access: Accessible.

Following an audiovisual presentation, you see exhibits that depict the history of wool textile manufacturing. They emphasize the transition from hand to machine production during the Industrial Revolution. But the demonstrations are the most exciting part of the visit. You watch carding, spinning, and weaving, and hear (the noise is deafening) the equipment in motion. From time to time, special traveling exhibits are booked. And the museum has an extensive library on textiles and textile history.

Peabody Museum of Salem Page 89.

Wenham Museum 132 Main Street, Wenham 01984

Phone: 508/468–2377.

Location: 25 miles north of Boston.

Directions: Route 128 north, exit 20 north to Route 1A north for 2.3 miles. Across from town green.

Open: Monday–Friday 10–4, Saturday 1–4, Sunday 2–5. Closed major holidays and early February.

Admission: $3 adults, $2.50 senior citizens, $1 children 6–14. Under age 6 free.

No wonder this is sometimes called "the doll museum." There are dolls—1,000 of them, from all over the world—made of wood, wax, china, cloth, papier-mache, rubber, metal, leather, and bisque. One dollhouse is a Victorian mansion with parquet floors, stained-glass windows, and hand-painted murals. It all started with the collection of Elizabeth Richards Horton; she lived in the 1600s Claflin-Richards House, now home to this small museum with its four period rooms, quilts, costumes, needlework, and woodenware. Also here: two "10-footer" shoe houses, an herb garden, and tools used when Wenham Lake ice was sent to India and Australia. The museum has become popular for ★ little girls' birthday celebrations (reservations required): A paper game, a treasure hunt of sorts, and a party across the street in another old house, the Wenham Tea House, can be arranged.

South of Boston

SEE "DAY TRIPS" TOO

Blue Hills Trailside Museum (Massachusetts Audubon Society) 1904 Canton Avenue (Route 138), Milton 02186

Phone: 617/333–0690.

Parking: Free.

Open: Year round, Wednesday–Sunday 10–5. Some vacation weekdays. Closed Thanksgiving, Christmas, and New Year's.

Admission: $3 adults, $1.50 ages 3–12, free under age 3. Massachusetts Audubon members free with cards.

Average stay: Up to an hour, longer if you climb the hill.

Handicapped access: Accessible.

Picnicking: At the top of Blue Hill or across the parking lot at ski area.

This family-sized museum—especially well attended on weekends and vacation days—is an all-weather place with indoor and outdoor activities, including live animal demonstrations and even night owling (learn to call and to listen), for all ages. Inside there are some "touch" items, along with displays of plants, trees, minerals, meteorites, birds, mammals, amphibians, reptiles, and fish. Outside exhibits (free) include a river otter (sometimes in action), foxes, turtles, mallard ducks, and geese. Marked hiking trails start from here.

Chickatawbut Hill Educational Center, about 5 miles up on the second highest hilltop in the Blue Hills Reservation, is the site of many day and overnight programs.

Trailside Museum Coffee House: First and third Saturday nights each month, in transformed auditorium with candlelit tables and nonalcoholic beverages. $5 per person.

Foxboro Museum of Discovery 26 Chestnut Street, Foxboro 02035

Phone: 508/543–1184.

Directions: (About 40 minutes from Boston.) Route 128 south to 95 south, exit 8. Turn right off exit onto Mechanic Street to first light. Right onto Chestnut Street; follow it to a stop sign. Turn right and take an immediate right to parking lot. (Check ahead! Some time in 1993, they may move to another Foxboro location.)

Parking: Free.

Open: Tuesday–Saturday 10–5, Sunday 1–5.

Average stay: 2 to 2½ hours.

Admission: $3 per person. Under 18 months free. Discounts for groups; please reserve.

Strollers: "We welcome them."

Handicapped access: "We are ramped."

Eating: A snack bar in museum with homemade cookies and muffins, some prepacked items. Two picnic tables, near the 25-ton sandbox and a rabbit family.

Gift shop: Items from $.10 to $100.

★ Birthday parties held in private area of snack bar.

Parents not only react to their children's reactions but are responsible for some of the most successful exhibits here. When one young visitor told his mother that it was impossible for "all that" to fit inside of him, the parent and staff came up with the Velcro anatomy apron for the body awareness exhibit. There's a TV room that inspires role playing (produce a show) as well as curiosity (how does the camera work?). A father and his son designed the

Not sure where the town is? Check the map on page 2.

nature trail with about thirty stops where you learn about trees, plants, and rocks. And then there was the time that children were measuring peas and lentils while their parents, who had never met before, communicated over their own activity, a town emerging from 1,000 Lincoln Logs.

About fifty interactive exhibits are in the rooms off the one long corridor in this former Foxboro State Hospital building. Many high school and graduate students volunteer. Most of the audience is between ages 2 and 11.

Fuller Museum of Art 455 Oak Street, Brockton 02401

Phone: 508/588–6000.

Location: 25 miles from Boston.

Directions: I–93 south to Route 128 north, to Route 24, to exit 18B, Route 27 north. First right onto Oak Street; the museum is 1 mile up, on the left.

Parking: Free and plentiful.

Open: Tuesday–Sunday 12–5. Closed Thanksgiving, Christmas, and New Year's. Air conditioned. Admission: $3 adults, $2 senior citizens, $1 age 16 and under. Family rates available.

Programs: Include lectures and children's series.

Courses: Museum school has them for all ages.

Handicapped access: All galleries are wheelchair accessible.

Cafe: Open 12–2 Tuesday–Friday.

★ Weddings and other social events. Auditorium and gallery space.

Although a special exhibition or performance may bring you here, the setting alone is worth the trip. The contemporary cedar-shingled structure is built around a courtyard with sculpture, fountains, ferns, and a view of a pond complete with ducks. Shows range from collections of nineteenth- and twentieth-century American masters to contemporary multicultural works.

What else is here? A large, beautiful wooded park. You can walk a half mile around Upper Porter's Pond to the observation tower and climb the tower for a good southerly view. Or ride a bicycle over 4 miles of trails (shared with motor vehicles) near the museum. Or fish in the ponds. There's something for everyone.

Whaling Museum 18 Johnny Cake Hill, New Bedford 02740

Phone: 508/997–0046.

Directions: (About an hour from Boston.) From I–95 in New Bedford, take exit 15 for 1 mile to "Downtown" exit. Right on Elm Street, left on Bethel. Parking garages nearby.

Open: Year-round, daily 9–5, Sundays 1–5; Sundays in July and August 11–5. Closed Thanksgiving, Christmas, and New Year's.

Admission: $3.50 adults, $3 senior citizens, $2.50 ages 6–14. Group rates by appointment.

Film: July and August, shown once in morning and again in early afternoon. September–June, weekends at 2.

Average stay: "At least 90 minutes; some people spend the whole day."

Handicapped access: Elevator available.

"The children absolutely loved that film!" exclaimed one visitor. The next reported that 22 minutes of an actual whale chase was too much for her youngster. One guaranteed hit: A climb aboard the deck of the world's largest ship model, the *Lagoda,* a half-scale full-rigged whaling bark, where you can touch harpoons, anchor chains, and blubber hooks. Then climb to the balcony of the museum for a topside view.

Journals of seamen show sperm whale stamps on the days when a whale was caught. The shortest trip on record lasted six months; the longest, eleven years. Also on display in the most comprehensive collection of artifacts from the American whaling industry: scrimshaw, ship models, paintings, dolls and toys, and early household items.

Nearby (on foot): Opposite the museum is the Seamen's Bethel with ship-shaped pulpit and wide-planked floor. . . . New Bedford Visitor Center at 47 North Second Street provides takeaway map of cobblestoned waterfront district and information about Buttonwood Zoo and Park, factory and designers' outlets, walking tours. . . . Two blocks from Whaling Museum is the East Coast's largest fishing fleet. Today, scallopers predominate. . . . Three blocks away: Year round, the restored 1923 vaudeville Zeiterion Theatre at 684 Purchase Street schedules professional concerts, theater, and children's performances, all at prices less than the big city.

Restaurants: Salads, burgers, steaks in converted 1833 bank building: Freestone's Restaurant and Bar, 41 Williams Street, steps from Visitor Center. Ethnic specialties and more formal: Portofino's, attached to the Durant Sail Loft Inn (at the south end of the waterfront), and Candleworks at 74 North Water Street. Perfect for families: Reasonably priced seafood at Davy's Locker at 1480 Rodney French Boulevard, on the water near the Martha's Vineyard ferry landing.

West of Boston

SEE "DAY TRIPS" TOO

Cardinal Spellman Philatelic Museum 235 Wellesley Street (adjacent to Regis College), Weston 02193

Phone: 617/894–6735.

Location: 18 miles from Boston.

Directions: Mass. Pike west to exit 15. Follow Route 30 (Commonwealth Avenue) west for about a mile. Right at light onto Wellesley Street for a few hundred feet on your left.

Parking: Free.

Open: Sunday 1–5; Tuesday–Thursday 9–4. Closed holidays. Air conditioned.

Admission: Free, but donations are welcome.

Handicapped access: Rear entrance has one step; elevator inside.

This is the only museum in the country designed and built expressly for the display and preservation (an emphasis here) of stamps. The nucleus of the museum's collection is the famous collection started by Cardinal Francis Spellman in his youth. Among three million items are rarities, stamp design errors, forgeries, and the Dwight D. Eisenhower Collection (received by Eisenhower when he was president of the United States). On the third Sunday of each month, a free collectors' bourse (market) supplements items from the museum shop with those from dealers. A Ben Franklin Stamp Club for elementary and middle school–age students meets the second Sunday of each month.

Charles River Museum of Industry 154 Moody Street, Waltham 02154

Phone: 617/893–5410.

Location: Located in the former Boston Manufacturing Company mill complex in Waltham.

Directions: Route 95/128 to exit 26/Route 20. Follow Main Street to Central Square. Cross river, turn left on Pine Street to municipal parking lot. Take footbridge over Charles River to driveway to museum.

Train: Take the Fitchburg/Gardner commuter rail line from North Station (617/722–3200 or 800/392–6100) to Waltham Station. Walk left on Moody for 1 block, then left into first driveway and then right into museum driveway.

Open: Thursday and Saturday 10–5, other weekdays by appointment.

Admission: $4 adults; $2 seniors, students, children, and unemployed.

Ring a 1,000-pound tower bell by rocking it back and forth on its cradle. Play a player piano. Control and ride a miniature train. Observe a noisy paper-bag machine in operation. And then gasp. Well, that's what most people do when they enter the 50-foot-high boiler room that now houses a steam and automobile exhibit, an educational room, and a workshop for machine tools. When the steam engine is demonstrated, you see lots of moving parts. There are antique cars, watchmaking tools, photos, and memorabilia. Volunteer guides at this museum—a national historic site, home of many firsts—have helped and are still helping to restore equipment and machines that were developed or used by manufacturers located along the Charles River since the 1800s. Tours vary in length and topic, depending on your interests. Mechanical engineers seem to stay for hours. Many children are fascinated for at least one hour, maybe two.

Danforth Museum of Art 123 Union Avenue, Framingham 01701

Phone: 508/620–0050 office, 872–0858 school.

Location: 21 miles from Boston.

Directions: Mass. Pike to exit 13 (Route 30 west), to Route 126 south. Follow Route 126 for about 2 miles. Turn right at traffic circle onto Union Avenue, to museum on your right.

Open: Wednesday–Sunday, 12–5. Closed most holidays.

Admission: $3 adults, $2 senior citizens and students. Free to Framingham State College and children under 12.

Handicapped access: Elevator from parking lot to galleries.

Take one part old school building. Add grass-roots support, lots of work, and nineteenth- and twentieth-century American and European prints, drawings, photographs, paintings and sculpture along with special loan exhibitions. The result? A good small museum, fine arts library, and museum school. The Ballou Junior Gallery ties hands-on activities and gallery games to exhibits. Members include forty-three schools that represent thirteen

Museum hours and prices change. Call for today's information.

towns in the area. Beyond that, it's an active place with extensive programming for all ages.

Outdoor combination idea: Garden in the Woods, page 198.

DeCordova Museum and Sculpture Park Sandy Pond Road, Lincoln 01773

Phone: 617/259–8355.

Location: 15 miles from Boston.

Directions: Route 2 west to Route 128 (I–95) south, to exit 28 (Trapelo Road). Follow Trapelo Road for about 3 miles, across Lincoln Road, to Sandy Pond Road.

Parking: Free.

Open: Tuesday–Friday 10–5, weekends 12–5. Closed Mondays, New Year's Day, Easter, July 4, Thanksgiving, and Christmas.

Average stay: About an hour.

Admission: Museum: $4 adults; $3 seniors, students, and ages 6–12; under 6 free. No charge for sculpture park.

Picnicking: Allowed.

★ Special events: corporate, private, and nonprofit events; weddings. (No proms or political or fund-raising events.)

Handicapped access: Grounds and main floor accessible; many steps to upper galleries. Sign-language interpreter available by arrangement. Some touch exhibition and sculpture park tours arranged for visually impaired.

Local residents and out-of-towners alike drive and pedal along the tree-lined entrance roadway to this magnificent setting—to the turreted building built in 1880, to museum exhibits that often focus on contemporary New England artists, to an Art in the Park festival in June, and to summer jazz and folk concerts in the large outdoor amphitheater. The 35-acre park, one of a kind in New England, is perfect for the approximately thirty (they change from time to time) contemporary and modern sculptures. There's plenty of space and manicured lawn, interesting topography, and paths, bordered by wildflowers, to the quiet pond below. The educational department offers something for toddlers on up, a children's summer art camp, tours, classes, and workshops.

"We tell the kids that you can let your parents play a little too."

The Discovery Museums 177 Main Street, Acton 01720

Phone: 508/264–4200; 264–4201 (group reservations). TDD: 508/264–0030.

Story phone: 508/264–4222 (3 minutes, changed weekly).

Experiment phone: 508/264–9592. A new at-home experiment each week, contributed in part by kids.

Location: 40 miles northwest of Boston.

Directions: From Route 128, take Route 2 west. Continue on Route 2 as you go around the Concord rotary; continue for about 2 miles. Take Route 27 exit and travel south toward Maynard (not Acton). Museums are 1 mile down on the left. Watch for Bessie, the green dinosaur, out front.

Open: *The Science Discovery Museum:* Tuesday, Thursday, Friday, 1–4:30; Wednesday 1–6; Saturday and Sunday 9–4:30. *The Children's Discovery Mu-*

seum: Tuesday, Thursday, Friday 1–4:30; Wednesday, Saturday, Sunday 9–4:30. Both museums closed Mondays except during school vacation weeks. Summer hours, both museums: Tuesday–Sunday 9–4:30; Science Museum until 6 on Wednesday.

Admission: $8 per person covers both museums, same day. $5 per person for each museum separately. Under age 1, free.

Birthday parties: A special workshop, but no facility for food and drink.

The Children's Museum in the converted Queen Anne Victorian came first—with use of every nook and cranny, every ceiling, wall, and floor space. What was a closet is open space with a video of a whale watch. There are costumes to put on, quiet corners for reading alone, rooms with themes. In the water room you can make a bubble big enough to encircle you. The Safari Room is nature related, with puzzles, sounds, stuffed animals, a bridge and a tunnel. The Discovery Ship has steering wheel, water bed, captain's quarters, and a sick bay. *Strollers?* "We recommend backpacks in the Children's Museum." *Handicapped access:* First floor.

In 1987 the custom-designed, not-too-big, activity-filled Science Museum opened for school-aged children. Set in a wooded area, it features much light and an octagonal-windowed tower. At the entrance "whisper dishes" direct the energy of sound, whispered conversations, from one parabolic dish to another. In the inventors' workshop you use recycled materials or take apart toasters, radios, typewriters, or computers. Create a mist tornado in a bottle, a sand design with a pendulum. *Strollers?* Allowed. *Handicapped access:* Entire Science Museum.

The Discovery Museums have been discovered. If you arrive at a busy time, you take a number and either wait here (climb on Bessie, whisper near the whisper dishes, and picnic on the grounds) or go to the nearby family-style Candlewood Restaurant or fast-food places. If the number has been called upon your return, you go right in to the museum. *Hint: Note that the two museums have different hours.* Both museums are open to all ages. Because adult accompaniment is required, if you are coming with two age groups that wish to be separate, plan on coming with two adults.

Fruitlands Museums 102 Prospect Hill Road, Harvard 01451

Phone: (508) 456–3924.

Location: 30 miles from Boston.

Directions: From Route 495, take Route 2 west 4 miles, exit at Routes 110/111 toward Harvard, right onto Old Shirley Road (at Fruitlands sign) for 1½ miles on the right.

Parking: Free and plentiful. Reception center, where you buy tickets, is at middle parking lot. Restaurant is at top lot.

Open: Mid-May to mid-October, Tuesday–Sunday and Monday holidays 10–5. Museum shop is open during museum hours and Thanksgiving–Christmas.

Admission: $5 adults, $4.50 seniors, $2.50 students with valid ID, $1 ages 7–16, free under 7. Advance reservations required for groups of 15 or more.

Recommended: A guide, available upon request, to introduce children to Picture Gallery's portraits, with suggested home follow-up activities.

Programs: Include concerts, demonstrations, and workshops—some designed especially for adults and/or children (age 5 and up) and school groups.

Eating: Sorry, no picnicking allowed on grounds. Cafe, at top parking lot, has lovely terrace overlooking the valley, with mountains in the distance. Open 10–4 for snacks, lunch, tea.

★ Rooms, not the grounds, available for social events, weddings, rehearsal dinners, some business meetings.

Strollers: Allowed.

Handicapped access: Partial—with plans to increase.

Some visitors just sit and enjoy the peace at this Massachusetts and National Historic Landmark. Some walk on the 2 miles of trails through woodlands, pine groves, and meadows with mountain vistas. And there are some who see all the exhibits in the five small manageable buildings set along a rolling hill, with Mount Wachusett and Mount Monadnock in the background. Check in at the reception center for the schedule of events. Feel free to ask questions of the interpreters, helpful folk who range from high school age to retirees.

All four Alcott children lived for a time in the eighteenth-century **Fruitlands Farmhouse** where Bronson Alcott strove to establish a new social and religious order. Now the building serves as a museum of the transcendentalist movement and contains memorabilia of Emerson, Thoreau, Alcott—even framed locks of Louisa's hair. Displayed farm and kitchen items illustrate the pre-Fruitlands community days. The **Shaker House,** built in 1794, was used as an office of the Harvard Shaker Society, which flourished until 1918. It houses a good collection of Shaker handcrafts and products. Herbs, weaving, and shoe repair were among community industries. The **Indian Museum** has a ceremonial buffalo robe, pottery, baskets, arrowheads, artifacts from tribes across the country. In the **Picture Gallery** are collections of American folk portraits by itinerant artists and nineteenth-century landscape paintings.

Nearby: Apple country with pick-your-own possibilities (see page 277).

John Woodman Higgins Armory 100 Barber Avenue, Worcester 01606

Phone: 508/853–6015.

Location: 45 miles from Boston.

Directions: Mass. Pike to I–495 north, to I–290 west, to exit 20. Turn right onto Burncoast Street, then left onto Randolph Road, ½ mile to museum.

Parking: Free.

Open: Tuesday–Saturday 10–4, Sunday 12–4. Open Mondays 1–4 in July and August. Closed most holidays.

Average stay: 2½ hours.

Air conditioned: All but great hall.

Admission: $4.25 adults, $3.50 senior citizens, $3.25 ages 6–16, under 6 free. Group rates available.

★ Birthday parties here include the knighting of the celebrant. Scouts who stay overnight start out as pages, have a feast and lots of activities, and leave as knights.

Restaurants: Can be seen from front door: Barber's Crossing on West Boylston Street, a family place with salad bar. Next door: Eddie's Pub, a

Higgins Armory Museum photo © Don Eaton

diner with soup and sandwiches. Five minutes away: Charlie's Eating and Drinking Saloon.

Handicapped access: Accessible. Programs arranged for mentally and physically challenged visitors.

Knights in armor line the exhibit hall in a castlelike Renaissance setting. Centuries-old artifacts, arranged chronologically, tell the story of arms and armor from antiquity to modern times. There are helmets with facial features (even mustaches), armor for children and hunting dogs, swords and other weapons, furniture, tools, stained glass, paintings, and tapestries. No touching in the exhibit areas (perspiration and oil from hands can cause rust); but there's an orientation program—held in a new auditorium—that involves suiting a member or two from the audience and a discussion about how protection has changed through the years. In the Quest (hands-on) Gallery, there are costumes that allow a child to become king, queen, Robin Hood, a jester, or a princess. Adults, too, try on authentic reproduction heavy metal helms. Or play chess and checkers. David Macauley's *Castles* and *Cathedral* are among the most popular videos.

Museum of Our National Heritage 33 Marrett Road (corner of Route 2A and Massachusetts Avenue), Lexington 02173

Phone: 617/861–6559, recorded message 861–0729.

Location: 12 miles from Boston.

Directions: Route 2 west to Waltham Street exit. Right at second lights onto Marrett Road (Route 2A), and up the hill. (One mile from the Minuteman Statue on Lexington Green.)

Parking: Free in museum lot.

Ⓣ: Alewife on the Red Line; then bus 62 (Bedford) or 76 (Hanscom) to museum. No bus service on Sundays or holidays.

Open: Monday–Saturday 10–5, Sunday 12–5. Air conditioned.

Admission: Free to individuals and guided (prearranged) school tours. Other groups, $1 each, $10 minimum charge.

Handicapped access: Full. Museum is all on one level.

The contemporary brick and glass building with central open courtyard was built and is supported by the Scottish Rite Masons. Exquisite displays in the four galleries may include clocks, quilts, folk art, photographs, books, paintings, or prints—all tied to America's growth and development.

Museum of Transportation Larz Anderson Park, 15 Newton Street, Brookline 02146

Phone: 617/522–6140 recorded information; 522–6547 office.

Location: An expansive, beautiful park with playground and pondside picnicking facilities.

Directions: Route 9 west to Lee Street at end of reservoir. Take sharp left onto Lee Street; Lee merges with Clyde; stay on Clyde to the end. Left at lights onto Newton Street. At immediate fork, bear right on Newton Street and follow signs to museum on the left.

Parking: Free.

Open: Year round, 10–5 Wednesday through Sunday including holidays.

Admission: $4 adults. $2 seniors, students with ID, children 12 and under. Under 3 free. Group rates available.

Picnicking: Allowed on park grounds.

★ Special events: everything from weddings to corporate functions to private parties.

Handicapped access: Accessible.

Brick walls, handsome beams, railings, arches, and wonderful open spaces provide the backdrop for exhibits in this 1888 carriage house, modeled after a French castle. Main-floor exhibits change annually; they have included cars of the future and, most recently, muscle cars—autos of the rock and roll era. A sense of time and place is evident in the lower-level permanent exhibit where restored classic cars and antique carriages are seen with videos, period fashions, and household goods. Although almost all are no-touch exhibits, you may step aboard a trolley. Or design your own car in the inventors' workshop stocked with wooden wheels, cardboard, dowels and other materials. Or use a special software package to design a car on the computer. Sometimes there are opportunities to take a vintage fire engine ride.

Worcester Art Museum 55 Salisbury Street, Worcester 01609–3196
Phone: 508/799–4406.

Location: 45 miles from Boston.

Directions: Mass. Pike, exit 11A. Follow I–495 north to I–290 west to exit 18. Bear right at light at bottom of exit ramp (Lincoln Street). Turn right at next traffic light on to Concord Street. Go straight at next light and bear immediate right onto Salisbury Street for 2 blocks on left.

Parking: Free in lots on Tuckerman Street.

Open: Tuesday, Wednesday, and Friday 11–4. Thursday 11–8. Saturday 10–5. Sunday 1–5. Closed Mondays, New Year's Day, Easter, July 4, Thanksgiving, and Christmas.

Admission: $4 adults, $2.50 seniors and full-time college students with ID. Free to age 18 and under; free to all on Saturdays 10–noon. Additional charge for some special previews and events. Group tours, arranged 3–4 weeks in advance, available free with admission.

Cafe: Tuesday–Saturday 11:30–2; beverages and desserts 2–3. Sunday noon–4 for brunch, desserts, teas. Thursday 5–8 for dinner. Good and reasonably priced.

Strollers: Allowed. Helpful guards direct you to elevators.

Handicapped access: Accessible. Wheelchair available upon request.

Art of fifty centuries, from a Sumerian stone figure to paintings by Gauguin, Matisse, and Picasso. The collection, arranged chronologically, includes noteworthy Egyptian, classical, pre-Columbian, Oriental, and medieval sculpture; mosaics from Antioch in the two-story-high central court; frescoes from Spoleto; a dark, cool Romanesque chapter house, moved stone by stone from France and rebuilt here; Italian and other European paintings of the thirteenth to twentieth centuries; and English and American art from the eighteenth century to today. It's very much a traditional museum setting, and it's lovely.

Open Space

- What's here? Staffed sanctuaries, huge public parks and lands, and small (almost hidden) treasures.
- Generally, it's a good idea to go with at least one other person.
- A reminder (at the request of staffers): Wear appropriate footwear for unpaved paths.
- Another reminder (from tired kids and some of their parents): The return part of a hike often seems longer.
- Picnicking may be allowed even where there is no designated area—if you carry your trash away.
- What else? Guided walks, field trips, workshops, demonstrations, and/or classes are scheduled at almost every one of the described areas. They take place morning, noon, and nighttime too—for adults, families, and children.
- Where else? Town forests and conservation lands. Chances are that there are paths throughout. A map may be available too.

Boston Harbor Islands State Park

Getting There

Many of the seventeen islands in the park are now open to the public. Comprehensive information is available from the Department of Environmental Management, 349 Lincoln Street, Building 45, Hingham 02043, phone 617/740–1605. The MDC (617/727–5250) sets rules and regulations for Georges, Lovells, and Peddocks. For all travel information, including the water taxi schedule, contact Bay State Cruises, 617/723–7800.

- **Georges Island:** See page 235. The longest day trip by commercial ferry from Boston's waterfront allows for a maximum of 6 hours on one or more islands.
- **Bumpkin, Gallops, Grape, Lovells, and Peddocks:** All are reached from Georges Island—there is no direct ferry from Boston—on a free water taxi that runs daily in the summer. The taxi allows for several hours on one island or for island hopping. Some years the boat runs weekends in June and September. Schedules vary.
- **Thompson Island:** Reached by Bay State Cruise boats Memorial Day through Labor Day. Please see page 234.

What's Where

Free guided walks: On Georges, Bumpkin, Gallops, Grape, Lovells, and Peddocks during the summer. Enthusiastic staff members share their knowledge of the islands' botany and history.

Drinking water: Bring plenty! It's available on Georges Island only.

Refreshment stand: Only on Georges, during the summer.

Picnicking: Allowed on all. Only Georges has barbecue pits.

Marked trails: On all the islands.

Fishing pier (catch-and-release recommended): On Georges, Bumpkin, Gallops, Grape, and Lovells.

Camping: On four islands (see page 240). Reservations required.

Supervised swimming: Sorry, on none.

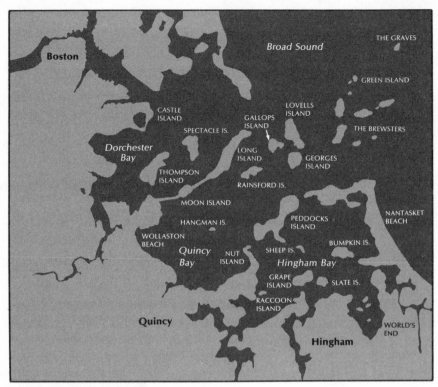

Boston Harbor Islands

Rest rooms: Available on all. Most are primitive, though.

Reminder: Dress for the occasion. Proper footwear helps.

Georges, open to the public for thirty years, is a popular outing site with plenty of open space and shade, barbecue pits, a refreshment stand. Explorers like to find their way around old Fort Warren, a defense of Boston Harbor in all U.S. wars and a prison for military and civilian personnel during the Civil War. With tunnels (bring flashlights), parapets, and steps to investigate, it can be a long hike. Take a guided tour or explore on your own. (Children are not allowed in Fort Warren without adult supervision.) In summer the information booth is staffed by the Friends of the Boston Harbor Islands.

 Bumpkin is the quietest island. A noticeable solitude. Trails with lovely wildflowers lead to stone arches of a farmhouse that was, for a time, part of a children's hospital.

 On **Gallops** are many different plants, remains of old foundations, a gazebo built over the water, and picnic tables. The high bluffs offer wonderful views of harbor activity.

 Lovells still has remains of World War fortifications. In addition to walking trails through meadows, dunes, saltmarsh, and woods, there are beautiful beaches. (Reminder: No supervised swimming.) Picnic tables. Shade shelter. Small gazebo.

 Peddocks has the longest shoreline of the islands. You are not on your own here: All visits are guided tours that highlight Fort Andrews, built in 1900.

Thompson Island, home to Outward Bound Education Center and the only private island in the harbor, is open to visitors on weekends, Memorial Day through Labor Day. The island, farmland for over two hundred years, is pastoral. The 2-mile northeast trail takes you into a wooded area, along the bluff, beach, fields, and coves, and into meadows with abundant bird life and wildflowers. The southwest trail focuses on history, old farm buildings, a weather station, and school sites. About a third of the paths are roadways, accessible to strollers and wheelchairs. Bring a picnic!

In or Very Near Boston

Arnold Arboretum (Harvard University) 125 Arborway (Routes 1 and 203), Jamaica Plain 02130

Phone: 617/524–1718 or 524–1717 (recorded information).

Directions: *To main gate:* Route 1 south (Riverway/Jamaicaway). A little beyond Jamaica Pond at a rotary take 203 east and gate is almost immediately on your right. *To Peter's Hill* and "the view": Route 1 south. Pass Faulkner Hospital and take first left turn left onto Walter Street, and left on Bussey. Park on Bussey or Walter.

Ⓣ: Orange Line to Forest Hills, then 2 blocks northeast to the main gate. E (Arborway) Green Line to Arborway, then 4 blocks to the Jamaica Plain gate. Or Arborway (number 39) bus from Boston Public Library at Copley Square to Monument stop in Jamaica Plain; walk 100 yards to entrance near junction of Route 1 south and Route 203/Arborway.

MY POEM 松の木
松の木が風にゆられて
さわさわさわいている.
松の木は木の中でつよいといっている
冬でも緑の衣をたっぷり着て
ほかの木たちのまん中に
ドシッとすわっている.
松の木は風が運んでくる話を聞くのが好きだ
アメリカの風が来たら
英語で話し,
日本の風が来たら
日本語で話し,
外国の風が来たら
たくさんの外国の言葉を話す.
だからこそ松の木はぼくのことを
理かいしてくれる.

MY POEM Pine Tree
The wind sways
The pine trees rustling through its branches,
Of all the trees that brag
The pine tree is the strongest,
Even in the winter,
It wears green clothes,
In the middle of other trees,
Sitting steadily,
The pine tree likes to listen to
The wind bringing conversation,
If an American wind blows,
It hears English.
When a Japanese wind blows,
It hears Japanese
If the oversea's wind blows,
It hears many languages.
So the pine tree understand me.

Arbor Day poem by Arnold Arboretum tree poetry competition winner Tadashi Tamaoki (visiting student from Tokyo, Japan, at Lawrence School, Brookline, grade 4).

Open: Year round, dawn to dusk.

Admission: Free. Visitor center at the Jamaica Plain gate closed until fall 1993, when it will reopen with "a new look," new exhibits, a model of the grounds. (Portable bathrooms until then.)

Tours: Drop-in van tours Sunday afternoons at 2, May, June, September, October. $4 adults (nonmembers); free for children under 16. Call to arrange for other guided tours.

Handicapped and elderly access: When visitor center reopens, special automobile permits issued on weekdays.

Dogs: Must be on a leash (and bring your pooper scooper).

Climbing: Sorry, not allowed.

Programs: Extensive. Year round. For children and adults.

A big beautiful place, most colorful in May and June. The 265-acre site was designed by Frederick Law Olmsted to simulate a natural landscape with open spaces and ponds, ravines and hills. (There's a wonderful view of the city from Peter's Hill.) Paths wind among six thousand different kinds of native and ornamental trees and shrubs labeled with common and scientific names, ages, and origins. Some of the bonsai collection are over 200 years old. In May the blooms on the dove tree, the oldest in America, look like doves' wings fluttering in the breeze. There are crabapples, a hemlock dell, a dawn redwood that was planted "from a seed we found in China." Favorites vary. Find your own.

Beaver Brook Reservation (MDC) Trapelo Road, Belmont

Phone: 617/662–5214.

Directions: Storrow Drive to Mount Auburn Street in Cambridge. Pass Star Market in Watertown and turn right at light onto Belmont Street for 3–4 miles, where it becomes Trapelo Road. Continue about another 4 miles and follow signs.

Parking and admission: Free.

Ⓣ: Harvard on the Red Line; then bus 73 to Waverly Square and a 5-minute walk.

In the duck pond area, walk across the bridge over the waterfall. Find a rock to fish from, or continue on the short path through the woods around the pond. Shaded picnic tables complete this pleasant spot. (Parking's available at the crest of the hill on Mill Street.)

The larger Trapelo Road area has a wading pool, playground, tennis courts, softball fields, woodland and a brook, and a pretty park with new swings and a slide.

Boston Common Bounded by Beacon, Park, Tremont, Boylston, and Charles streets

Ⓣ: Park Street on the Red or Green Line.

The oldest public park in the country, once the site of public hangings, stocks and pillories, cow pasture, and a British troop station; today it's an open area with big old trees, the Shaw Memorial (page 106), the Frog Pond (used for wading in summer), and the Central Burying Ground (1753) on

Boylston Street. Through the year, the Common is a place for concerts, festivals, demonstrations, lunch on a bench, maybe sledding in winter. Suggestion: If you're walking through the Common, to or from the Boston Public Garden, stay toward Beacon Street.

Across Charles Street **Boston Public Garden** Page 129.

Castle Island (MDC) Day Boulevard, South Boston

Directions: Southeast Expressway to exit 15. Then follow Day Boulevard to the end.

Parking and admission: Free.

Ⓣ: Broadway on the Red Line; then City Point bus to the island. Less frequently: bus 7 (10-minute ride) from South Station (617/723–3200).

Groups: For tours of Fort Independence (1801), call 617/727–5218.

Those "in the know" bring out-of-town guests to this historic fort, which has a marvelous circular walkway enjoyed by everyone—whether on foot or on bicycle, on roller skates or in a stroller. There's a great vantage point from the fishing pier that juts out into the ocean. Plenty of grass. Picnic sites. Barbecue pits. A small beach for swimming and a sailing program in the summer, when the parking lot fills early. Rest rooms, Memorial Day through Labor Day.

Charles River Reservation (MDC) Boston and Cambridge along the Charles

Parking: The Massachusetts Eye and Ear Infirmary lot on Storrow Drive, near Charles Street Circle, charges $3 for the first hour, $7 for 3–5 hours.

Ⓣ: Charles on the Red Line; then cross the footbridge to the Esplanade. Or Arlington on the Green Line; then along the Public Garden to the river.

If you start along the Boston shore at Community Boating, across from the Massachusetts General Hospital, you'll pass Back Bay townhouses built long before Storrow Drive, dozens of sailboats, and the Hatch Shell. From here you can walk the Arthur Fiedler Footbridge (passing the oversized sculpture of Fiedler's head) into the Back Bay (page 126). There are several enclosed children's playgrounds, and a lagoon along the 2½-mile stretch up to Harvard Bridge (at Massachusetts Avenue).

On the Cambridge side near Harvard is open space, with little to shade the well-used weed-and-grass banks of the Charles. At JFK Street, across from the venerable sycamores that shade the benches perfectly placed for taking in the river scene: the John F. Kennedy Park, page 141, with fountain and acres of grass—good for running and touch football.

The Fenway

The Back Bay Fens parkland, established in 1877, is bordered by the Museum of Fine Arts and the Gardner Museum. The area is full of paths, benches, short rustic bridges and dog-walkers. Just over the footbridge in back of the Museum of Fine Arts is the rose garden, beautiful in season. Neighborhood gardeners grow flowers, beans, corn, tomatoes, pumpkins,

even peanuts in 15- by 30-foot plots. The ball park, sometimes flooded in winter for skating, is busy with local competitions.

Franklin Park (MDC) Blue Hill Avenue and Columbia Road, Dorchester

This is the largest park—527 acres—in the Emerald Necklace, Frederick Law Olmsted's park design for Boston. There are woodlands, native and exotic plants, and open space—a surprise to many who think of the park only as the zoo (page 28). The golf course and stadium have been refurbished recently. In 1992 the World Cross-Country Championships were held here. The Kite Festival is attended by thousands. Throughout the year Boston Park Rangers (page 125) conduct many programs, including walking tours, orienteering, and cross-country skiing. On a daily basis, like many open space areas, the park is used mainly by neighborhood residents.

Fresh Pond Park Fresh Pond Parkway (at Route 16) Cambridge
Ⓣ: Harvard on the Red Line; then bus 74.

"An oasis in the city," says one daily power walker. A popular place for joggers, cyclists, dog-walkers, birdwatchers, stroller-pushers. A path encircles the reservoir. There are shaded areas, picnic sites, swings for children, and a large open area for playing ball or just running. In winter the slopes are good for skiing (no tows) and sledding. The only drawback: no rest rooms.

Jamaica Pond Pond Street and the Arborway (Route 1), Jamaica Plain
Directions: Route 1 south.
Ⓣ: Pond Street on the Arborway/Green Line; then a 1-block walk west.

The beautiful 65-acre pond, Boston's first reservoir, is circled by a shaded and paved pathway—a fitness course for joggers and cyclists. A good place to picnic or explore water life. Rowboats and sailboats for rent (page 230). Children can fish the stocked water (no license needed under age 15) from the shore. The refreshment stand is open in the summer. Rest rooms available.

John F. Kennedy Library and Museum Page 155.

Larz Anderson Park Goddard Avenue and Newton Street (two entrances), Brookline
Phone: 617/730–2083.
Directions: Route 9 west to Lee Street on the left (at the end of reservoir). Left at the lights, and follow the signs at the fork for parking. The left fork goes to the Goddard Avenue entrance and playground; the right, to the Newton Street entrance, the hill, and skating.
Parking and admission: Free.

Sixty acres of beautiful fields and hillside with a panoramic view of Boston and plenty of running space. Bring bread for the ducks in the picturesque pond, located near the Museum of Transportation, page 176. Facilities include a well-equipped tot lot, large picnic area (permits required for use of grills), and baseball diamond. The hill offers good kite flying in warm weather, sledding in winter. Rest rooms at the playground area.

Near Brattle Street

Mount Auburn Cemetery 580 Mt. Auburn Street (Route 16 on the Watertown-Cambridge line), Cambridge

Phone: 617/547–7105.

Ⓣ: Harvard on the Red Line; then a 5-minute ride on the Watertown bus.

Open: Year round, daily. April 8–6, May–October 8–7, November–March 8–5. The greenhouses on the Grove Street side are open weekdays and most summer Saturdays.

Maps: Indicate the graves of famous people and locations of some of the plantings. Available in the office near the main gate, Monday through Saturday, 8:30–4.

Rules: No cycling or dogs allowed.

From the first crocus to the last chrysanthemum, the 164 acres blossom with about a thousand varieties of flowers, shrubs, and trees. Many people come just to walk along Tulip, Honeysuckle, Hollyhock, and Camellia paths, past azaleas and dogwood, beech, and Japanese cherry trees; to discover a lake or pond bordered by velvet lawn; or to climb the tower for views of Boston. The cemetery is a marvelous spot, too, for birdwatchers; hundreds have their own keys ($3 at the office) for early-morning entrance through the Egyptian gates.

    The plants and trees—labeled—date back to 1831, when the Massachusetts Horticultural Society established an experimental garden in what was to become the first garden cemetery in the country.

Christopher Columbus/Waterfront Park Page 145.

North of Boston

Bradley Palmer State Park Route 1, Topsfield

Phone: 508/887–5931.

Location: 24 miles from Boston.

Parking: In the picnic area, $5. No charge for cars in the horse van area.

Interesting terrain, beautiful trees and flowering bushes, brooks, open space, hiking trails, and footpaths—all in this large, well-kept park, a former estate. A paved road (cars allowed) takes you through variegated flora, a botanic delight. Watch the Ipswich River flow while you fish or canoe (bring your own). The picnic area is set in a lovely pine grove.

Breakheart Reservation (MDC) Saugus and Wakefield

Phone: 617/233–0834.

Location: 10 miles from Boston.

Directions: Tobin/Mystic Bridge to Route 1 north, to the Lynn Fells Parkway. The Saugus entrance is on Forest Street, just west of Route 1. Pine Tops

Road begins at entrance and loops for 2 miles to picnic areas, ponds, and trails.

Brochure with map: Free at 177 Forest Street, Saugus 01902.

Many marked trails—some quite strenuous—for hiking in one of the loveliest wooded spots in the Boston area. Several of the picnic sites ($7 permit for 25 or more people) have fireplaces and shelters. This reservation has a very active Friends organization and interpretive program.

Halibut Point Reservation (The Trustees of Reservations) Rockport

Halibut Point State Park (Department of Environmental Management) Rockport

Phone: 508/546–2997.

Location: 46 miles from Boston; the reservation and the state park abut each other.

Directions: Tobin/Mystic Bridge to Route 1 north, to Route 128 north, to Route 127, to Gott Avenue at the Old Farm Inn.

Parking: $5 or $30 season pass to all state parks.

Open: Year round, 8 a.m. to sunset.

Picnicking: Allowed.

In headquarters: On weekends, a videotape about the quarry.

Rest rooms: The portable kind.

Guided tours (90 minutes): June–October, most Saturdays at 9:30. Topics include the quarry, tidal pools, edible wild plants.

A very special place at the outermost tip of Cape Ann where you stand at the edge of a granite quarry—it functioned until 1929—and see the greenish water below with the blue of the ocean beyond. You can walk (20 minutes) around the quarry. Or follow trail signs to the overlook with its three-state view on a clear day. Or connect with path lined with blueberry bushes (picking in late July) to an open ocean view from huge sheets of granite rock. In summer, lobstermen are hauling traps. Sailboats dot the coastlines of Plum Island, New Hampshire, and Maine. The tide pools are magnificent. Kids seem to find the ones covered by rocks, big enough to crawl under, where the light patterns are wondrous. (Wear sneakers.) When the tide is coming in, you might sit in the pockets of the rocks and let the waves splash on you. Many people fish for perch and mackerel—sometimes bluefish. Birders come here year round. A great place for spring and fall trips when the sun is warm. Keep an eye out for poison ivy. Always bring jackets.

Ipswich River Wildlife Sanctuary (Massachusetts Audubon Society) Perkins Row, Topsfield

Phone: 508/887–9264, Tuesday–Sunday 9–5.

Location: 24 miles from Boston.

Directions: I–95 to Route 1 north, Route 97 south at lights. Second left onto Perkins Row for 1 mile to sanctuary on right.

Open: Dawn to dusk. Closed Mondays, except for major holidays.

Admission: $3 adults, $2 ages 3–15 and senior citizens.

Rules: No dogs allowed.

Handicapped access: Program barn is handicapped accessible, rest rooms are not.

Walk on paths of pine needles, pebbles, moss, and wood chips; cross bridges (are there any two alike?); look at enormous gnarled trees, rhododendrons, yews, greenery, wildflowers, a partially frozen pond in spring, and acres of waterfowl nesting grounds; clamber over and under and in and around the magnificent rockery. A fantastic place with 25 miles of well-marked trails. Somewhat buggy on warm May and June days.

An hour from Boston

Maudslay State Park Curzon Mill Road, Newburyport
Phone: 508/465–7223.

Directions: Route 95, Newburyport exit 57. Right on Route 113, left at cemetery onto (unmarked) Noble Street, where you'll see signs to the park. Left on Ferry Road, left on Pine Hill to the park entrance on Curzon Mill Road.

Rest rooms: The temporary variety.

A jewel. On the Merrimack River. Bucolic, rolling estate grounds—the 1920s mansion was taken down in 1955—with dogwoods, extraordinary rhododendrons and azaleas, a natural stand of mountain laurel. Tall pines for shade. Ponds. Stone bridges. A bald eagle habitat. (Sorry, none to be seen.) About 8 miles of carriage roads and trails. There's a spring festival: Maudslay in Bloom. And a fall festival with hayrides, pumpkins, and lots of fun. And a children's theater in residence in the summer. Hike. Fish. Picnic. Birdwatch. Spread a blanket. Enjoy.

Middlesex Fells Reservation (MDC) Winchester, Stoneham, Medford, Malden, and Melrose
Phone: 617/662–5214. (Also for Friends of Middlesex Fells Reservation.)

Location: 11 miles from Boston.

Parking and admission: Free.

Maps: Available for $2 at headquarters, 1 Woodland Road, Stoneham 02180, weekdays 9 to 5.

The best way to explore the miles of varied carriage paths and hiking trails here is with a map. There are several entrances to the reservation. **Sheepfold,** one of the main entrances, is off Route 28, next to I–93, on the Stoneham-Medford line. Here are large open recreation areas and parking facilities. Suitable for brown bag picnics.

Enter from South Border Road in Medford to the **Bellevue Pond** area for parking facilities and picnic tables. Walk up to Wright Tower, and follow the marked **Skyline Trail.** The entrance off the Fellsway East in Malden also leads to the Skyline Trail, as does the Winchester entrance off South Border Road, opposite Myrtle Terrace.

Parker River National Wildlife Refuge Plum Island, Newburyport 01950
Phone: 508/465–5753. Office hours Monday–Friday, 8–4:30; at other times, taped information about beach accessibility for public.

Location: 32 miles from Boston.

Directions: See page 215.

Parking and admission: Year round: $5 per car, $1 walk-in, free 62 and up or handicapped persons. Season pass for a year (running July 1 through June 30), $15 per car.

Open: Year round, dawn to dusk.

Greenhead fly season: July and early August. Less troublesome on cool, cloudy, windy, dry days.

Rules: No pets, vegetation picking, or alcohol. And please, no dune climbing.

Hike on nature trails (watch out for poison ivy); walk along the 6-mile beach (sometimes closed for nesting plovers). Sunbathe, swim, picnic, barbecue, go surf fishing. The gravel road, an hour's round trip, is a dusty ride in dry weather. The refuge—a birdwatcher's delight year round—is a resting and feeding area for migrating waterfowl. (Peak migration periods for ducks and geese are in March and October.) Thousands of acres of dunes, freshwater bogs, and fresh and tidal marshes. Ripe beach plums and cranberries can be picked after Labor Day.

Phillips Academy Bird Sanctuary Page 166.

South of Boston

Ashumet Holly Reservation (Massachusetts Audubon Society)
Route 151, East Falmouth

Phone: 508/563–6390.

Location: 77 miles from Boston, adjacent to Barnstable County fairgrounds.

Directions: From Routes 28 and 51 in North Falmouth, take Route 151 east for 4 miles. Turn left on Currier Road, 100 yards to the sanctuary.

Open: Most holiday Mondays and Tuesday–Sunday dawn to dusk. Closed Mondays except for major holidays.

Admission: $3 adults; $2 ages 3–15 and senior citizens.

Rules: No dogs allowed.

A quiet place. The paths (you can walk them all in an hour or two) take you completely around the pond, among heather, wild flowers, dogwood, rhododendrons, and sixty-five varieties of hollies (spectacular in early winter). Bamboo grows near the greenhouse. Rest rooms available.

Blue Hills Reservation (MDC) Canton, Quincy, and Milton

Phone: 617/698–1802.

Location: 8 miles from Boston.

Directions: I–93 south to Route 128 north, to exit 3 (Houghton's Pond/Ponkapoag Trail). Turn right at the top of the ramp for about a mile. (Reservation headquarters is ahead, next to MDC Police Station.)

Parking: Free, in many areas, including the Trailside Museum (page 167).

This is a huge (6,000 acres) reservation, the highest ground in the metropolitan area. There are woodlands, open spaces, outdoor education centers,

well-marked nature and hiking trails from the Blue Hills Trailside Museum, picnic areas, outdoor ice-skating areas and an indoor rink, and cross-country trails and ski slopes (page 248). In Houghton's Pond area—children's playgrounds, swimming and fishing, tennis courts, two athletic fields, tables and fireplaces, and rest rooms.

Borderland State Park Massapoag Avenue, Easton

Phone: 508/238–6566.

Directions: Route 3 to Route 128 north to Route 106. Take 106 toward Mansfield, crossing Route 138, and then Bay Road to park signs on your right.

Parking and admission: Free.

Picnicking: Allowed. Bring your own grill for designated area.

The sweeping lawns of the former Oakes Ames estate are bordered with big old trees that provide shade for picnics. Wonderful marked trails lead through oak, beech, and pines, and by ponds and meadows. Occasionally, tours are given of the imposing 1910 mansion of this estate, which the state acquired in 1971. Sometimes there are summer concerts. Or bird walks scheduled for 7 a.m. Often, there are many people of all ages who appreciate the beauty and tranquillity.

It's a drive from one area to another

Cape Cod National Seashore Eastham, North Truro, and Provincetown

Phone: 508/349–3785, headquarters; 508/255–3421, Salt Pond Visitors' Center.

Parking: Charge for beach areas (page 217) in summer only.

Admission: Free.

Visitor center: Main center at Salt Pond, Route 6 in Eastham, is open year round. Schedule varies from year to year, but usually weekends in January and February; daily rest of year. March–Memorial Day 9–4:30, June 9–5, summer 9–6.

Programs: In summer, wonderful guided walks daily; some at night and in off-season too.

Handicapped access: Most of the park is accessible. Short braille trail at Salt Pond Visitors' Center.

Determined adventurers make the round trip from Boston in a day. Some exotic highlights: Provincetown has the longest (8 miles) seashore bicycle trail, a paved path by ponds and through bogs, forests, and dunes. The South Wellfleet parking lot near the Marconi Station area has an entrance to Cedar Swamp Trail, a don't-miss short one that leads over a boardwalk. For a more arduous exploration, the 4-mile Great Island Trail starts in the woods at the end of Chequesset Neck Road in Wellfleet and crosses sandbars. (Watch the tides!)

Moose Hill Wildlife Sanctuary (Massachusetts Audubon Society) Sharon

Phone: 617/784–5691.

Location: 24 miles from Boston.

Directions: I–95 south, exit 10. Left off ramp. Right onto Route 27 north toward Walpole for ½ mile. Left onto Moose Hill Street for 1½ miles. Or I–95 north, right onto Main Street for about a mile to Moose Hill Street on left.

Open: Year round. Closed Mondays, except for Thanksgiving, Christmas, New Year's.

Visitor center: Tuesday–Saturday 9–5, Sunday noon–5.

Admission: $3 adults, $2 senior citizens and ages 3–15. Under 3 free.

★ Facilities available for rent.

Rules: No dogs allowed.

Some less-than-a-mile loops as well as a portion of the AMC Warner Trail are among the 12 miles of trails here in the state's oldest (1916) Audubon sanctuary. From a granite bluff, there's a good view of Providence. In 1991 a garden was planted to attract butterflies spring through fall. Maple sugaring and Halloween Prowl are long-standing traditions. And now, year round, there's a wide variety of programs for adults and children. In the visitor center: a library with deck, art gallery and rest rooms.

Myles Standish State Forest, South Carver. Camping, cycling, fishing, and hiking. Please see pages 219 and 240.

Less than a mile off Route 3

South Shore Natural Science Center Jacobs Lane, Norwell

Phone: 617/659–2559.

Location: 26 miles from Boston.

Directions: I–93 south to Route 3 south, to exit 13 (Route 53) toward Norwell. At the first intersection, right on Route 123 for ¼ mile to Jacobs Lane on the left.

Open: Monday–Saturday 10–4, Sundays and most holidays 12–4. Closed New Year's, July 4, Thanksgiving and Christmas.

Admission: Free.

Picnicking: Allowed. Some picnic tables provided.

Handicapped access: Visitor center and rest rooms are accessible. One sensory trail for visually impaired.

A great family place. An outdoor smorgasbord. A rural pocket where you walk—not really hike—the short trails. You look and listen near marsh, woodlands, fields, and freshwater pond. Take a workshop or see a demonstration. Visit in the nature shop. Attend programs in the auditorium.

Stony Brook Wildlife Sanctuary (Massachusetts Audubon Society)
North Street, Norfolk

Phone: 508/528–3140.

Location: 34 miles from Boston.

Directions: From intersection of Routes 1A and 115 in Norfolk, take Route 115 north for 1½ miles to the third left onto North Street. (Bristol-Blake State Reservation is part of Stony Brook.)

Open: Year round, dawn to dusk. Closed—including trails—Mondays from Thanksgiving until April vacation. Office hours: Monday–Friday 9–5, Saturday 9–4, Sunday 10–3.

Admission: $3 adults, $2 senior citizens and ages 3–15. Under age 3 free.

Handicapped access: Parking, nature center, gift shop, rest rooms.

Picnicking: Under trees near the parking area but not on trails.

Rules: No dogs allowed.

★ Auditorium available to rent for nonprofit groups. Birthday parties with advance arrangements.

Trails and a boardwalk lead visitors over a marsh and along Kingfisher Pond (where you might see great blue herons and painted turtles or hear the croak of a frog) in a 1-hour, 1-mile walk for all ages. Near smaller Stony Brook Pond, part of the Charles River Watershed (and home to a resident family of geese), are ruined foundations of several mills. In and around the nature center: exhibits and a butterfly garden. This is a good place for young children. There's always something to see (and do) here. Extensive programming includes vacation walks, a summer day camp, and an annual fall fair.

Known for its natural spring

Wompatuck State Park Union Street, Hingham

Phone: 617/749–7160.

Location: 14 miles from Boston.

Directions: I–93 south to Route 3 south, to Route 228 (toward Nantasket). Follow Route 228 for 4.2 miles to Free Street, on the right. Left on Union Street, and first right to the park.

Parking and admission: Free except for camping (page 241).

Picnicking: Spread a blanket; no tables or fireplaces.

Visitor center: Daily 8–4. Maps. Rest rooms. Information about walks, slide presentations, and other programs.

Once a military station, now a wooded area open to the public. You'll find good hiking among the geological formations, many dating back to the glacial period. The 15 miles of paved trails (no cars allowed) make this a popular place for Sunday cyclists. And there are designated areas for horses.

If you drive the 2-mile road through the park, you'll come to Mt. Blue Spring (there's a sign), with its delicious water.

A little lost? Check the map on pages xvi–xvii.

Boston's skyline from Hingham Bay

World's End Reservation (The Trustees of Reservations) Hingham

Directions: From Route 3A in Hingham, go around the rotary to Summer Street, which branches to the left, toward Nantasket. Follow Summer ¼ mile to the lights, and turn left on Martin's Lane (drive slowly please). If that route didn't please you, coming back cross Route 3A onto Summer Street, right on East Street to Main Street, to Route 228, to Route 128. (Reminder: Nantasket traffic is heavy on weekends.)

Parking: Fills weekend afternoons in good weather.

Ⓣ: Red Line to Quincy Center, bus 220 to Star's Restaurant. Walk straight past traffic circle (be careful) to light at top of hill. Turn left on Martin's Lane for about ½ mile.

Open: 10–sunset, summer; 10–5 off-season.

Admission: $3 adults. Free under age 12.

Rules: Strollers allowed. No picnicking, swimming, fires, firearms, camping, or organized sports and games. Dogs must be under owner's control.

Put on your walking shoes and explore several of the winding 8-foot-wide gravel trails. More than 200 acres of wildlife and magnificent landscaping dating back to 1890. The peninsula is actually two drumlins: the outer elevation, World's End, and the inner elevation, Planter's Hill. Connecting the two is a narrow strip of lowland, about a 40-minute walk from the entrance.

What's "to do" here? Play hide and seek in the tall grass, look for horseshoe crabs in the water, or examine shells on the shore. Bring an art box and draw or paint. A good vantage point too for the Boston skyline, harbor islands, sailboats (possibly racing), yachts, unusual birds, and a panorama of the South Shore. No rest rooms.

West of Boston

Ashland State Park. A family place, popular for picnics and swimming. Please see page 220.

Broadmoor Wildlife Sanctuary (Massachusetts Audubon Society)
280 Eliot Street (Route 16), South Natick
Phone: 508/655–2296 or 617/235–3929.
Location: 22 miles from Boston.
Directions: Route 9 west to Route 16 in Wellesley for about 5 miles (1.8 miles beyond South Natick Center) to sanctuary on your left.
Open: Dawn to dusk for grounds. Closed Mondays, Thanksgiving, Christmas, New Year's Day.
Admission: $3 adults, $2 senior citizens and ages 3–15. Under 3, free.
Rules: No dogs allowed. Picnicking not allowed here, but there's a very nice area (with ducks waiting to be fed) on the Charles River at South Natick Dam, in South Natick Center on Route 16 (see page 225).
Handicapped access: Parking, nature center, observation area, and rest rooms are handicapped accessible.

"Watch for parents feeding insects to young swallows."

—POSTED HINT

View wildlife from a spectacular 110-foot-long footbridge that crosses Indian Brook. That's a highlight along 9 miles of marked trails (a single trail could be covered in an hour) that wind along the Charles River—through wetlands, woods, and field. Of particular interest are the stone foundations of one of the first gristmills in America, and a sawmill. The solar-heated visitor center, a barn renovated in 1983, has natural history exhibits and extensive programming (and public composting toilets).

Cochituate State Park Page 221.

Drumlin Farm Education Center and Wildlife Sanctuary (Lincoln) Page 27.

Walking your dog? In consideration of your fellow walkers, please use a leash. Most places that allow dogs require the use of a leash. Generally, dogs are not allowed on beaches in summer months.

Garden in the Woods (New England Wild Flower Society) Hemenway Road, Framingham

Phone: 508/877–7630 or 617/237–4924; recorded information 508/877–6574.

Directions: Route 128 to Route 20 west for 8 miles to Sudbury. Go through first Sudbury traffic light at Mill Village and take second left on to Raymond Road for 1.3 miles to Hemenway Road. *Or* Mass. Pike, exit 12 (Route 9/Framingham). East on Route 9 for 2.4 miles to Edgell Road exit. At top of ramp at lights, left on Edgell Road for 2.1 miles to first traffic light. Right on to Water Street. First left after railroad tracks onto Hemenway Road.

Open: Tuesday–Sunday 9–4, April 15 through October; until 7 p.m. in May. Closed Mondays except Memorial Day.

Admission: $6 adults, $5 age 60 and up, $3 ages 5–15, under 5 free. Fee includes informal guided walks on Tuesday, Friday, and Saturday mornings at 10.

Rules: Please—no dogs, picnicking, or smoking.

More than a thousand varieties of wildflowers and native plants grow in this rare and beautiful garden. On the 45 acres are 3 miles of woodland paths, dry wooded slopes, shaded brooks, sunny bogs, open spaces, interesting rocks, even a hemlock dell—a wealth of local natural history. Tall azaleas and lady's slippers bloom during May and June, the most colorful months. To protect fragile plantings, all visitors—including active youngsters—should stay on the paths. Bring insect repellent. Wear walking shoes.

Over 100 courses offered year round for adults and children. Rest rooms are accessible.

Great Brook Farm State Park 841 Lowell Street, Carlisle 01741

Phone: 508/369–6312.

Location: Rural. 15 minutes from downtown Lowell, 15 from historic Concord, 40-minute drive from Boston.

Directions: Route 128 north to Route 225 west, to Carlisle Center. Turn right on Lowell Street for about 2 miles to park. Turn right on North Road to parking area. Canoe launch is past the parking lot, at a pretty dam about ½ mile down on your right.

Parking and admission: Free.

Open: Park is open daylight hours. Ice-cream stand, April–October 11–dusk.

Horse jumps: 25 in the park. (Bring your own horse.)

"It is as rustic as nature intended it, as old as creation itself. Its design is as splendid as a tall pine forest and as elegant as any respectful wildlife tenant could dream it to be. It is simply beautiful, with a pond surrounded by grass, majestic fields, and serene streams. There are ten miles of hiking trails with marvelous views and hideaways."

—Ray Faucher, senior forest park supervisor, Great Brook Farm State Park, Carlisle

Picnicking: Bag lunch picnics (no fires) allowed. Tables by pond.

Rest rooms: Portables.

On the working dairy farm here, visitors are welcome to stand at the fence to view cows as well as some sheep and goats. From the ice-cream stand you can almost always see a calf right next to the visitors' window, a viewing spot for the evening milking (6:30) in warm weather. There's good bass fishing in the lightly stocked trout pond. And to the west of the farm is a 2-mile trail around a town-owned cranberry bog. Cross-country skiing, page 247.

Great Meadows National Wildlife Refuge Weir Hill Road (visitor center), Sudbury 01776

Phone: 508/443–4661.

Location: 24 miles from Boston.

Directions: *To visitor center:* Route 20 west to Wayland Center. At light, right onto Routes 126/27 north for .1 mile. Bear left and stay on Route 27 north for 1.7 miles. Right onto Water Row Road to end. Right onto Lincoln Road. Left onto Weir Hill Road. Follow signs. *To Concord impoundment:* From Concord Center go east on Route 62 for 1.3 miles. Left on Monsen Road for .3 mile on left.

Parking and admission: Free.

Open: Grounds, sunrise to sunset daily.

Programs: Guided weekend walks in spring and fall for families, nature sketching workshops, much more. Newsletter available.

Picnicking: Allowed. No sites. Please leave with your trash.

Canoe landing: Canoeists along the Sudbury River are welcome to land (no launching) at Weir Hill.

Great places for walks—not really hikes. The *Concord entrance* brings you to the 1½-mile Dike Trail, which divides a submerged meadow from the Concord River. What's to see? There may be turtles and muskrats nesting in the banks of the dike; rabbits, raccoons, ducks, geese—and birdwatchers using the photo blind. From the tower there's a view of waterfowl, migratory song-birds, great blue heron, and occasionally a peregrine falcon or osprey. Off the Dike Trail are two smaller loops, the Black Duck Creek Trail and the Timber Trail, bringing the total to a little over 2 miles.

From the visitor center in Sudbury there's a 1-mile loop trail over Weir Hill, through a red maple swamp, and around a small pond, with views of the Sudbury River.

Habitat Institute for the Environment 10 Juniper Road, P.O. Box 136, Belmont 02178

Phone: 617/489–5050, Monday–Friday 9–5.

Directions: Take Storrow Drive and follow Belmont/Watertown signs to Route 2 west to Route 60 (Pleasant Street)/Belmont. Turn toward Belmont to second set of lights. Turn right onto Clifton (Leonard is on your left). Take first left onto Fletcher Road. Follow signs.

Open: Formal garden and lawn areas usually open daily; call to check. Trails open all the time. Rest rooms available, usually 9–5.

It's an environmental education/nature center with a formal garden, rose gardens, wildflowers, and a trail through pine woods and meadows and by a pond. It's free the first visit, but membership ($25 per year for a family) is requested the second time.

Hammond Pond Woods Chestnut Hill, Newton

Phone: 617/552–7120 (Newton Recreation Department).

Location: 7 miles from Boston.

Directions: Look for sign to one entrance on Hammond Pond Parkway across from Congregation Mishkan Tefila. Or enter MDC land from parking lot in back of Bloomingdale's (Lower Mall) and follow signs to adjoining Webster Conservation area. Houghton Garden entrance between Beacon Street and Route 9, on Suffolk Road, west of Hammond Street.

Ⓣ: Chestnut Hill stop on Riverside/Green Line; walk on along Hammond Street to Suffolk Road on left.

Several miles of paths (some are color-coded) are all connected in this hidden jewel. They lead across a bog bridge, through woods, and among interesting rock formations (some good for climbing). In the Webster Conservation Area you might see deer. Thanks to the Chestnut Hill Garden Club, the Houghton Garden is beautifully maintained, complete with manicured lawn.

A little lost? Check the map on pages xvi–xvii.

Hemlock Gorge–Echo Bridge Newton

Phone: 617/239–0659.

Location: 8 miles from Boston.

Directions: Route 9 west to the Chestnut Street ramp on the right. Cross Chestnut Street, and turn left onto Ellis Street (Quinnobequin is on your right) to the small parking area. *Or,* to the main parking area at the main trailhead: Continue ahead on Route 9 to light at Eliot Street. Turn right, and just as you cross the river (Eliot becomes Central Avenue) are Hamilton Place spaces on your right, facing a meadow (former fish-drying area) that is still deeded to Indians.

Ⓣ: D (Riverside) Green Line to Eliot stop. Walk up Chestnut Street to a walkway on your right to the bridge. Missed it? Take first right, almost a U turn, and you will arrive at base of bridge.

Admission: Free.

Picnicking: Allowed.

This is more of a visit—and a good picnic spot—than a serious hike. It's "just right" for being outdoors, for young children, for all ages.

Stand on the platform below the 120-year-old bridge (a nineteenth-century aqueduct), and call out. On a still day, your voice may echo thirteen times. Walk along the recently resurfaced 50-foot-long, 21-foot-wide bridge (its main arch is 70 feet above the water) for a wonderful view of the falls—on the way to a small, beautiful wooded area and another view of the falls, often captured through the years by artists. This 23-acre area was Frederick Law Olmsted's last project—executed by Charles Eliot.

If you approach the bridge from the main trailhead (see Directions above), it's about a ten-minute walk on a cleared, flat path.

Also here: A path toward Route 9 that leads via a footbridge to a stone building, a pond (which can be seen from Route 9) enjoyed by skaters in winter, and a cave. Last used as a nail factory, the stone building, part of the mill complexes that flourished here at the turn of the century, may soon be a museum or nature center. Periodically, MDC interpreters schedule guided walks with an historic and geological perspective.

Highland Farm Wildlife Sanctuary (Massachusetts Audubon Society) Belmont

Rock Meadow (Belmont Conservation Commission) Belmont

Directions: From Belmont Center, follow Concord Avenue uphill through Pleasant Street. Turn right at the fieldstone gateposts, just before the Belmont Hill Club, and go along the land to the sanctuary.

Parking and admission: Free.

Ⓣ: Harvard on the Red Line; then a 15-minute ride to Belmont Center on bus 72. From Belmont Center follow Concord Avenue to the foot of the hill. Enter Rock Meadow through the fields beyond the Mill Street stop sign.

Up to 6 miles of easy hiking in these two adjacent areas of wide open grassland and trees. The sanctuary with marked trails is at the top of the hill; Rock Meadow, at the foot. No rest rooms.

Menotomy Rocks Park Off Jason Street, Arlington Heights

Phone: 617/641–5492 (weekdays).

Location: 10 miles from Boston.

Directions: Massachusetts Avenue to Arlington Center, then left on Jason Street. The park is ¼ mile beyond Gray Street, on the right. Unloading allowed, but park on Spring Street.

Parking and admission: Free.

A great view of Boston, trails through woods, rocks to climb on, fireplaces and a picnic area, baseball and soccer fields, a children's playground, and a skating pond. No rest rooms.

Noanet Park (The Trustees of Reservations) Dedham Street, Dover

Directions: From intersection of Routes 135 and 128, take Route 135 west for .7 mile. Left on South Street just after crossing Charles River. Left onto Chestnut Street. Right on Dedham Street after crossing Charles River again, almost a mile to entrance at Dover's Caryl Park on your left.

Parking and admission: Free. $1 for map from ranger on duty.

Dog walkers love this place. (Bring a leash.) Mountain cyclists who are considerate of hikers are welcome too. Sometimes there are guided walks in this property, which has four ponds, a 387-foot peak, and wonderful views of Boston.

Prospect Hill Park Totten Pond Road, Waltham

Phone: 617/891–9343.

Location: 16 miles from Boston.

Directions: From Route 128 take Totten Pond exit toward Waltham, ¼ mile on the right.

Parking and admission: Free. Donations appreciated for farm.

Picnicking: Some sites have fireplaces and/or shelters. Grills allowed. Swings, merry-go-round, slide, sandbox. Reservations (fee for groups) taken weekdays, 8:30–4:30, 617/893–4040 extension 3110 or 617/891–9343.

Most people come to picnic at this high point with a beautiful view; a few, to walk the steep paved road through the wooded acreage. At the base of the hill is a small farm, a 15- to 30-minute visit, depending on the time you spend looking through a high chain-link fence at the horses, goats, sheep, chickens, deer, pigs, a rabbit, donkeys, and ducks. Sometimes, a pony ride is available. Sorry, no feeding allowed.

Always cool

Purgatory Chasm State Reservation Purgatory Road, Sutton

Phone: 508/278–6486.

Location: 50 miles from Boston.

Directions: Mass. Pike to exit 11, to Route 122 north, to Route 20 west, to Route 146 south. Then follow the signs.

Parking: $5 per car. $30 season pass (to all state parks).

Open: Year round, dawn to dusk. Very busy spring and fall weekends.

The chasm, awesome and beautiful—and cool in the summer—is a half mile long and at least 60 feet deep in parts. Climbing and exploring may be difficult for children younger than 9 or 10. A marked route suggests a path along the jagged rocks, past new trees sprouting through the steep walls and older trees with huge exposed roots. Bring insect repellent!

Outside the chasm, in the park: durable playground equipment (the old-fashioned kind of swings, seesaws, and push-go-rounds). A 1-mile marked trail through the woods is appealing and little traveled. Picnic sites are throughout the large pine-groved area. Bring wood if you want to use fireplaces; grills permitted. The "rest rooms" are not the permanent variety.

Well used

Walden Pond State Reservation Route 126, Concord

Phone: 508/369–3254.

Location: 21 miles from Boston (1¼ miles from the railroad station in Concord).

Directions: Route 2 west to Route 126 south.

Parking: $5 per car. $30 season pass (to all state parks). Charged 8 a.m.–7 p.m. weekends, Mother's Day to Memorial Day and Labor Day to Columbus Day, and daily, Memorial Day to Labor Day.

The 1½-mile, well-worn path around the pond leads, near the north end, to the site of Thoreau's hut. Other paths go through woodlands. Memorial Day to Labor Day there is supervised swimming (fills early) and rest rooms are open. Sometimes, guided walks with Thoreau readings. Ice fishing in winter.

Wellesley College 106 Central Street (Route 135), Wellesley
Phone: 617/235–0320.

Location: 17 miles from Boston.

Directions: Route 9 west past Wellesley Hills to Weston Road (toward Wellesley). In Wellesley Square, turn right on Route 135 to the campus, on the left.

On this lovely campus is a wonderful combination of outdoor and indoor attractions. There are acres of grass and trees, miles of paths, and a good view of the Hunnewell estate's shaped evergreens (topiary) across Lake Waban.

An inside highlight: the fourteen Margaret C. Ferguson Greenhouses, open daily 8:30–4:30, which were built in 1922 and restored in 1983. The collection in the Cryptogram House includes mosses and ferns. You stand on a small rustic bridge and are sure that some youngster (yours?) has touched something when the automatic mist sprays every few minutes. In other houses you'll see cacti, orchids, orange and lemon trees, tea plants, coffee trees, passion flowers, leaves big enough to hide under, magnificent blossoms, even banana tees and pineapple plants.

Also on campus are the Jewett Arts Center (closed summers and school vacations), the recycled Victorian Schneider Center, Houghton Memorial Chapel (1899) with the only Renaissance organ in the country, an ultramodern science center, and a small arboretum behind the greenhouses. Lost? The campus police office can orient you.

Organizations

American Youth Hostels Page 11.

Appalachian Mountain Club 5 Joy Street, Boston 02108
Phone: 617/523–0636.

AMC is a great resource for outdoor information. Mountain climbing, canoeing, snowshoeing, skiing, hiking, camping, or just being outside are all included in its offerings. Family trips and outings (day, weekend, or longer) are open to nonmembers. March is the month when details are published about AMC campgrounds (self-service and full-service facilities in beautiful areas near Boston and up-country) and about the AMC hut system (page 246) and its junior naturalist program.

At headquarters, a townhouse on Beacon Hill, there is a knowledgeable staff, a library with books on camping and sharing the environment with children, extensive map and photographic collections, and guidebooks.

Massachusetts Audubon Society South Great Road, Lincoln 01773
Phone: 617/259–9500.

A nonprofit educational organization dedicated to the conservation of the Commonwealth's natural resources, and a leader in environmental concerns. Mass. Audubon's sanctuaries offer a tremendous range of experiences (field trips, courses, summer camps) and habitats—from hiking paths in Sherborn, to blueberry hills and swamp in Princeton, to rustic bridges and a rockery in Topsfield. All are open Tuesday through Sunday and most

Monday holidays, sunrise to sunset. Closed other Mondays, Thanksgiving, Christmas, and New Year's. Directions to each sanctuary are listed in a descriptive folder available at headquarters.

The society itself is an informational gold mine. Naturalists answer questions galore. They even identified the Bostonian Hotel house finch (page 135) on the phone. The library, focused on natural history and environmental issues, has a special collection for teachers. And it lists environmental jobs.

Massachusetts State Parks and Forests Massachusetts Department of Environmental Management, 100 Cambridge Street, Boston 02202
Phone: 617/727–3180.

There are over a hundred state parks and forests in Massachusetts. Write for a complete list of places and facilities. Almost all offer picnic areas and trails, and several schedule interpretive programs through the Historic and Preservation Department. The season varies according to weather and personnel, but generally sites are open April through mid-October and are busiest during the summer, particularly on weekends.

Metropolitan District Commission (MDC) 20 Somerset Street, Boston 02108
Phone: 617/727–0460 (information), Monday–Friday, 9–5.

Since its creation with reservations, ocean frontage, riverbanks, and parkways in 1893, this state agency has acquired and preserved thousands of additional Boston area parkland acres that fit into Frederick Law Olmsted and Charles Eliot's original landscape design. It has also built new parks and recreational facilities, and has developed a Reservation and Historic Sites Division. For current programming, call the numbers listed with each MDC area described in this book.

National Park Service Boston National Historical Park Visitor Center, 15 State Street, Boston 02109
Phone: 617/242–5642.

NPS issues a Golden Eagle annual pass ($25), which admits holders to both urban and natural area parks that are NPS fee-collecting sites (in contrast to cooperating sites—as some are on the Freedom Trail) without charge. Senior citizens (ages 62 up), the blind, and the permanently disabled can receive free passes by applying in person at 15 State Street or at many NPS sites.

Sierra Club 3 Joy Street, Boston 02108
Phone: 617/227–5339.

The wide variety of day and overnight trips offered year round includes backpacking, canoeing, cycling, birdwatching, beach walks, and issue-oriented city tours. The minimum age depends on the trip; mostly adults attend, but entire families are welcome. The details are announced in a newsletter that also lists information about environmental awareness, conservation, education, and other club concerns.

The Trustees of Reservations 572 Essex Street, Beverly 01915
Phone: 508/921–1944.

Founded in 1891 by Boston landscape architect Charles Eliot as a private organization for preserving land. Since that time, it has acquired for public use and enjoyment seventy-three properties of scientific, historic, and ecological value throughout the state. Halibut Point, World's End, and Crane Beach are Trustees reservations included in this book. Admission and parking fees and policies are different at each location. Many reservations schedule special events and activities.

Recreation

Amusement Parks

They're not making new ones any more. And the old-timers are getting rarer. By the time the next edition of this book is released, it is possible that Lincoln Park on Route 6 in North Dartmouth will have been revived. Carousel (only) rides are available in Fall River, page 61, and Hull, page 65.

Canobie Lake Park Salem, New Hampshire
Phone: 603/893-3506.

Location: 28 miles north of Boston.

Directions: I–93 north to New Hampshire exit 2.

Open: April and May, weekends only; June–Labor Day, daily. Amusements open at noon; closing times vary.

Admission (covers all rides, shows, and huge swimming pool): $14 adults, $9 for senior citizens and anyone under 48 inches tall. After 8 p.m. $8 for all ages. Age 2 and under free. Group rates available.

Picnicking: None allowed in park. (Hint: Stop at rest area 2 miles from Canobie just over the New Hampshire line on I–93.)

The rides—everything from a carousel to kiddie rides, from a corkscrew roller coaster that goes upside down to a boat trip around the lake—are spread throughout this attractive 90-year-old park. It offers a pleasant setting with lots of shade and evergreen groves. Canobie is a big place that holds many people without feeling crowded. Stage performances and children's shows are presented every day from mid-June through Labor Day. Fireworks are scheduled on Saturday nights in July and August.

Riverside Park Agawam
Phone: 413/786-9300 or 800/370-7488.

Location: 100 miles west of Boston.

Directions: Mass. Pike west to exit 6. Ask at the toll booth for a direction sheet.

Open: At 11 a.m. every day mid-April through October 12. Closing times vary.

Admission (includes rides and shows): $17.95 for everyone who is at least 54 inches tall, $9.95 if less than 54 inches. Age 3 and under, free.

Picnicking: Not allowed.

Huge. Fifty rides. Many, like the log flume, are spectacular. Another highlight: simulated parachuting in the theater. Lots of live shows—from a strolling musician to Punch and Judy—daily.

Rocky Point Amusement Park Warwick, Rhode Island
Phone: 401/737-8000.

Location: 62 miles south of Boston.

Directions: I–93 south to Route 128 north, to I–95 south, to Rhode Island exit 14. Bear left on ramp. Take first exit (Post Road, south). Left at third traffic light; follow signs.

Open: Weekends in May and September. Daily Memorial Day through Labor Day, Sunday–Thursday 11–10:30, Friday and Saturday 11–midnight. Other times, subject to attendance and weather.

Admission (includes admission and all rides): $12.95 for those more than 4½ feet tall. $8.95 if less than 4½ feet. $3 less on Thursday. General admission only (no rides): $2.50; free to senior citizens and under age 8. $5.75 for a book with 20 tickets. Group rates for 20 or more.

Eating: In large dining hall—chowder, clam cakes, watermelon, steamers, fish, and chicken. No picnic facilities.

The second oldest amusement park in the country, established 145 years ago, still has the 1910 carousel (which in part was painted in the 1950s). There are ten kiddie rides and twenty major rides, including the log flume and the one known as a Free Fall. Flower barrels are sprinkled throughout this park. It's a family place most of the time, except Friday nights.

About an hour's drive
from Boston

Whalom Park Route 13, Lunenburg
Phone: 508/342–3707.
Location: 50 miles northwest of Boston.
Directions: Route 2 west to Route 13 north.
Open: Mid-June through Labor Day, Tuesday–Sunday noon–10.
Admission: General admission: $2.99 anytime. All rides, all day, $6.99 April through mid-May and fall weekends after Labor Day. Memorial Day through Labor Day, $9.99 for an all-day ticket; $12.99 includes water slide. Kiddie Land only, $6.99 high season. After 5 p.m., $5.99 Memorial Day through Labor Day.
Picnicking: In picnic groves with trees and grass. Reserve a grill or bring your own.

You can't get lost in this century-old park; it is rather contained, not spread out. The midway has twenty-three adult rides. There are twenty-two kiddie rides, a miniature golf course, games, an arcade, and paddleboats. The lake (with beach) is open to swimming on weekends. Daily, June through August, there are clowns, a parade, and performances including a puppet show.

AIRPORT

Some parents report that **Kidport** at Terminal C of Logan Airport (see page 263) is an interesting change, especially for young children, during school vacations. Plan to miss the rush-hour traffic.

Ballooning

Aeronauts Unlimited 27 Skyview, Lexington 02173
Phone: 617/861–0101.

Individuals or families can just watch or join in (as ground crew members) the inflation, launching, and chase—all without charge. For a ride, there is a fee—and teenagers are the youngest allowed.

Balloon Adventures of New Bedford, Inc. 564 Rock O'Dundee Road, South Dartmouth 02748
Phone: 508/636–4846.
Fee (reservations required): $200 per person. $225 May–October weekends. $125 ages 6 (the youngest permitted) to 11.

"Year round, when the weather is good, we fly from anywhere in southeastern Massachusetts or in Rhode Island, over natural areas with ocean, marshes, rivers, ponds, wildlife. Most of our flights begin about sunrise; others are in late afternoon. The launch site, determined by the wind and weather, is not known until about an hour or two before flight time. It's not a ride; it is an experience—a way to stop and smell the roses."

Until 15 years ago, David Gifford was a textile designer. On each flight, he shares his love of ballooning with two to six passengers for 60 to 90 minutes. Landings in a yard or field become a neighborhood happening with chilled champagne in French crystal, freshly squeezed orange juice, and homemade apple cake.

Beaches

Sorry, no dogs allowed on beaches, May–September.

In Boston

Boston Harbor Islands State Park Page 181

Beaches on Lovells (sandy), Gallops (sand and stone), and Grape (stone) are without lifeguards because of the budget crunch.

MDC Saltwater Beaches

All accessible by Ⓣ. The water quality of these urban locations is often affected by storms. In **Dorchester:** Malibu, Savin Hill, and Tenean Beach are on Morrissey Boulevard. 617/727–9547 or 727–8865. **East Boston:** Constitution Beach is near the airport. 617/727–9547 or 662–8370. **South Boston:** Carson Beach is on Dorchester Boulevard. Along Day Boulevard are City Point, Pleasure Bay, M Street Beach, and Castle Island (page 185) with its old fort, grassy area, picnic area, and fishing pier. 617/727–9547 or 727–8865.

North of Boston

North Shore beaches tend to be much cooler—sometimes colder—than South Shore areas. Two outstanding places are Crane's in Ipswich and Plum Island in Newburyport.

Gloucester

ALL SALTWATER
SWIMMING

Location and day trip information: Page 61.
Nonresident parking: Memorial Day through Labor Day, $10 per car.

Stage Fort Park
Directions: Tobin/Mystic Bridge to Route 1 north, to Route 128 north, to exit 13. Turn right to the beach.

Swings and equipment to play on, an old fort to explore, and rocks to climb. One beach is sandy; the other, with round beach stones, is scheduled for clearing. Closed fires allowed in the shaded, grassy picnic area. Bathhouse. Leashed dogs and those under command are allowed.

Off-season parking, at least September through May, is usually free at beaches.

Wingaersheek Beach

Directions: Tobin/Mystic Bridge to Route 1 north, to Route 128 north, to exit 13, to long, winding (careful, please) Atlantic Street.

Small, scenic beach, with sand and dunes, at the mouth of the Annisquam River. A good place for young children. Smooth rocks to climb on. Relatively short beach at high tide. Sorry, no dogs allowed. Parking lot fills early.

Good Harbor Beach

Directions: Tobin/Mystic Bridge to Route 1 north, to Route 128 north, to the extension. Left on Eastern Avenue, then right onto Thatcher Road after the Cape Ann Market.

Small, sandy, and populated. Parking lot fills early.

Ipswich

Crane Beach (The Trustees of Reservations) Argilla Road

Phone: 508/356–4354 (beach information, including greenhead fly presence); 508/356–4351 (office).

Location: 30 miles from Boston.

Directions: Tobin/Mystic Bridge to Route 1 north, to Route 128 north, to Route 1A north, to Argilla Road (on the right), 4.2 miles to the beach.

Parking (beach admission included): Memorial Day through Labor Day, $6 weekdays (Mondays and Tuesdays half price), $10 weekends. Many summer weekends the lot fills early. Spring and fall, $3.25 weekdays, $3.75 weekends. Winter, $2.75 weekdays, $3.25 weekends. Buses $20 year round.

Rules: Hibachis allowed; no open fires, no dogs, and no camping.

Walk-in admission: $2.

Lifeguards, bathhouse, and snack bar: Memorial Day through Labor Day.

A showplace. About 4 miles of beautiful clean sand. Mid-July through mid-August, insect repellent may help with the greenhead flies. (They are very bothersome, particularly on hot, humid, muggy days when there is little breeze.)

Walking possibilities: It's a good hour's round trip to Castle Hill, an estate with rolling lawns and sculpture and magnificent views of sea, sand, and marsh. Or follow Pine Hollow Interpretive Trail—a 1-mile path over dunes, into pine hollows, and onto a boardwalk in a red maple swamp. (A booklet is available for $2 at the beach gate or from the patrolling ranger in winter.)

Traditional stop: Goodale Orchards, 123 Argilla Road, 2 miles from beach. Organic herbs and vegetables. Apples, berries. Homemade doughnuts. Sweet and hard cider. Animals.

Manchester-by-the-Sea

Singing Beach

Location: 31 miles northeast of Boston.

Directions: Tobin/Mystic Bridge to Route 1 north, to Route 128 north, to exit 15. Turn right (to the center), and left on Central Street to the beach.

Parking: At the beach, $15 weekdays for a few nonresidents' cars; weekends and holidays for residents only. A few free all-day parking spots on Beach Street (Masconomo Park) across from train depot. At the depot, the Boy Scouts charge $15 for all-day parking.

T: It's a 51-minute commuter rail ride from North Station (617/722–3200), followed by the 1-mile walk to the beach.

Walk-in admission: Friday–Sunday and holidays, $1 per person, $7.50 season pass.

Lynn and Nahant

Nahant Beach (MDC) Nahant Road

Phone: 617/727–5380.

Location: 10 miles north of Boston.

Directions: Callahan Tunnel to Route 1A north. Turn right on Route 129.

Parking: $2, Memorial Day through Labor Day.

T: Commuter rail from North Station (617/722–3200) to Lynn station, then a 10-minute walk. Go east to the rotary; cross parkway and walk beyond Port Hole Restaurant to the beach.

Nearby: Smaller Coast Guard Beach. No parking. On Nahant Beach, face ocean; turn to right. Walk to end of beach and continue for about ¼ mile.

Newburyport (Plum Island)

Parker River National Wildlife Refuge Page 191

Phone: 508/465–5753. (Office hours 8–4:30 Monday–Friday; taped message at other times.)

Location: 35 miles north of Boston.

Directions: Route 1 north, I–95 north to Route 113 east, to High Street in Newburyport. Continue along High Street until you come to a light with a pond and ballfield on your right. Turn left onto Rolfe Lane and follow refuge signs.

Parking and admission: Year round, $5 per car; $1 walk-in, free 62 and up or handicapped persons. Season pass (July 1 through June 30), $15 per car. Park in one of several areas along the 6-mile road and then take a boardwalk to beach.

Open: Generally, year round, dawn to dusk. But when endangered birds are nesting on the beach, usually April 1 until at least June—and even into the summer months—the beach (not the refuge, see page 191) is closed.

Beautiful. Cool-cold open ocean, strong surf (watch the undertow), and dunes along 6 miles of magnificent beach. A good place for walking and picnicking. July through early August is greenhead fly season. On hot days, parking areas tend to fill early and reopen about every two hours. No lifeguards.

Salem

Location and directions: Page 85.

Forest River Park

Parking: In summer, Monday–Friday, $4 nonresidents. Weekends and holidays, residents' parking only.

Two beaches and an outdoor pool that is open weekdays until 6.

Salem Willows Park

Parking and admission: Free.

A busy, pleasant place with grass and trees on a stretch overlooking the water, a small amusement area with merry-go-round, and a big pier. Pavilions and picnic tables jam-packed with cookouts on hot Sundays. Large groups can reserve the sports facilities. Contact the Recreation Department, 27 Fort Avenue, 508/744–0733.

Winter Island Park

Directions: From Maritime Site (page 87), continue toward Salem Willows along Derby Street, which becomes Fort Avenue (at power station), to Winter Island Road on the right.

Parking: $4 for nonresidents.

A recently updated recreational area, site of seafood festival, with two rocky beaches, picnic sites, and camping (page 239).

Salisbury State Beach Ocean Front

Phone: 508/462–4481.

Location: 40 miles from Boston.

Directions: Tobin/Mystic Bridge to Route 1 north, to I–95 north, to Route 110 east, to Route 1A.

Parking: Memorial Day weekend through Labor Day, $5 per car. Day-use season pass for all state parks, $30.

Handicapped access: Accessible.

Rules: No surfing or open fires on beach.

Clean sandbar beach, 4 miles long. Surf swimming (undertow when surf is heavy). Also here: a boat ramp; a camping area (page 239); and, across the street, a small amusement park.

> Off-season parking, at least September through May, is usually free at beaches.

Saugus

Pearce Lake (MDC) Breakheart Reservation (page 189)

Phone: 617/727–9547 or 662–8370.

Location: 9 miles north of Boston.

Freshwater swimming, a bathhouse, and a picnic area. Crowded.

Swampscott

King's Beach (MDC) Lynn Shore Drive

Phone: 617/727–9547 or 662–8370.

Directions: Callahan Tunnel to Route 1A north, to Route 129 east.

Ⓣ: Haymarket on Orange or Green Line; then Humphrey bus to beach.

Winchester

Sandy Beach (MDC) Mystic Valley Parkway (on Upper Mystic Lake)

Phone: 617/727–9547 or 662–8370.

Location: 8 miles north of Boston.

Freshwater swimming, a bathhouse, picnic areas, and a tot lot. Crowded.

South of Boston

Cape Cod National Seashore (508/349–3785) beaches, 100 miles from Boston. (See page 194.) Long, clean, sandy, and beautiful. All with lifeguards in summer. All with rest rooms. Eastham has Nauset Light (parking area fills as early as 10) and Coast Guard Beach (follow signs to Little Creek parking area; $5 per car includes shuttle to Coast Guard Beach). Marconi Beach is in South Wellfleet; Head of the Meadow (usually the last to fill) in Truro. Provincetown has Race Point Beach and Herring Cove Beach (the most accessible for wheelchairs). Mid-June through Labor Day parking: per car, $5 per day or $15 season pass.

Duxbury

Duxbury Beach Route 139

Location: 38 miles from Boston.

Directions to entrance for nonresidents: I–93 south to Route 3 south, to exit 11 onto Route 14 east. At Duxbury Police Station, Route 14 forks. Take Church Street fork (which becomes Route 139). Cross Route 3A, continuing to a Catholic church in Marshfield, where you turn right (follow beach sign) onto Canal Street; this veers to the right and becomes Gurnett Street to the beach.

Parking: $6 weekends, $4 weekdays.

Six miles of beach, narrow at high tide, with dunes, beach grass, and bayberries. Reestablished after being battered by a no-name 1991 storm. Bathhouse and snack bar. Great place for out-of-season walks—when nonresidents, too, can enter via the country's longest wooden bridge.

Hull

Nantasket Beach (MDC)

Phone: 617/727–9547 or 727–8865.

Location: 16 miles from Boston.

Directions: I–93 south to Route 3 south, to Route 228. It's bumper to bumper on summer weekends.

Parking: $2 Memorial Day through Labor Day.

Ⓣ: Quincy on the Red Line; then the Nantasket bus.

Boat: In summer, from Long Wharf. See page 234.

Three miles long, but can be crowded on hot days. Popular with all ages. Surfing in restricted area only. Near carousel, old fort, Lifesaving Museum (page 65).

Milton

Houghton's Pond (MDC) Blue Hills Reservation, Hillside Street

Phone: 617/727–9547 or 727–8865.

Location: 8 miles from Boston.

Directions: I–93 south to Route 128 north, to Route 138 north. Right at the first set of traffic lights.

A freshwater pond, tot lot, tennis courts, baseball fields, picnic areas, and a bathhouse. Crowded.

Scusset State Beach

Sandwich

Phone: 508/888–0859.

Location: 59 miles from Boston.

Directions: I–93 south to Route 3 south, to South Sagamore Circle (don't go over the bridge).

Parking: Memorial Day weekend through Labor Day, $5 per car. Day-use season pass for all state parks, $30.

A popular place for its sandy beach and cool, calm Cape Cod Bay water. About a mile away: fireplaces, snack bar, playground, fishing pier jutting out into Cape Cod Canal.

Myles Standish State Forest

South Carver

Phone: 508/866–2526.

Location: 41 miles from Boston.

Directions: I–93 south to Route 3 south, to exit 5. Turn right on Long Pond Road and follow signs to forest.

Parking: Memorial Day through Labor Day, $5 for College Pond.

A big forest with miles of roads. Swimming area with sandy beach fills to capacity on warm days. Bathhouses. Rest rooms. Lifeguards.

> All Massachusetts state beaches are handicapped accessible.

Demarest Lloyd State Park Barney's Joy Road

South Dartmouth

Location: 60 miles from Boston.

Directions: I–93 south to Route 128 north to Route 24 south; then 195 east to Faunce Corner exit. Turn right onto Faunce Corner Road and cross Route 6 onto Chase Road. Turn right on Russells Mills Road, left on Barneys Joy Road, and follow signs to park.

Parking: Memorial Day weekend through Labor Day, $5 per car. $30 day-use season pass for all state parks.

Pretty. Relatively undiscovered. Perfect for families. Calm, warm water. Huge sandbars. Bathhouse. Lifeguards. Many picnic tables and fireplaces in wooded area. Walking trail. Views—of ospreys, terns, and Cuttyhunk.

Horseneck State Beach Route 88

Westport

Phone: 508/636–8816.

Location: 55 miles from Boston.

Directions: I–93 south to Route 128 north, to Route 24 south, to I–195 east, to single-laned Route 88.

Parking: Memorial Day weekend through Labor Day, $5 per car. $30 day-use season pass for all state parks.

Three miles of gorgeous sand. Surf, slight undertow, and warm water. Picnic tables. A great place for camp groups, families, all ages. (Caution:

There's usually a sharp drop at low tide.) Bathhouse. **Lifeguards. Rest rooms.** Snack bar.

Ashland State Park Route 135

Phone: (Seasonal number; or call Hopkinton State Park, 508/435–4303, for information.)

Location: 22 miles from Boston.

Directions: Route 9 west to Route 16 (toward Wellesley), to Route 135 west.

Parking: Memorial Day weekend through Labor Day, $5 per car. $30 day-use season pass for all state parks.

Still relatively undiscovered. Small (freshwater) swimming area in a lovely setting, surrounded by woods and picnic areas (with barbecues). Good family place. New bathhouse. New ramp for handicapped into water.

Walden Pond State Reservation Page 203

Phone: 508/369–3254.

Too popular. Seek another place! Parking area often filled by 9 a.m.

Douglas State Forest Wallum Lake Road

Phone: 508/476–7872.

Location: 50 miles from Boston, where Massachusetts, Rhode Island, and Connecticut meet.

Directions: Mass. Pike (Route 90 west) to 495 south, Route 16 west, follow signs. Entrance on Wallum Lake Road.

Parking: Memorial Day weekend through Labor Day, $5 per car. $30 day-use season pass for all state parks.

A gorgeous day-use area. A big forest, 3,700 acres, with outstanding beach, wooded picnic sites, grills, fishing. Motorboats on the 322-acre lake do not interfere with day-use swimming area. Interpretive center with bird blind is a short walk from the beach. Bathhouse. Lifeguards.

Dunn's Pond Route 101 south

Phone: 508/632–7897.

Location: 59 miles west of Boston.

Directions: Route 2 west, Route 140 north to Route 101 south for about 2 miles; entrance on the left.

Parking: $5 per car.

Considered special enough for some Bostonians to drive the extra hour beyond Walden Pond. Clear water in gorgeous pond, recently excavated and scientifically designed, with smallish sandy beach. Bathhouse with granite fireplace in lobby (used by skaters in winter). Picnic area under pine trees. Delightful half-hour trail around the pond. Fitness course. Changing rooms. Lifeguards. And paddleboat rentals available.

Bonus: It's about a mile to (free) Gardner Heritage State Park Visitors Center, a converted firehouse that has interesting exhibits about furniture making—and information about factory outlets in Gardner.

Hopkinton State Park Route 85

Phone: 508/435–4303.

Location: 26.2 miles from Boston (by Boston Marathon measurements!).

Directions: Route 9 west to Route 85 south for 3 miles.

Parking: Memorial Day weekend through Labor Day, $5 per car. $30 day-use season pass for all state parks.

The long, straight freshwater beach gets very crowded. Lot fills very early on weekends. Cars often in line by 8. Many picnic tables in a wooded setting. Grills provided; some under pavilions. New rest rooms. Boat launching ramps for canoes, rowboats, and sailboats with plenty of parking.

Nearby: Weston Nurseries on Route 135. Vast display of trees and shrubs. Closed Sundays. Phone: 508/435–3414 or 800/322–2002. Groups: Reservations (100 people minimum) for a special area are accepted as of March 1.

Cochituate State Park Route 30 (near turnpike interchange)

Phone: 508/653–9641.

Location: 15 miles from Boston.

Directions: Mass. Pike west to exit 13 (Route 30 east).

Parking: Memorial Day weekend through Labor Day, $5 per car. $30 day-use season pass for all state parks.

A very busy place with a well-used freshwater swimming area and boating. Picnic tables and fireplaces in wooded areas. New rest rooms.

> Sorry, no dogs allowed on beaches, May–September.

Bicycling

Cyclists are everywhere, in and out of the city. For help in charting routes, there are active organizations and helpful publications; please see page 223.

Paths

In town, the major path (5- to 25-mile loops, depending on the bridge you cross) is along the **Charles River.** From Massachusetts General Hospital it's about 2½ miles to Massachusetts Avenue on the Boston side, another mile to the BU Bridge, another 2½ miles to the Larz Anderson Bridge. Less traveled is the area beyond here to Watertown. Around the Esplanade and Back Bay the bike path can be an obstacle course among joggers, skaters, strollers, and other cyclists. Pedal with caution. The signed Watertown-to-Cambridge side is quiet and pretty, and then it's straightforward all the way to the Charles River Dam.

Other MDC paths: Trails at **Stony Brook Reservation** start at West Roxbury Parkway and Washington Street in Roslindale and lead through 2 to 5 miles of forest. In Somerville, the **Mystic River Reservation** offers a couple of miles.

Wompatuck State Park (page 196) has 15 miles of trails (no automobiles allowed) without crossroads.

Currently under construction: A path from Arlington to Bedford. Other planned paths are waiting for funding.

Cape Cod Rail Trail

Parking: Free for trail users. At the trailhead off Route 134 in South Dennis, at Headwater Road in Harwich, at Route 137 in Brewster, at Nickerson State Park in Brewster, and at the Cape Cod National Seashore Headquarters (page 194) in Eastham.

Everyone you pass greets you with a smile on this 20-mile-long, 8-foot-wide paved path, a former railroad right-of-way that passes through more of the "real Cape" than you would see in a day of driving. It was exotic even one December weekend, when walkers, too, admired freshwater ponds, salt marshes, pine woods, wildlife. Almost flat, this treasure runs from Dennis to Eastham, where it ends across Route 6 from the Cape Cod National Seashore's Salt Pond Visitor Center.

Reminder: If you are round-tripping in a day, a head wind could make the return pedal a bit longer.

Bikes on the Ⓣ

A FEW AT A TIME

Phone: 617/727–4400.

Permits (photo ID): Required. Minimum age: 16. Ages 12–15 receive permits if application signed by child's parent or guardian; child must be accompanied by a responsible adult when bringing bicycle on the Ⓣ. Purchase permits at the Senior and Access Pass Office, Monday–Friday 8:30–4:15 at the Downtown Crossing (Ⓣ: Red and Orange Lines) subway concourse. Valid for four years. Cost: $5.

Hours: *Commuter rail:* Saturdays and Sundays, all day, both directions. Monday–Friday, any time except during the morning rush inbound and evening rush outbound. *Subway:* Red, Blue, and Orange Lines only. Saturday 5:30–8:30 a.m. Sunday all day. Monday–Friday after 8 p.m.

Limitations: Maximum of 6 bicycles allowed on each commuter rail train, 2 on last car of rapid transit train at any one time. Bicycles never allowed on Green Line or on buses. Bicycles not allowed on subways and trains between Thanksgiving and Christmas, or on days or evenings of Boston Garden events and Red Sox games. And check information line for special events which change the schedule.

Reservations: Strongly suggested (617/722–3600 until midnight) for Rockport/Ipswich commuter rail line on weekends.

Books

Highly recommended

Short Bike Rides in Greater Boston and Central Massachusetts by Howard Stone (Old Saybrook, Conn.: The Globe Pequot Press, updated frequently). My husband and I have followed just about every one of the more than 100 rides. From suggested parking places to "don't miss" sites to commentary, the author hits the mark.

Very popular

25 Mountain Bike Tours in Eastern Massachusetts by Robert S. Morse (Woodstock, Vt.: Countryman Press). Maps are included with the described routes, which are in parklands from the Connecticut River to the Atlantic Coast.

Maps

The Explorer Recreational Map and Guide ($3.50), P.O. Box 1040, Boston 02117, is very useful for make-your-own day trip routes. Sites such as parks, lakes, and beaches are included along with selected roads inside Route 495.

The Boston Bike Map ($6.00), Great Circle Productions, 163 East Lothrop Street, Beverly 01915, covers roads in communities inside Route 128.

New

Bike Map Massachusetts ($4.95) is published by Bikemaps New England, P.O. Box 1035, Porter Branch, Cambridge 02140; phone 617/868–8948. Cycling advocate Andy Rubel has embellished and computerized an out-of-print state bike map to give much more detail on the *Eastern Massachusetts map,* first in a series, released in 1992. (The *Western Massachusetts map* is due in 1993.) Printed in five colors, it includes commuter rails, mountain biking trail areas, state parks and campgrounds, youth hostels, some B&Bs, and swimming and picnic spots.

Repairs

Consult the yellow pages or your neighbor for bicycle repair shops. Watch newspaper listings (under "Bicycles") for repair clinics held by organizations, museums, and bicycle stores.

Of particular interest is the one-of-a-kind, staff-owned **Broadway Bicycle School,** 351 Broadway, Cambridge 02139. It has three price levels (all reasonable): for space and tools, for bicycle maintenance sessions, and for mechanics' work. New and used bikes, parts, accessories, and tools are sold. Open Tuesday–Saturday year round plus Sundays in summer. Hours vary. Phone 617/868–3392.

Rentals

Inventory varies—sometimes from season to season. In **Boston:** Community Bike Shop, 490 Tremont Street (South End), 617/542–8623. **Lincoln:** Lincoln Guide Service, 151 Lincoln Road (at the railroad tracks) rents tandem, road, and mountain bikes. They also lead day and overnight bicycle trips. **Cohasset** (20 miles south of Boston): Cohasset Cycle Sports, 739 Chief Justice Cushing Highway, 617/383–0707.

Organizations

Day trips

For a full schedule of day trips (no membership needed) that are scheduled every weekend year round, check Thursday's "Calendar" section in the *Boston Globe.*

American Youth Hostels Greater Boston Council, 1020 Commonwealth Avenue (across from Eastern Mountain Sports), Boston 02215
Phone: 617/731–5430 for worldwide hostel information; 617/730–8AYH (8294) for trip hotline, changed weekly.

Programs are open to all ages. This office has information about day trips, hosteling, and group trips here and abroad. Activities include cycling, mountain climbing, skiing, sailing, and canoeing.

Hostels in the United States average $10 per person per night, depending on place and season. Family rooms (one for the whole family) are available in many locations. All have kitchen facilities. Some duties are expected of hostelers. Reservations suggested. Boston hostel, page 11.

Boston Area Bicycle Coalition 214A Broadway, Cambridge; mailing address, P.O. Box 1015, Kendall Branch, Cambridge 02142
Phone: 617/491–RIDE.

Office hours: Sunday 1–4 p.m.

BABC is a volunteer organization primarily interested in the bicycle as transportation. They focus on state legislation, secure bike parking, bicycle-friendly streets, more bike paths and lanes, more access for bikes on the ⓣ. They conduct bike maintenance workshops, have a library, and publish a very informative newsletter.

Boston Park Rangers Page 125

The rangers conduct monthly cycling day trips along the Emerald Necklace, from Boston Common to Arnold Arboretum.

Charles River Wheelmen 19 Chase Avenue, West Newton 02165
Phone: 617/325–BIKE (recorded information line).

Group rides along well-marked routes are open to all—members and non-members, individuals and families—without charge. Everything from short 15-mile loops to 100-mile jaunts are scheduled on most Sundays, year round.

New England Mountain Bike Association 69 Spring Street, Cambridge 02141
Phone: 617/497–6891.

This volunteer organization is interested in having trails available for mountain bikes. As an educational organization, it advocates responsible riding and is concerned about the environment. Members—about four hundred currently—receive a newsletter that includes upcoming events, rides (suggested for age 14 or 15 and up), and races.

Birdwatching

A serious activity that's enjoyed by many. (Some get "hooked" at a very young age.) Field trips (no charge), an hour or a day long, start as early as 5 in the morning. Leaders act as narrators, identifying sounds and finding species in marsh, woods, or wherever. They also give directions to beginners. A good clearinghouse for birding information is the Conservation Department of the Massachusetts Audubon Society (page 204).

Boating

Lessons

Safety courses are offered someplace in the area year round. Families are welcome, and often there are special sessions for young people. Check with Massachusetts Environmental Law Enforcement, Boat Division, 100 Nashua Street, Boston 02114 (617/727–0882 or 727–8760), or with the U.S. Coast Guard, Boating Safety Division, 408 Atlantic Avenue, Boston 02110–3350 (617/223–8310).

Free summer **sailing lessons** offered through the MDC, through the Harry McDonough Sailing Program, Day Boulevard, Castle Island, South Boston. Call for this year's schedule: 617/268–8556.

The Charles River Canoe and Kayak Center, page 231, offers lessons in **canoeing, kayaking, and rowing.**

Launching Areas

There's no charge for most public ramps, including those along the Charles in Brighton on **Nonantum Road** (near the skating rink) and in Cambridge at **Magazine Beach** (off Memorial Drive, near Stop & Shop). For other launching sites under MDC jurisdiction, call 617/727–5215. Statewide locations are compiled in *Public Access to the Waters of Massachusetts,* available for $3 from the Commonwealth of Massachusetts Public Access Board, 100 Nashua Street, Room 915, Boston 02114, 617/727–1843.

Brighton

Christian Herter Center area, across from WBZ studios on Soldiers Field Road. Canoe and kayak rentals. Check with MDC, 617/727–5033, for this year's arrangements.

Carlisle

Great Brook Farm State Park, page 198, has a launch on North Road near dam. Five-acre pond with islands and inlets to explore.

Dover-Needham

At the **Charles River Village Falls,** canoeists travel downstream of the dam. Park at the end of South Street, off Route 135. To paddle upstream of the dam, take a right here onto Fisher Street.

Hopkinton

Hopkinton State Park on Route 85 (see page 221) has boat launching ramps for canoes, rowboats, and sailboats with plenty of parking. Opportunities to explore islands in the upper reservoir. No motorboats allowed. Phone 508/435–4303; parking $5 per car; $30 season pass for all state parks.

Milton

For canoeing on the Neponset River. At **Paul's Bridge** on the Milton-Readville line at the junction of Brush Hill Road and Neponset Valley Parkway.

Natick

At **Cochituate State Park** on Route 30, near turnpike interchange (see page 221), there's no charge for use of launching ramp on the reservoir. Call about rentals of canoes and/or windsurfers. Phone 508/653–9641; parking $5 per car; $30 season pass for all state parks.

Newton

Nahanton Park, Nahanton Street, is adjacent to the Kendrick Street bridge on the Needham-Newton line. On the Charles River. Launching area, small dock (April–October), lovely open space appreciated by birdwatchers, one soccer field, building with small meeting room (some nature programs and fishing clinics run by the city of Newton), and rest rooms. Park (no charge) adjacent to canoe launch area or with trailer, in lot off Nahanton Street, above canoe launch area.

South Natick

On the Charles River, at the **South Natick Dam,** a photographer's paradise. In South Natick Square, at Route 16 and Union Street (which becomes Pleasant Street once you cross Route 16). There on Pleasant Street, near the pine grove with picnic tables and grills, you can launch a canoe for paddling below or above the falls. On the opposite bank: a picturesque park by the waterfall with a small grassy area, shade trees, benches, and views of arched stone bridge, ducks, Canada geese, ever-changing vegetation, sunsets.

Before you go out, check marine weather by calling 617/569–3700.

Topsfield	**Bradley Palmer State Park** Page 189.
Weston-Newton	On the Charles River. From Routes 30 and 128, take **Recreation Road** to free parking lot. Launch platform is upriver of footbridge.

Rowing

Community Rowing Daly Rink, Nonantum Road, Brighton (on Newton line); mailing address, Box 2064, Cambridge 02238

Phone: 617/455–1992.

Open: April–October.

Rates: $15 annual membership fee plus program fees (minimum of a month). $25 per hour for private lessons by appointment. Group lessons and rates arranged.

You too can join the sweep rowers in eights or single scullers in those graceful boats on the Charles River. Lessons offered for beginners, for recreational and competitive rowers, for children (12 and older) and adults. There are opportunities to row on your own. Everyone is required to pass a swim test. Programs available for visually challenged and physically impaired. Free introductory lessons on summer Sunday mornings; call for time.

Rentals

CANOES,
PADDLEBOATS,
ROWBOATS, AND
SAILBOATS

Although there are no sailboat rentals at Community Boating (see box), it may be the best local deal for sailors. Lessons, charters, and memberships—but no rentals—are available at private sailing clubs, listed in the Yellow Pages.

Concord

South Bridge Boat House Main Street (just beyond Concord Center, on the Concord River), Concord 01742

Phone: 508/369–9438.

Location, directions, and train: See page 55.

Open: April–October. Weekdays 10–6, weekends 9:30–dusk. Reservations made for groups only.

Rates: Canoes (for 2, 3, or 4) or rowboats: Weekdays, per hour, $6.50; $5.50 for students. Per day, $25; $23 for students. Weekends, per hour, $7.40; $36 maximum. Rates include life preservers; all sizes available.

The Rohans, owners for almost forty-five years, have just celebrated the 100th birthday of the original boathouse. They encourage you to bring lunch for a riverbank stop (no fires allowed), perhaps at Old North Bridge (page 55) or Great Meadows National Wildlife Refuge (page 199). You can paddle up to 50 miles and see ducks, turtles, birds, a lot of wildlife. Reminder: One way is against the current.

Dedham

Tropicland Marine and Tackle 100 Bridge Street, Dedham 02026

Directions: Route 128 to Route 16A to Route 109 east for 2 miles on the right.

Open: Late April through September. Monday–Saturday 9:30–3 (be back by 5).

SAILING

Harry McDonough Sailing (MDC) Castle Island, page 185, South Boston

Phone: 617/727–9547.

Open: Late June through Labor Day, 10–6 daily.

Free instruction and use of sailboats. Open to the public. Swim test required.

Community Boating 21 Embankment Road (near the Hatch Shell), Boston

Phone: 617/523–1038 or 523–7699. TTY: 617/523–7406.

T: Charles on the Red Line; then cross the Storrow Drive footbridge.

Parking: Off-hours parking at a discount at the Mass. Eye and Ear Infirmary visitors' lot.

Open: April–October daily.

Junior program: Mid-June through late August. For ages 11 to 17—the biggest bargain in town—$1 for entire season. (Donations welcome.) Juniors have their own shore school, racing program, social program (outings and canoes), and hours (weekdays 9–3).

This centrally located, well-equipped facility on the Charles offers everything to everyone at reasonable rates. Open membership—by the month or season—includes the use of sailboats and all instruction. And members who pass the sailing test have interchangeable benefits with Regatta Point Community Sailing, North Lake Avenue, Worcester, 508/757–2140.

Rates: On location: $5.50 per hour, 2-hour minimum. $25 per day. Takeaway (includes cartop foam): $35 per day, $100 security deposit. Advance reservations permitted.

Minimum age: 18 unless accompanied by an adult.

Go downriver almost 9 miles to a waterfall in Newton, or upriver about 14 miles to a waterfall in Dover—all along a section of the Charles River where only hand-carried boats are allowed. Canoes can hold three people. Plenty of places to stop for lunch. Preservers and paddles provided. Fishing tackle, rods, reels, lures, and live bait sold.

Hopkinton

Hopkinton State Park Route 85 Page 221.

Phone 508/435–4303 for this year's arrangements.

Ipswich

Foote Brothers 356 Topsfield Road, Ipswich 01938

Phone: 508/356–9771.

Location: 32 miles north of Boston, at Willowdale Dam on the Ipswich River.

Directions: Tobin/Mystic Bridge to Route 1 north. At the second light after the Topsfield fairgrounds, take Ipswich Road (which becomes Topsfield Road) for a couple of miles to the landing.

Open: April–October. Reservations advisable.

Rates: Canoes (per day): Weekdays $18, weekends $22 leaving from Foote Brothers dock. Shuttle trips: up to Salem run (a 4-hour paddle), $25; Thunder Bridge run (6–7 hours), $28. Paddles and personal flotation devices provided with rentals. Overnight rentals available.

Camping: Ask about overnight arrangements on an island within a wildlife sanctuary.

Paddle through scenic protected watersheds. Bring a lunch. There are many places to stop along the river.

Jamaica Plain

Jamaica Pond Boat House 507 Jamaicaway (Route 1), Jamaica Plain 02130

Phone: 617/522–6258.

Directions and ⊤: See page 188.

Open: March until mid-December, 9–5 spring and fall, until 8:30 in summer. (Reminder: All renters must be able to swim.)

Rates: *Rowboats:* $6 per hour, $3 with Massachusetts fishing license. *Sailboats:* Spindrifts available in summer. Call for rates and information on individual and group lessons for adults and children.

Fishing: Bring your own rod. The 50-foot-deep pond is stocked.

Bonus: The boathouse is also a center for classes in environmental education and nature study. Free sessions—in the nature study room or in the park—are by appointment with public and private schools for grades 1–12.

Lynn

Seaport Landing Marina 154 Lynnway, Lynn 01902

Phone: 617/592–5821.

Open: June–August. Wednesdays, 4–dusk. Saturdays and Sundays, 8 a.m. until dusk.

⊤: Commuter rail to Central Square/Lynn. Cross Lynnway and you're there.

Rates: For about 20 minutes: $3.50 age 13 and over, kids free.

Pedaling these paddleboats is more exercise than you may think. An instant hit when introduced in 1991, they hold two adults or two adults and two children. You pedal in a designated area of the cove. Everyone wears life preservers that are provided. A lifeguard is on duty. The landing is complete with picnic pavilion, boardwalk, and grass, all within minutes' walk from the (free) Lynn Heritage State Park, page 71.

Millis

Upriver Outfitters Route 109, Millis 02054

Phone: 508/376–1288.

Location: 45 minutes west of Boston, on Route 109 at the Charles Restaurant, on the Millis/Medfield line. On a little cove.

Directions: Route 128 to exit 16B for about 8 miles.

Open: April–November, *weather permitting,* Friday, Saturday, Sunday, and Monday, 8–6. "Because the wind tends to be lighter in the morning, with children especially, we recommend an early start." Reservations required for groups.

Rates: $15 for up to 3 hours. $20 all day for solo or tandem canoes. $20 for 3 hours or $25 for all day for family-sized canoes (4 adults or up to 900 pounds). Folding chairs, cushions, life jackets, paddles, option of cartop carrier, and litter bag included.

Rules: At least one in the party has to be 18. Solo canoes rented to under age 18 if one or more supervising adults is in party.

Food: Bring a picnic. Get takeout from, or eat at, reasonably priced Charles Restaurant (traditional American menu; kitchen closes at 4 p.m.).

"Our most popular trip is about four hours, a one-way paddle for many, from here along the Charles River to South Natick Dam, through marvelous winding flatwater, through open marshes, Rocky Woods Reservation, rural areas, and large estates. For younger children, we suggest a downstream route to a small pond or upstream to the Stop River confluence that has nice views."

> "Canoeists comment on the muskrats, ducks, red-tailed hawks, red-winged blackbirds, sometimes deer in the early morning. The great blue heron has been called a pterodactyl by some kids. And then there was the anxious child who was calmed when we suggested that he count the number of turtles. Two hours later, from round the bend, we heard: '131 . . . 132 . . .'!"
>
> —Larry McCarthy, Upriver Outfitters

Natick

Cochituate State Park Page 221.

Call for this year's arrangements.

Newton

Charles River Canoe and Kayak Center 2401 Commonwealth Avenue (Route 30), Newton 02166

Phone: 617/965–5110.

Ⓣ: Riverside on D Green Line; then a 20- to 30-minute walk.

Open: April–October, 10–7 weekdays, 9–7 weekends.

Rates: *Canoes*: Weekdays, $6 an hour, $24 maximum. Weekends, $7 an hour, $28 maximum. *Kayaks*: Weekdays, $8 an hour. Weekends, $9 an hour. Shells: $15 an hour. *Car racks*: Off-premise rentals available.

Rules: Under 18 without an adult, signed permission form needed.

Canoes can take three people; four if two are young children. Most day-trippers paddle 6 miles or so. Bring a picnic lunch or call ahead to have one provided.

In addition to instruction in canoeing, kayaking, and rowing, the center offers takeaway rentals and day trips along the Massachusetts coast.

Not sure where the town is? Check the map on page 2.

Kings Landing Marina 80 Kings Landing, Norwell 02061

Phone: 617/659–7273.

Location: 30 miles southeast of Boston.

Directions: From Norwell Center on Route 123, past Bridge Street, to a dirt road on the right, follow sign.

Open: Tuesday–Sunday, March through September. *Suggestions:* On weekends, call about canoe availability. Telephone reservations taken; call on Thursday or Friday—earlier for holiday weekends—to reserve a canoe and for the tide schedule.

Rates (include life jackets and paddles): $20 deposit. $10 first hour, $15 for 2–4 hours, $20 maximum for more than 4 hours. Group rates available.

Rules: Renters should be at least 17 years old or accompanied by an adult canoeist.

"Most people go out for 4–6 hours. If you leave on an incoming tide and go beyond the low bridge ½ mile upriver, there's no traffic. If you leave on an outgoing tide, you're going toward the ocean. Often, people call to check the tides of the North River, a designated scenic waterway that has wonderful foliage in the fall. Regardless of your direction, there's a swimming beach. Our canoes can hold three adults or two adults with up to three small children."

The Lincolns have owned this boatyard for over forty years. They provide canoeists with a map that shows distances from one point to another. It also shows brooks, roads, beaches, and Blueberry Island. And along the river there are plaques that tell where shipyards were and the names of ships built there.

Boat Trips

From Boston Harbor

BRING A JACKET!

Several companies sail from the waterfront:

- **A.C. Cruise Lines**, Pier 1, 28 Northern Avenue, Boston 02210 (at bridge between James Hook Lobsters and Museum Wharf). Ⓣ: South Station on the Red Line; then a 5-minute walk. Phone 617/426–8419 or 800/422–8419.

- **Bay State Cruise Company Inc.**, 67 Long Wharf, Boston 02110. Ⓣ: Aquarium on the Blue Line. Walk to red ticket booth half way down the wharf beyond the Marriott Hotel, facing the Aquarium. Phone 617/723–7800. *Note:* To request (no charge) a Cruiser Card, write—please do not call—during April or May. Season card provides individual discounts for all regularly scheduled cruises.

- **Boston Harbor Cruises**, One Long Wharf, Boston 02110. Ⓣ: Aquarium on the Blue Line and you are right there. Phone 617/227–4321.

- **Massachusetts Bay Lines,** 67 Rowes Wharf, Boston 02110. Phone 617/542–8000. Currently, a charter service only.

Group discounts may be available with advance arrangements.
Long Wharf is at Marriott Hotel. **Rowes Wharf** is behind the Boston Harbor Hotel.

Boston By Sail 66 Long Wharf, Boston 02110

Phone: 617/742–3313.

Season: Spring through late fall, 90-minute sails depart daily, every two hours, 10 a.m. to 10 p.m.

Rates: $30 per person, 15 percent less for senior citizens and children under 10. Romantic evening schooner sails, $75 (include hors d'oeuvres) per couple.

All ages partake of day sails. Young couples enjoy the evening sails. The sloop can take up to 6 people, the schooner up to 49. And arrangements can be made for private day, overnight, weekend or weekly charters.

Bay State Cruise Company sails late May through mid-October with a stop at Georges Island. Several sailings daily spring and fall. Weekends and daily summer schedule: Leave Long Wharf at 10, 11, 1, 2, 3, and 4. Fares: $6 adult; $4 group member, senior citizen, child under 12.

Boston Harbor Cruises leave 10–4, every hour on the hour, July through mid-October; and at 11, 1, and 3 Memorial Day through June. Fares: $8 adult, $6 senior, $4 under age 12.

Harbor tours plus

Science At Sea: The New England Aquarium's *Doc Edgerton* accommodates a maximum of 80 passengers on 90-minute narrated harbor trips with hands-on possibilities. School groups book spring and fall excursions; if there's room, individuals may join them. Open to the public, July and August, leaving from New England Aquarium, page 162, daily at 10:30, 12:30, 2:30, 4:30, and 7. Participate as much or as little as you want. Pull up a lobster trap. Net some plankton for microscopic viewing. Measure salinity, temperature, depth. Use a chart to see what course the boat is on. Combination tickets (with aquarium admission) $10 adults, $8.50 seniors, $8.50 ages 12–18, $8 children under 12. Phone 617/973–5200.

Spirit of Boston Rowes Wharf, Boston 02110

Phone: 617/569–4449; 569–6867 for groups of 20 or more.

You know it when you see it. Sleek and gleaming. Can take up to 600 passengers. Three huge climate-controlled enclosed decks plus outdoor decks. Close to 3-hour cruise with narrated harbor tour, buffet lobster clambake luncheon or evening dinner cruise—both with Broadway revue by wait staff, and a dance band ('40s and golden oldies) too. Daily April–December. Lunch $27.25–$29.75; $15.15 age 12 and under. Dinner/dance $39.95–$45.95 per person.

Airport water shuttle

Logan Airport Water Shuttle runs to and from Rowes Wharf. Call 800/23–LOGAN for schedule. $8 adults, $4 senior citizens, children under 12 free if accompanied by an adult. Free van to terminals.

Charlestown Navy Yard (USS *Constitution*)

Passengers have the option of staying on board for a total of 45 minutes or spending 1–6 hours in Charlestown before returning on narrated inner harbor tours that leave from Long Wharf:

Bay State Cruise Company, 617/723–7800. In summer, every hour on the half hour, 10:30–4:30; less frequently in spring and fall. Rates include return trip: $5 adult; $3 group member, senior citizen, child under 12.

Boston Harbor Cruises, 617/227–4321. Memorial Day through Labor Day, every hour on the half hour, 10:30–4:30 daily. Return trips are every hour on the hour 11–5. Round-trip fare: $5 adults, $4 seniors, $3 for children ages 3–12, free under age 3.

Great for Freedom Trail

Navy Yard Commuter boat service (10-minute ride)

ⓣ **two-way service,** April–October, docks at Navy Yard Pier 4.

Boston Harbor Cruises leave Long Wharf weekdays every 15 minutes 6:30–9 a.m.; every half hour 9:30–3:30; every 15 minutes 3:45–6:30; every half hour 7–8. The shuttle leaves Charlestown Navy Yard for Long Wharf every 15 minutes 6:45–9:15 a.m., every half hour till 3:45, then every 15 minutes till 6:45. Last boat leaves Charlestown at 8:15 weekdays. Weekends and holidays: every half hour 10–6 from Long Wharf; every half hour 10:15–6:15 from Navy Yard. $1 per person; pay as you board. 60-day pass, $45.

Bay State Cruise Company sails from Navy Yard's Pier 1 (where USS *Constitution* is docked), April–October, usually at 10 past hour, 11:10–4:10 daily. $1 per person.

Lunch Cruises

Bay State, 617/723–7800, sails from 12:15 until 12:45 weekdays, mid-May through mid-September from Long Wharf. $1 per person.

Music Cruises

Water Music summer cruises are very popular—especially with singles, but all ages are welcome. The Cabaret Jazzboat sails mid-June through August, 7–9 p.m. and 9:30–11:30 p.m., and features traditional and contemporary jazz, blues, reggae, and calypso. Food and liquor available on board. Tickets: $12.50–$16.50. For this year's schedule, call 617/876–8777.

To Thompson Island from Boston

Bay State Cruises, 617/723–7800, sails weekends, Memorial Day through Labor Day, from Long Wharf at 11, 2, and 4. Last boat leaves Thompson Island at 4:30. $8 adults, $6 senior citizens and children under 12.

To Nantasket from Boston

90 MINUTES EACH WAY

The boat is the best way to get to Nantasket Beach, but on warm Sunday afternoons it's not a relaxing cruise—it's busy! **Bay State,** page 232, sails from Long Wharf on weekends Memorial Day through September at 10, 1, and 5:30; leaves Nantasket at 11, 3:30, and 7. Weekdays, late June through Labor Day, 10 and 2 to Nantasket, 12 noon and 3:30 from Nantasket. $8 adult, $5 group member or senior citizen, $3 child under 12. $1 bicycle each way.

Sunset Cruise

90 MINUTES

Boston Harbor Cruises, page 232, leaves Long Wharf late May through Labor Day at 7. $8 adults, $6 seniors, $4 children under 12.

Bay State, page 232, leaves Long Wharf daily at 5:30, returns weekdays at 7:15, weekends at 8:15. $6 adult, $5 group member or senior citizen, $3 child under 12.

Charles River Excursions

Boston Harbor Cruises, page 232, offers a 2-hour narrated river excursion, mid-June until Labor Day. They sail through the locks and upriver as far as the Massachusetts Avenue bridge. Snack bar on board. Leaves Long Wharf at 10:15 and 1:15. $10 adults, $9 seniors, $8 children under 12.

To Georges Island via Bay State Cruises, 617/723–7800. $6 adult, $4 group, senior citizens, children under 12. Rates include the option of taking the summer water taxi *from Georges to Bumpkin, Gallops, Grape, Lovells, and Peddocks Islands.* On Georges Island, check at the information booth about specific schedules and destinations. Although you could just ride on the water taxi (holds 49 passengers), most people spend about an hour on one or two smaller islands, either exploring on their own or learning from the interpreter on duty.

From Boston: A 45-minute harbor tour (page 233 includes rates). The last boat leaves Georges Island at 4:45 summer weekdays, 5:45 summer weekends.

From Hingham: Call for schedule.

From Nantasket Beach/Hull: Half-hour ride. Weekdays only. Leave Nantasket at noon. Leave Georges Island at 2:45.

From Lynn: Monday, Tuesday, Wednesday in July and August. One round trip per day.

Charles River Boat Company, 100 CambridgeSide Place, Suite 320, Cambridge 02141. Phone: 617/621–3001. Single-deck boat built for this cruise leaves October–May from CambridgeSide Galleria lagoon, every hour on the hour, 12–5, weekends in spring and fall, daily Memorial Day through Labor Day. (Full-service bar. Catering and evening cruises arranged for groups.) The 50-minute narrated cruise picks up and drops off passengers at the Museum of Science. Travels up Cambridge side of river and turns at the Hyatt Regency Hotel area to return on Boston side. Flexible seating. Awning. Fully enclosed in inclement weather. $6 adults, $5 senior citizens, $4 ages 3–12. Age 2 and under free.

To JFK Library

Boston Harbor Cruises, page 232, runs this water shuttle July through September plus weekends in October. Leaves Long Wharf 10–5 on the hour. Leaves the library on the half hour. About a 30-minute trip. $2 per person each way.

To Gloucester

TWO AND A HALF
HOURS EACH WAY

The boat docks for 2½ hours at Rocky Neck (page 64), the oldest art colony in the country, an area in East Gloucester filled with art galleries and restaurants. **A.C. Cruise Lines** sails from Boston at 10 a.m., Memorial Day weekend and weekends in June, daily late June through Labor Day. $18 round trip, $16 senior citizens, $12 children under 12; under 1 no charge. Bicycles $1 each way. Group rates available.

To Provincetown

Bay State (page 232) sails from Commonwealth Pier (World Trade Center), adjacent to Anthony's Pier 4 restaurant, weekends Memorial Day through Columbus Day, plus daily late June through Labor Day. The boat leaves Boston at 9:30, docks in Provincetown for 3 hours, and returns to Boston at 6:30. (From Long Wharf in Boston there is a 9 a.m. shuttle, $1 per person, to Commonwealth Pier.) Three decks (music and dancing on covered middle deck) and two galleys on board. Fare: $25 adult round-trip, same day ($15 one way). $18 group member, senior citizen, or child under 12 ($13 one way). $5 bicycle, each way. Master Card or Visa accepted for advance reservations.

The 7- by 3-mile island has fantastic beaches, gorgeous hiking trails, and views from dramatic bluffs. Cyclists will find the few roads hilly. Year round, boats leave from Port Judith, Rhode Island—a 1¼-hour drive from Boston. Boat trip is about an hour and ten minutes. Adults $6.60 one way, $10.50 same-day round-trip. Children under 12 $3.15, $5.50 same-day round-trip. Bicycle $1.75 each way.

In summer boats also leave from Providence (a 3-hour sail) and Newport (a 2-hour sail). Phone Interstate Navigation at 401/783–4613 for schedules.

A 1- by 2-mile haven (two-thirds is undeveloped) with 1.3 miles of paved road, beautiful beaches (less crowded away from the dock), a general store, a couple of gift shops and two restaurants in summer, one inn, a library, a one-room schoolhouse, a church, and a lookout. Recommended: Hiking boots and long-sleeved clothing for a walk. Wildlife (deer, for sure), vegetation (huckleberries and bayberries), and great views.

Alert II (Cuttyhunk Boat Lines) leaves from New Bedford's Pier 3, next to the Coast Guard lightship (a couple of blocks from the Whaling Museum), at 10 weekdays, at 9 weekends. Round-trip fare: $15 same day, $10 each way. Age 11 and under $10 same day, $8 each way. Arrive at least a half hour ahead of time so that you can park in nearby garage, $2.50 per day. Telephone reservations accepted: 508/992–1432.

Greyhound (page 6) provides bus connections from Boston to all boats.

From Falmouth (77 miles south of Boston): The **Island Commuter Corporation,** Falmouth Heights Road, sails daily May through October. The

SWAN BOATS

Boston Public Garden; mailing address, P.O. Box 1487, Boston 02130–3003

Phone: 617/522–1966 (April through mid-September).

Ⓣ: Arlington on the Green Line.

Season: First Saturday before April 19 until mid-September, except when it's rainy or windy. If in doubt, call. Hours April through late June and fall: 10–4. Late June through Labor Day: 10–5.

Rates: $1.25 adults, $1 senior citizens, $.75 children age 12 and under. Group rates available Monday–Friday.

Handicapped access: Accessible.

A young captain sits between the wings of a model swan in back of benched passengers and pedals one of the boats that have been a Boston tradition since Robert Paget created them in 1877. Paget's wife, Julia, carried on when she became a widow in 1878. Today the business, run by third- and fourth-generation Pagets, is getting help from the fifth generation.

Bring feed for the ducks, and try to spot Mrs. Mallard and her ducklings (made famous by Robert McCloskey's *Make Way for Ducklings*) during the 12-minute ride. The setting also has special meaning for *Trumpet of the Swan* readers.

Children will remind you that the ducklings' names are:
Jack,
Kack,
Lack,
Mack,
Nack,
Ouack,
Pack,
and Quack.

ferry docks at Oak Bluffs. It's a 40-minute trip each way. Round-trip fare: $9 adults, $4.50 under age 13. Under age 5 free Friday–Monday. Bicycles $6 round trip. Phone 508/548–4800.

From Hyannis (84 miles south of Boston): **Hy-Line** leaves daily, early May through late October, from Ocean Street Dock; docks at Oak Bluffs. It's a 1¾-hour trip each way. Round-trip fare: $21 adults, $10.50 age 12 and under. Bicycles $4.50 each way. Phone 508/775–7185.

From New Bedford (58 miles south of Boston): **Martha's Vineyard Ferry** sails daily mid-May until mid-September from Billy Wood's Wharf; docks at Vineyard Haven. It's a 1½-hour trip each way. Same-day round-trip fare: $15 adult ($8.50 one way); $7.50 child under 12 ($4.50 one way). Bicycles $2.50 each way. Phone 508/997–1688.

From Woods Hole (74 miles south of Boston): The **Steamship Authority** operates ferries to Vineyard Haven year round, to Oak Bluffs in summer. It's a 45-minute trip each way. Parking $7 a day, in two lots. The one in Woods Hole fills as early as 9 some mornings; the other lot is 4 miles away in Falmouth. Free shuttle bus to the wharf. Same-day round-trip fare: $9 adults, $4.50 ages 5 to 12, free under 5. Cars (reservations required): extra charge. Bicycles $2.75 each way. Phone 508/540–2022.

To Nantucket from Hyannis

Greyhound (page 6) provides bus connections from Boston to all boats. The **Steamship Authority** services Nantucket Island year round (from Hyannis only) for the 2¼-hour trip. Same-day round-trip fare: $19.50 adults, $9.80 ages 5 to 12, free under 5. Cars (reservations required): extra charge. Bicycles $4.50 each way. Phone 508/540–2022.

Hy-Line sails for Nantucket spring through fall. Schedules for their 2-hour trip allow for up to 8 hours on the island. Round-trip fares: $21 adults, $10.50 ages 5–12, free age 4 and under. Bicycles $4.50. Phone 508/775–7185.

To Star Island

A treeless, rocky island with birds, plants, and places to think. Leave Portsmouth, New Hampshire, page 82, at 11 on the **Isles of Shoals Steamship Co.** boat, mid-June through Labor Day. During three hours on the island, you can take a guided tour (included in boat fare); explore on your own (map provided); sit on a rocking chair on the porch of the Oceanic Hotel (site of Unitarian Universalist conferences); picnic (bring your own) under a pavilion; let the kids cavort in the playground; swim in the small, life-guarded area. To the island, it's 1 hour; the return trip is longer, 3–4:45 p.m., complete with a narration as you sail by eight other islands. Fares: $15 adults, $9 ages 3–11. Phone 603/431–5500.

To Thacher Island from Rockport Page 83.

Camping Areas

Massachusetts

Season: May–October (some campsites available mid-April).

Fees: Camping: $8–$12 per night, plus utilities (at four parks where there are hookups). Off-peak times, $2 less, Monday–Thursday.

A full list of public campgrounds is available from the Department of Environmental Management, Division of Forests and Parks, 100 Cambridge Street, Boston 02202 (617/727–3180). Check with them, too, for current winter camping conditions and arrangements.

In season, all campsites are available on a first-come, first-served basis and are often filled by Thursday for the weekend. Groups must make arrangements at least a week in advance. Leashed dogs are allowed.

All Massachusetts state camping areas are handicapped accessible.

Private campgrounds: Listed in directory available from the Massachusetts Association of Campground Owners, RR1, Box 3040, Kennebunk ME 04043. Phone 207/985–4864.

Cabins, all in the Berkshires, are available year round at:

Berkshires Savoy Mountain State Forest, RFD 2, North Adams 02147 (413/663–8469). Near South Pond, three one-room cabins, each with wood stove and four cots. No water or electricity. Reservations may be made up to six months in advance. Summer reservations should be for at least one week and not more than two. Rest of year, minimum reservation is for two nights. Hiking, boating, swimming, fishing, cross-country skiing, snowmobiling, ice fishing.

Mohawk Trail State Forest, P.O. Box 7, Route 2, Charlemont 01339 (413/339–5504). Log cabins, $16 or $20 depending on size. Reservations accepted up to six months in advance.

Below are several areas in eastern Massachusetts:

North of Boston

Island camping Pages 84 and 230.

Harold Parker State Forest Route 114, North Andover
Phone: 508/686–3391.
Location: 29 miles from Boston.
Directions: Tobin/Mystic Bridge to Route 1 north, to Route 114 north. Left on Harold Parker Road, right on Middleton, and left on Jenkins.
Facilities: 130 campsites. Both tent and trailer sites. Extensive hiking trails. Fishing.

Salisbury Beach State Reservation Page 216
Phone: 508/462–4481.
Facilities: 500 campsites. Both tent and trailer sites. Hookups. A camping and a beach area. Boating, swimming, and fishing. Weekend campers should arrive by Friday morning.

Winter Island Park Salem Page 216
Phone: 508/745–9430.
Facilities: May–October. 28 RV hookups; some with water and electricity. 18 tent sites on grassy ground. Water views everywhere.
Fees: Per night, $18 with electricity; $15 without. Advance reservations with one night's deposit.

Horseneck Beach State Reservation Page 219

Phone: 508/636–8816.

Facilities: 100 campsites. Ocean swimming and fishing.

Massasoit State Park Taunton

Phone: 508/822–7405.

Location: 38 miles from Boston.

Directions: I–93 south to Route 128 north, to Route 24, to Route 44 east. First right on Orchard, then left on Middleboro Road.

Facilities: 126 campsites. Electrical and sewage connections for trailers. Cartop boating. Pretty entrance. Nice pond for swimming. Relatively undiscovered.

Myles Standish State Forest Page 219

Facilities: 274 campsites. Freshwater swimming, fishing, hiking, and cycling (15 paved bicycle trails).

R. C. Nickerson State Forest Route 6A, Brewster

Phone: 508/896–3491.

Location: 90 miles from Boston.

Facilities: 420 campsites. The 8 miles of bicycle trails in park connect with 20 miles of Cape Cod Rail Trail.

Two public areas in or close to Boston where you can camp:

Boston Harbor Islands (page 181): Reservations required. Caution: Plenty of poison ivy! For *permits* to camp on *Grape* or *Bumpkin islands,* first call 617/740–1605 to see if a site is available. Then follow up with a letter and fees to the Commonwealth of Massachusetts, Department of Environmental Management, Boston Harbor State Park, 349 Lincoln Street, Building 45, Hingham 02043. *Fees:* $5 per night for up to 5 at a site. $16 for a group site. Available July through Labor Day; also off-season for those who can provide their own transportation.

For *Lovells* or *Peddocks islands,* send a letter to MDC, 98 Taylor Street, Dorchester 02122 (617/727–5290). Include dates requested, name of island, number (adults and children) in group, means of transportation. Available July Fourth weekend through Labor Day. Maximum stay: two weeks. Total of 70 campers allowed on each island. No facilities; bring everything you need. No alcohol or dogs allowed. No charge.

Reminder: Lovells, Grape, and Bumpkin (and maybe Peddocks) do not have drinking water. None of the islands have lifeguards. In the summer, all have interpreters who give informal tours.

Camp Nihan (MDC), Walnut Street (Route 129), Saugus. Permits: 617/727–5151. The site is separated from *Breakheart Reservation,* page 189, by the Saugus River. Overnight camping, September–June, for adult-supervised, chartered (registered with state) youth organizations. Swimming, canoeing, hiking, fishing, and winter sports.

Beach (not in the forest) nearby

Shawme-Crowell State Forest Sandwich
Phone: 508/888–0351.
Location: 65 miles southeast of Boston.
Directions: I–93 south to Route 3 south, to Route 6A, to Route 130.
Facilities: 280 campsites. Pretty. No swimming here, *but* campers are not charged for parking at Scusset Beach, a 5-minute drive.

Nearest swimming is a 15-minute drive

Wompatuck State Park Page 196
Phone: 617/749–7160.
Facilities: 400 campsites (140 with electricity) plus 10 miles of bicycle (pretty) trails.

Connecticut

Call 800/CT BOUND for vacation guide that includes all **public and private campgrounds.** They will also take requests for the more detailed "Connecticut Campground Directory" (mostly private campgrounds), which is sent separately from Connecticut Department of Economic Development, 865 Brook Street, Rocky Hill, CT 06067. At state campgrounds the season varies according to location. Maximum stay at shoreline is 21 consecutive days; at inland campgrounds, 14 days. Reservations required; must be received at least ten days before stay. Day-trippers swell the population at Hammonasset Beach in Madison and Rocky Neck in Niantic, where there's saltwater swimming.

Maine

State Parks: Maine Bureau of Parks and Recreation, Station 22, Augusta, ME 04333; phone 207/289–3821. *Reservations* with Visa or MC: 207/289–3824, in-state 800/332–1501; 9–3 Monday–Friday, starting first working day after January 1, reservations taken for June 15 through Labor Day. **Acadia National Park:** 207/288–3338. **Baxter State Park:** 207/723–5140. **Maine Campground Association** (private campgrounds): 207/782–5874, or request their directory from 800/533–9595.

New Hampshire

State campgrounds (first-come, first-served) are listed in the vacation kit sent with state map from the New Hampshire Office of Travel and Tourism, P.O. Box 856, Concord, NH 03302–0856; phone 603/271–2343. Groups (only) can make reservations. **Private campground directory:** New Hampshire Campground Owners' Association, 800/822–6764. **White Mountain National Forest:** P.O. Box 638, Laconia, NH 03247; phone 603/528–8271.

Rhode Island

Camping kit available from Rhode Island Department of Economic Development, 7 Jackson Walkway, Providence, RI 02903; 800/556–2484 or 401/277–2601.

Vermont

State parks: Department of Forest, Parks and Recreation, 103 South Main Street, Waterbury, VT 05671–0603; phone 802/244–8711. Minimum of three nights for reservations. Openings filled by first-come, first-served. Can stay up to two weeks. **Green Mountain National Forest:** P.O. Box 51, Rutland, VT 05671; phone 802/773–0300. Five developed campgrounds with 94 campsites.

Clam Digging

Every coastal city and town has its own shellfish regulations. Check with town hall for license and contamination information before you dig. . . . Children can help, and add excitement to the quest. . . . Bring a digging fork, sneakers, a strong back—and patience.

Folk and Square Dancing

Thriving! Sessions—often with terrific live music—are scheduled every day of the week somewhere in the Greater Boston area. Some are for all levels, with lessons for beginners at the start; others are just for beginners, families, or experienced dancers. Admission is about $5 per session. For this week's extensive schedule, see the *Boston Globe*'s Thursday Calendar; or call 617/491–6084, the recorded information line of the **Folk Arts Center of New England,** 1940 Massachusetts Avenue, Cambridge, MA 02140. The active organization also sells records, CDs, tapes, and sheet music.

Golf Courses

Boston

George Wright Golf Course, 420 West Street, Hyde Park. The 18-hole course opens daily at dawn. Rates: Weekdays $16, weekends $19. Call on Thursday to make weekend reservations. Phone 617/361–8313.

Cambridge

Thomas P. O'Neill Jr. Golf Course at Fresh Pond, 691 Huron Avenue. A 9-hole course, open to the public. Electric carts, pull carts, rental clubs, pro shop, food concession, lessons by PGA professionals for age 12 and up. Rates: Weekdays $12 for 9 holes, $14 for 18 holes. Weekends and holidays $15 for 9 holes, $17 for 18 holes. Phone 617/349–6282.

Canton

Ponkapoag Golf Course (MDC), Route 138. 18-hole courses. Lessons. From Route 128, follow Route 138 south, toward Stoughton. Rates: Weekdays $12, seniors $5, juniors $5. Weekends and holidays $14, juniors and seniors $5. After 5 p.m. every day, $5 for everyone. Always first-come, first served. Phone 617/828–5828.

Weston

Leo J. Martin Memorial Golf Course (MDC), Park Road. An 18-hole course. Lessons. From Route 16, turn right on Concord Road; from Route 30, turn left on Park Road. Always first-come, first-served. Rates: Weekdays $12. Weekends and holidays $14. Seniors and juniors (16 and under) $5 weekdays, $12 weekends. After 4 p.m. $5 for everyone. Phone 617/894–4903.

Horses, Carriages, and Sleighs

See also the Calendar section on pick-your-own crops (pages 277–278) for other hayride possibilities.

Agawam Stables 32 Shoemaker Lane, Agawam 01001
Phone: 413/786–1744.
Location: 90 miles west of Boston (near Springfield).
Rates: Pony rides: $5 for a half hour. Trail rides in woods: $10 per hour per person (tall enough to reach stirrups) with trail guide. Hay or sleigh rides: $80 for wagon that holds 20 adults or 25 children.

Hay or sleigh rides in woods and fields include a postride bonfire. Bring your own refreshments.

Beland Stables 17 Montgomery Street, Lakeville 02347
Phone: 508/947–6982.
Location: 60 miles southeast of Boston.
Rates (for groups only, advance notice required): $5 per person, with a minimum of $50 for sled that holds 10 or 12 people, $100 for hayride that can take up to 35.

Less than an hour from Boston, you can take a 1¼-hour hayride on country roads and then look around at this 23-year-old stable, which boards, stables and trains horses. Half-hour sleigh rides are in a pung, a farmer's work wagon.

Drumlin Farm (Massachusetts Audubon Society) Lincoln
Weekends, spring through fall. Please see page 27.

Lazy S Ranch 300 Randolph Street, Canton
Phone: 617/828–1681 or 821–5527.
Location: 14 miles south of Boston.
Rates: Hayrides, $100 per hour for up to 28 people. Pony rides here, $2 for quarter-mile ride on track.

What started out to be one business has become three—teaching, selling of riding clothes and horse equipment, and rides. The 1-hour hayrides here go into the woods and partially around Ponkapoag Pond in Blue Hills Reservation. The ponies also travel to schools and parties.

Point of View Farm 160 South Road, Deerfield, NH 03037
Phone: 603/463–7974.
Location: About 90 minutes north of Boston.
Rates: For groups: weekdays 10–4, $35 one wagon or sleigh; $70 two. Monday–Thursday 5–9, $50 one wagon or sleigh, $100 two. Weekends $70 for one, $140 for two. Individual rates: $5 adult, $3.50 age 12 and under, free age 2 and under. Capacity is 20 on a haywagon, 15 on a sleigh.
★ Birthday package: $30 cake, ice cream, and beverage for 15 (plus ride fee), $50 surrey ride and brunch for two. $125 couple, romantic evening.

Carriage (including a vintage surrey), hay, and sleigh rides have replaced the pigs and milk cows on Tyke and Sue Frost's farm between Concord, Portsmouth, and Manchester.

Two-hour children's birthday parties include a one-hour hay ride on the 60-acre property; a bonfire/marshmallow-toasting or hot dog stop; and time back in the wood-stoved gathering room, where everyone has a chance to crank ice cream (an old-fashioned maker) and eat it with cake. Groups can book the gathering room for hot chocolate or cider and apple crisp.

Romantic evenings include an hour-long coach ride on back roads followed by a complete dinner served in a private dining room. Brunch for two is served after an hour-long ride in a canopied surrey. Following group brunch rides, you have the opportunity to see the carriage collection, enjoy the flower and herb gardens, or take a nature walk.

Nearby: In fall, a pick-your-own apple orchard. In winter, Bear Brook State Park with groomed cross-country trails.

Silver Ranch   Route 124, Jaffrey, NH 03452

Phone: 603/532–7363.

Location: 55 miles north of Boston.

Rates: $80 for up to 10, then $8 per person for a 40-to 60-minute ride along wooded trails.

Horse-drawn hayrides, sleigh rides, and carriage rides through forest and fields. Night rides in winter by reservation only. For groups (up to 50), there's a package of ride, refreshments, and country dancing in the ranch hall. Will travel too. ★ Hilltop wedding site.

Valley Riders   Wayside Road, Natick 01760

Phone: 508/653–4656.

Rates: From the farm: $60 for an hour, 16 adults or 20–25 children.

From March through December John McHugh offers rides in a covered wagon pulled by two horses on quiet Natick roads (good for bicycling too) near his farm. ★ If you'd like, he'll bring it all to your place, fair, or party. "Some folks serve birthday cake and beverage in the wagon!"

Ice Skating

Skate Rentals

Skate rentals are available at most private rinks, at Brookline's Larz Anderson Park rink (page 188), and at some MDC rinks.

Lessons

A comprehensive list of places that give instruction is published in the sports section of the *Boston Globe*. Included are the **West Suburban Arena** in Natick and **Babson Skating Rink** at Babson Park in Wellesley (page 120). Also:

Bay State Ice Skating School, 30 Ransom Road, Newton Center 02159, offers lessons for ages 5 and up (adults too)—all levels—on either hockey or figure skates. Lessons given at local MDC rinks. Phone 617/965–4460.

Tom McGinnis Ice Skating School (617/332–7589) offers classes year round in recreational, figure, and hockey skating at the Skating Club of Boston, 1240 Soldiers Field Road, Brighton. Children's sessions begin at 6:30 p.m.; adults, later. Membership isn't necessary. Fees per session: adults $5, children $4. Skate rental $2.50.

Pilgrim Skating Arena, 75 Recreation Park Drive, Hingham, offers figure and hockey lessons for children and adults. Phone 617/749–6660.

Year-round (or Almost)

Summer sessions (rental skates available) are usually scheduled at these Boston area indoor rinks:

Boston: Skating Club of Boston, 1240 Soldiers Field Road, Brighton, 617/782–5900.

Natick: West Suburban Arena, Windsor Avenue, 508/655–1013, 655–1014 (recorded information).

Wellesley: Babson Skating Rink, 150 Great Plain Avenue, 617/235–0650, has public sessions mid-September until mid-June.

Winter

Rinks

For private rinks, look in the Yellow Pages under "Skating Rinks." Very few are limited to members. All are indoors, and almost all offer lessons and public sessions. Schedules vary from season to season and from year to year.

MDC rinks are open November through mid-March. Call the individual rinks (Blue Pages under "Massachusetts, Commonwealth of: Metropolitan District Commission") for schedule, rental, and lesson information. Rates are $3 adults, $.50 senior citizens, $1 children under 16.

Outdoors

Ponds and flooded playgrounds and tennis courts are used in many communities. Arlington, Needham, Newton, and Wakefield are among many that have good natural areas; check the regulations with town or city hall.

Boston: Skating in the **Boston Public Garden** is a tradition. Some years, depending on weather and funding, taped music is played, the ice is maintained, and vendors may sell hot chocolate and snacks. Areas may be set aside for beginners and small children, for families and couples, and for hockey. (And sledding is usually allowed on the Boston Common area that slopes toward Charles Street.)

Brookline: Larz Anderson Rink, 23 Newton Street; phone 617/730–2083 weekdays, 730–2080 nights and weekends. Open December through February—weather permitting. (This is an uncovered rink with warming house.) Rates for nonresidents: $4 adults, $2 age 17 and under. Half price for Brookline residents. $3.50 skate rental.

Mountain Climbing

To build stamina, many try Blue Hill (page 192) first—about an hour or so round trip, depending on your route—before going on to Mount Monadnock in Jaffrey, New Hampshire (see box), and eventually an overnight trip in the White Mountains. Reminder: May through early June is black fly season up-country. (See page 276.)

The best source for comprehensive information, guided trips, and workshops is the **Appalachian Mountain Club** (page 204). Reservations are required for the eight AMC huts, which are open to nonmembers and located a day's hike apart—most above the timber line—in the White Mountains. The huts may be used as a base for day hikes or as lodging facilities for hut-to-hut travel. Some have family rooms. All have bunk accommodations. Hot all-you-can-eat meals are served at 7 a.m. and 6 p.m. mid-June through early September. For kids, there are environmentally oriented activities.

Pinkham Notch is the AMC visitor center in the White Mountain National Forest; here individuals and families can stay overnight and also enroll in workshops focusing on the environment or outdoor activities.

Orienteering

New England Orienteering Club 9 Cannon Road, Woburn 01801
Phone: 617/648–1155.
Fees: $4 per meet, nonmember; $3 member.

Meets are very informal. Participants range from babes in backpacks to senior citizens. Some choose to stroll along the course through the woods. Others are quite competitive as they use a map to find specified points.

> **Mount Monadnock** (603/532–8862) in Jaffrey, New Hampshire, 65 miles from Boston, is a full day's adventure. Often it is called the most-climbed mountain in the United States. On nice spring and fall weekends and holidays (Columbus Day, for sure), you will find much company (crowds) enjoying the spectacular views from all trails. When it is clear, you can see Boston skyscrapers and maybe some of all six New England states. First-timers at this state park should go to the headquarters area, where rangers—on duty daily April through mid-November and on weekends and holidays in winter—will give you maps and describe various trails. (Regulars tend to use the more detailed maps that are for sale to crisscross the mountain on less-traveled trails.) Come prepared for climbing and cooler temperatures at the top of the mountain. Wear layers of clothing and supportive footwear. Bring food and water. Be aware that coming down can be much harder than going up. And get an early start. Fees: $2.50 per person age 12 and over; free under age 12. Sorry, *no pets allowed*. Directions: From Route 101 in Peterborough, Route 202 south to Jaffrey, to Route 124 west for 2 miles.

Special courses are set up for very young children. Instruction is available at all meets.

Roller Skating

Norwood: Roll-Land Skating Rink, 942 Route 1, Norwood. Open year round, Wednesday through Sunday. Phone 617/762–6999.

Waltham: Wal-Lex Recreation Center, 800 Lexington Street, Waltham. Open year round. "Lots of birthday and group parties." Phone 617/894–1527.

Skiing

Cross-country

Rentals are available at some cross-country ski centers and at sports stores including the following:

Belmont: Belmont Wheel Works, 480 Trapelo Road, 617/489–3577.

Boston: The Ski Market, 860 Commonwealth Avenue, 617/731–6100.

Brighton: Eastern Mountain Sports, 1041 Commonwealth Avenue, 617/254–4250.

Reading: REI (Recreational Equipment Inc.), 179 Salem Street, 617/944–5103.

Somerville: Ace Wheel Works, 145 Elm Street, 617/776–2100.

Weston: Weston Ski Track, page 248, 617/891–6575.

Nearby Areas

Where to go in the Boston Area? Almost anywhere—open space areas (pages 181–204), golf courses, even the banks of the Charles River—as long as there's enough snow.

Carlisle: Great Brook Farm State Park, page 198. Trails on two sides of the road. Warming hut with two wood stoves, hot drinks and soups, ski accessories and rentals. Phone 508/369–7486.

Lincoln: Lincoln Guide Service, 151 Lincoln Road (at the railroad tracks). Ski free (with lots of company on a nice day) on miles of nearby conservation lands. Lessons and rentals available. Phone 617/259–9204.

Malden/Medford/Melrose: Middlesex Fells Reservation (MDC). Directions and phone: See page 191. Free. Two loops offer a total of (ungroomed) 6 miles of trails created by Harvard Community Health Plan and the MDC. Trailheads are located at the Sheepfold and Bellevue Pond parking lots.

Princeton: Wachusett Mountain, 499 Mountain Road. This downhill area (see below) has 15 km of groomed cross-country trails when there is natural snow. Phone 508/464–2300.

Weston: Weston Ski Track at the Leo J. Martin Memorial Golf Course (page 242). Rentals, lessons for children and adults, evening lights, a cafe. Rates: $10 adults, $6 for 6–12, free under 6. Throughout several consecutive lean-snow winters, the Weston Ski Track has made enough snow (to cover 1½ km) to be open through at least January and February. Phone 617/894–4903.

Always, ski areas want to remind Bostonians who are looking at bare ground that there may be good skiing within driving distance. That's the time to discover Windblown (603/878–2869) in New Ipswich in the **Monadnock region of New Hampshire.** No snowmaking, but able to open with 4 inches of snow. Along the 30 km of 8-foot-wide groomed trails (some beginner, most intermediate; one steep wide slope for telemarking) are a warming hut with wood stove and one bunk room (for rent); three open-face shelters for picnicking; some outhouses; and fantastic views of Mount Monadnock and Vermont. Rentals, lessons, ski shop, restaurant for light meals.

In **Massachusetts:** Drive a couple of hours to the popular Northfield Mountain Cross-Country Ski Area (413/659–3713) in **Northfield** with 26 miles of trails. . . . The snowmaking equipment of the Swift River Inn (413/634–5751) in **Cummington** covers about 4 of their 23 km of trails. (Return in warmer weather for mountain biking on those trails, or for rock climbing, guided nature walks, or fly-fishing in a stocked pond.) . . . High on a hill in a beautiful undeveloped area: The Crawfords at Stump Sprouts Ski Touring Center (413/339–4265) in **West Hawley** cover 4 km and machine groom most of their 25 km of trails. Rentals, lessons, accommodations, and a cathedral-ceilinged barn/rec room too.

Downhill

Note (especially during a snowless winter): Because all these nearby ski places have snowmaking facilities, they are open (days and nights) as long as the temperatures are low enough.

Nearby Areas

Blue Hills Ski Area 4001 Washington Street, Canton 02168
Phone: 617/828–5070.
Location: 14 miles south of Boston.
Directions: I–93 south to Route 138 north, to exit 2B (Route 138 north).
Facilities: 7 trails with 100 percent snowmaking. 1 double chair, 2 J-bars, 1 pony lift. Open 7 days and nights a week. Rentals, cafeteria, ski school.

Wachusett Mountain 499 Mountain Road, Princeton 01540
Phone: 508/464–2300.
Location: 47 miles west of Boston.
Directions: Route 2 west to exit 25 onto Route 140 south.

Big Squaw Mtn.

201

Sugarloaf / USA

Saddleback

Eaton Mtn.

MAINE

Jay Peak

Balsams / Wilderness

91

Black Mtn.

2

Smugglers'
Notch

Burke Mtn.

Sunday River

New Hermon Mtn.

SEARSPORT, ME

Bretton Woods

Wildcat
Mtn.

Mt. Abram

Bromley Valley

Stowe

89

Camden
Snow Bowl

CAMDEN, ME

Mad River Glen

302

Cannon Mtn.

Attitash

Mt.
Cranmore

Black Mtn.

Lost Valley

Sugarbush

VERMONT

Loon Mtn.

King Pine

Shawnee Peak at Pleasant

Middlebury College Snow Bowl

Waterville Valley

302

7

Dartmouth Skiway

Lookout Mtn. Resort

95

Killington

Suicide
Six

93

Pico

Ragged Mtn.

Gunstock

Okemo Mtn.

King Ridge

89

Highlands

Bromley Mtn.

Mt. Sunapee

NEW

Stratton Mtn.

Pat's Peak

HAMPSHIRE

Mt. Snow / Haystack

Maple Valley

Temple Mtn.

12

Atlantic Forest

Brodie Mtn.

Berkshire East

Bradford

495

Jiminy Peak

2

Nashoba

Pine Ridge
Ski Area

Wachusett Mtn.

Bousquet

MASSACHUSETTS

Blandford Ski Area

Ward Hill

Blue Hills

128

Butternut Basin

Mt. Tom

Catamount

Otis Ridge

90

Klein Innsbruck

91

495

Mohawk Mtn.

Ski Sundown

R. I.

87

7

CONN.

395

Mt. Southington

84

Woodbury
Ski and Racquet

Powder Ridge

95

New England Ski Areas

Information courtesy of New England Ski Areas Council

Facilities: 17 trails (longest is 1½ miles), beginner to expert, with 100 percent snowmaking. 3 chair lifts, one rope tow. Open 7 days and nights a week. Rentals, cafeteria, ski school and shop, nursery, 2 lounges.

Nashoba Valley Ski Area Power Road, Westford 01886

Phone: 508/693–3033.

Location: 25 miles west of Boston.

Directions: Route 2 west to Concord Circle. Take Route 2A for 6 miles to Power Road on your right.

Facilities: 10 trails, 2 triple chair lifts, one double chair lift, 1 T-bar, 4 rope tows. 100 percent snowmaking and lighting 7 days and nights a week. Lessons for age 4 and up, for beginners through racers. Restaurant and lounge are handicapped accessible.

★ Surprise: "Weddings are our specialty."

Ward Hill Ski Area 1000 Main Street, Shrewsbury

Phone: 508/842–6346.

Directions: Route 128 to Route 9 to Route 20 to Northboro. Follow signs to Shrewsbury.

Facilities: 6 slopes, vertical drop of 180 feet, one chair lift, two T bars, 2 rope tows. Longest trail is 1,400 feet.

Ski Club

Massachusetts Ski Club 15 Oak Street, Needham 02192

Phone: 617/449–3074.

Pickup points: About a dozen Greater Boston communities.

The youth ski program, open to ages 8–17, provides transportation to New Hampshire and Vermont ski areas, lessons, and supervision. Inquire about memberships and supervisory possibilities.

Up-Country

There are many up-country areas within a two-hour drive. Favorites depend on facilities, costs (packages often available), crowds, distance, and conditions. Some years, states offer toll-free telephone reports. Call 800/533–9595 for trail conditions in Maine, 800/262–6660 for conditions in New Hampshire. Many individual areas, too, have a toll-free number for reports and/or conditions:

In Maine: State report: 800/533–9595. Sunday River: 800/543–2SKI.

In New Hampshire: State report 800/258–3608. Cannon: 800/552–1234. King Ridge: 800/334–1312. Loon: 800/745–8100. Wildcat: 800/552–8952.

In Vermont: Killington: 800 621–MTNS. Okemo: 800 78–OKEMO. Stratton: 800/843–6867. Sugarbush: 800/53–SUGAR. Waterville Valley: 800/468–2553.

Other areas: Check with 800/555–1212 to see if a toll-free information number is available.

Spectator Sports

Along with listings of all kinds of participatory sports from boomerang lessons to wind surfing, the *Boston Globe*'s Friday edition lists a full schedule of amateur, college, semiprofessional, and professional events.

Order tickets several weeks in advance. . . . Boston Garden recorded information: 617/227–3200. Final major league results are available 24 hours a day from the *Boston Globe* Telephone Scoreboard: 617/265–6600.

SPORTS ARENA SEATING PLANS

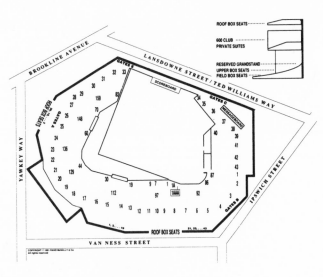

FOXBORO STADIUM

FENWAY PARK

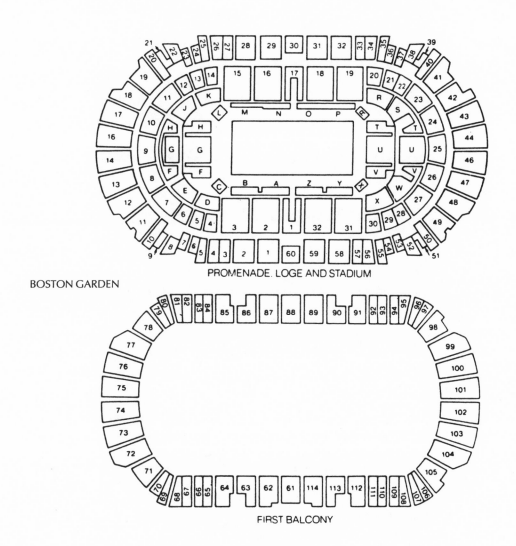

PROMENADE, LOGE AND STADIUM

BOSTON GARDEN

FIRST BALCONY

Baseball

Boston Red Sox 4 Yawkey Way, Boston 02215
Phone: 617/267–1700 (tickets), 267–9440 (office). TDD 617/236–6644.
Ⓣ: Fenway on the Riverside/Green Line.
Tickets: $7–$18. Discounts for designated family, senior citizen, and youth days.
Handicapped access: Listening devices for hearing impaired at information booth under section 19. Accessible areas are marked.

Basketball

Boston Celtics 151 Merrimac Street, Boston 02114
Phone: 617/623–3030 (tickets), 523–6050 (office).
Ⓣ: North Station on the Orange or Green Line.
Tickets: $12–$40. Individual tickets go on sale in September. Group rates available for some games.

Home games are played in Boston Garden October through April. Evenings only until the first of the year; then Sunday afternoons too. Special days with giveaways—perhaps posters or cards—for children under 14 are held a few times during the season.

Football

New England Patriots Foxboro Stadium, Route 1, Foxboro 02035
Phone: 800/543–1776 (tickets), 508/543–8200 (office).
Location: 25 miles south of Boston.
Directions: I–93 south to Route 128 north, to I–95 south to exit 9 onto Route 1 south.
Tickets: $18–$28.

Preseason in August; home games Sunday afternoons September through December.

Hockey

Boston Bruins 150 Causeway Street, Boston 02114
Phone: 617/227–3206.
Ⓣ: North Station on the Green Line.
Tickets: $16–$40.

Games are played at Boston Garden October through March, mostly on Thursday evenings and on Saturdays.

Train Excursions

A teaser Page 122.

Mystic Valley Railway Society P.O. Box 486, Hyde Park 02136
Phone: 617/361–4445.

The thrust of this nonprofit organization is to teach people about rail transportation through trips, including many on regularly scheduled trains. All fifteen annual day trips—as well as longer ones (as far as the West Coast)—are open to nonmembers. No alcoholic beverages are allowed. Most trips include meals on a train or boat or in a restaurant. The average number of riders per trip is fifty. Children are usually in the minority, and get plenty of attention.

Massachusetts Bay Railroad Enthusiasts, Inc. P.O. Box 8136, Ward Hill 01835.
Phone: 617/489–5277.

If you have ever wanted to ride the rails in a car borrowed from a museum or in cars specially chartered to travel for "rare mileage excursions"—on tracks now used only by freight cars—then contact this organization, which can boast of sponsoring the world's first "railroad fan trip" in 1934. Some passengers come from as far as California for the opportunity to ride on routes that are inaccessible to people in any other way. Every year the foliage day trip and snow country trip each attract eight hundred to a thousand people. Food service or box lunches may be offered; picnicking is allowed and even encouraged. Many of these trips are quite popular with families who have older children.

Whale Watches

You really see whales in and out (breaching) of the water. Most trips last 4 to 5 hours, have a naturalist/interpreter on board, and sail twice a day, May through October (some on April weekends). Adult fares range from $15 to $23; it's a little less for children under 12. Most offer group rates. Discounts are often announced in ArtsMail (page 50) mailings. Reservations suggested; sometimes required.

> Bring a jacket. Wear rubber-soled shoes. And as one fifth grade teacher says, "If, perchance, it is a bit rough leaving the harbor, ask the kids to wait before snacking."

The following lines have regularly scheduled trips.

Boston

A. C. Cruise Line: 28 Northern Avenue, Boston, 617/426–8419 or 800/422–8419.
Bay State Cruise Company: Leaves from Long Wharf and Commonwealth Pier in *Boston* and from Pemberton Pier (free parking) in *Hull*. ($1 water shuttle available from Long Wharf half hour before boat leaves Commonwealth Pier and to Long Wharf upon return.) Phone 617/723–7800.
Boston Harbor Cruises: One Long Wharf, Boston, 617/227–4321.
Boston Harbor Whale Watch: Rowes Wharf, 400 Atlantic Avenue, 617/345–9866.
New England Aquarium: Central Wharf, Boston, 617/973–5277 (recorded information) or 973–5281 (reservations). Senior citizens and college student rates offered. Children under 36 inches are not permitted on board.

North of Boston

From Gloucester

Cape Ann Whale Watch: Rose's Wharf, 415 Main Street, 508/583–5110 or 800/877–5110.

Captain Bill's Whale Watching: Rose's Wharf, 415 Main Street, 508/283–6995 or 800/22–WHALE (eastern Mass. only).

Seven Seas Whale Watching: Seven Seas Wharf, Route 127, 508/283–1776 or 800/238–1776.

Yankee Whale Watch: Cape Ann Marina, 75 Essex Avenue, 508/283–0313 or 800/WHALING (USA and Canada).

From Newburyport

New England Whale Watch: Hilton's Dock, 54 Merrimack Street, 508/465–7165 or 800/848–1111.

South of Boston

From Plymouth

Cape Cod Cruises: *Mayflower II* State Pier, 508/747–2400.

Captain John Boats: Town Wharf, 508/746–2643 or 800/242–2469 (Mass. only).

Massachusetts Whale Watching Center: Town Wharf, 508/833–0181.

*From Barnstable
(Cape Cod)*

Hyannis Whale Watcher Cruises: Millway Marina, 508/362–6088 or 800/287–0374.

From Provincetown

Leaves from Fisherman's Wharf:

Cape Cod Cruises: Fisherman's Wharf, 800/225–4000.

From MacMillan Wharf (off Commercial Street):

Dolphin Whale Watch: MacMillan Wharf (off Commercial Street), 508/349–1900 or 800/826–9300 (USA and Canada).

Provincetown's Portuguese Princess Whale Watch: MacMillan Wharf (ticket office: 309 Commercial Street), 508/487–2651 or 800/442–3188 (New England only). Refreshments include Portuguese specialties.

Provincetown Whale Watch, Inc.: MacMillan Wharf (off Commercial Street), 508/487–1582 or 800/992–9333.

Tours

"I'm tired! Sorry, no more," said one small-business owner who has had too much publicity about his willingness to give tours. That happens! Such experiences were taken into consideration for this updated version of an *In and Out of Boston* original.

Most of the suggested tours are free. . . . Many of the listings do not offer a formal tour, but they are happy to show you around and answer questions. . . . If the day seems just right for an inside visit, call to see if your family can join an expected group. (Notice the minimum age; it may denote interest level.) . . . Some visits are geared for people with a particular interest. If you're just looking for something to do, please shy away from those. . . . Group leaders find benefits are always greater with orientation and follow-up. . . . When parents supervise a group, it's usually better not to bring younger siblings along. . . . Often the guide makes a difference. If yours doesn't give adequate explanations, ask questions and explain details to the children. This is particularly important for those at the end of the line. . . . If a place you have suggested is among the missing, most likely it has occasional arrangements and prefers to have its name unpublished. . . . Please observe restrictions and plan more than enough supervision. . . . If you have a specific interest, check the category in the Yellow Pages, then call the public relations department. If a place hasn't been deluged with requests, it may take on a vocationally oriented group. . . . Also check tour information in Animals, Day Trips, Historic Sites, and Museums.

How was the tour? Acknowledgments with feedback are appreciated and helpful.

Local Suggestions

For almost any age, but particularly for young children, check safety regulations and double-check group size . . . and please make an appointment.

Architect's office: An awareness of space and how to use it.

Artist's studio: The medium. The time. The space.

Bakery: Make your own before you visit. *Reminder:* Bakeries start early in the day.

Bus ride: Let a child pull the cord for a stop.

Candy house: A small local shop.

Car wash: Some let children ride through the suds.

Cleaning plant or laundry: Maybe one with a shirt presser.

Construction project: A hard-hat site.

Craftspeople: A home studio.

Dairy: Find out when they milk the cows.

Doughnut shop: Watch the holes too.

Fast-food places: Often with samples.

Fire station: Sleeping quarters, communications system, engines and their gadgets, the firefighters' gear. Some nursery school groups have found this exciting; others report that a midvisit alarm has made it a frightening experience.

Greenhouse: Buy a plant or bring home seeds.

Hospital: Particularly for a youngster about to enter. Some hospitals have programs.

Kennel: Maybe a dog will be having a bath or a clipping.

Library: Any special programs?

Lumberyard: Take home an old piece from the scrap barrel.

Newspaper: Check ahead of time to see what there is to see.

Pet shop: Difficult to plan just a visit, not a shopping trip.

Photographer's studio: All the processes.

Police station: Its responsibilities. Is there an animal control department?

Post office: Busiest in the morning, but personnel may not be available then. (Send thank-you notes with artwork; these may get posted for all the world to see.)

Radio station: Where does the voice come from?

Theater: Backstage is most revealing.

Places

Animal Rescue League Page 33.

Boston Ballet 19 Clarendon Street (at Warren), Boston 02116–6110
Phone: 617/695–6950.

Ⓣ: Orange Line to Back Bay Station, 5-minute walk. Green Line to Copley, 10-minute walk.

Tours: 20 to 60 or more minutes, depending on interests of visitors. Wednesdays at 6 p.m., Saturdays at noon. July and August, by appointment only. Year round, groups of 10 or more should call ahead. For Wang Center backstage tours, limited to major donors or group ticket purchasers on a first-come, first-served basis, please see page 38.

A dream—for dancers, architecture aficionados, and visitors. Designed by Graham Gund and completed in 1991, America's largest building dedicated solely to dance is located in a neighborhood with the country's largest collection of Victorian brownstones. The Boston Ballet building is a magnificent five-storied air-conditioned home for the company, classes, and administration.

You meet in the dramatic lobby and (to the strains of music from studios) follow your guide up the theatrical central staircase, through the halls, and past state-of-the-art studios. What you see—maybe some classes or a company member who is practicing—depends on the schedule of the day. You are invited to enter a studio that is not in use and to step and spring on the special flooring. Among the seven professional studios equipped with sound and videotape for rehearsal and instruction purposes is the skylit grand studio that is the size of the Wang Center stage. Although it is not possible to tour the wardrobe department, where seven full-time and many part-time artists dye white fabric and cut, sew, and sequin all the company's costumes, you'll hear about the making of a tutu and have the opportunity to examine an elaborate gown.

Boston Edison Company Mystic Station Power Plant, Everett
Phone: 617/424–2577.

Tours: By appointment, 90-minute tours, Tuesday–Thursday.

Requirements: At least 10 days' notice. For groups (up to 25). Minimum age: 10. Telephone reservations accepted. To book by mail: Education Coordinator, 800 Boylston Street, Boston 02199.

Everyone wears a hard hat for a firsthand look at how electricity is generated from fuel. There's lots of interaction between visitors and staffers in the main control room, where the array of lights prompts questions. The tour includes boiler facilities, turbines, environmental control equipment, and the electrical operation control room too. Both men and women work here.

The Boston Globe 135 Morrissey Boulevard, Dorchester 02107
Phone: 617/929–2653.

Directions: Southeast Expressway to exit 15.

Ⓣ: Columbia on the Red Line, then a 10-minute walk.

Tours: By appointment, 90-minute tours, Tuesdays and Thursdays at 9:30, 11 and 2. Minimum age: 12.

Follow copy from reporter to the editorial department to the composition room, where it emerges, thanks to computers, on long sheets of paper. Other processes: Negatives turn into photoengravings. Aluminum plates are made. And, depending on the hour, you may see presses printing an edition that's on sale by the time you get home. Plenty of time for questions. How much paper is used? For a Sunday edition, about 2,000 miles' worth, enough to pave a path from Boston to Chicago.

Nearby: Minutes' drive to John F. Kennedy Library and the Commonwealth Museum, pages 155 and 156. Or for a National Park Service ranger's talk at Dorchester Heights Monument in South Boston, call 617/242–5688. Sometimes arrangements can be made to climb (for a view of the harbor) the monument, which commemorates the first major success of the Revolution —March 17, 1776, when the British left town.

Boston Public Library Copley Square, Boston 02117
Phone: 617/536–5400, extension 212 or 213.

Tours: 1 hour. Year round. Monday at 2:30, Tuesday and Wednesday at 6:30 p.m., Thursday and Saturday morning at 11 a.m. Other times arranged. All ages welcome.

Fascinating and far from staid. Your guide may play the role of librarian, artist, carpenter, cleaning person, or architect (complete with beret) while sharing anecdotes and facts—and the character's perspective too—about the extensive art, including murals and paintings, and the architecture and history of the world's oldest free municipal library (page 129), a National Historic Landmark. Currently, the century-old main building is undergoing a $50 million physical transformation. At the end of phase one (of three), in 1993, the Copley Square entrance is scheduled to be reopened with handsome new exhibition and lecture space.

The Butterfly Place at Papillon Park 120 Tyngsboro Road, Westford 01886

Phone: 508/392–0955. Winter phone, 617/893–7875.

Location: 40 miles northwest of Boston.

Open: April 15 through Columbus Day, 10–5 daily. Guided school field trips Monday through Friday, no holidays.

Tours: Last about 60 minutes; for groups of 10 to 60.

Requirement: One adult required for every 8 children.

Rates: Individuals $5 adult, $4 ages 3–12 and 65 or older. Season passes available. Groups $3 per person, plus $10 guide fee; 25 percent deposit required. From groups, each child receives a pass good for future visit (not another group tour).

Handicapped access: Accessible.

Ever since George Leslie was a 9-year-old lad living in Watertown, he had been enchanted by butterflies. Five decades later, in 1990, the successful businessman created his second career when he built the country's fourth and the Northeast's only living butterfly farm—and began to be featured at the New England Spring Flower Show.

Exterior landscaping is planned. Meanwhile, hundreds of butterflies flutter—especially on a sunny day—in the 27-foot-high, 75-foot-wide pesticide-free solar dome, which has at least 50 varieties of nectar-producing weeds, shrubs, and flowering plants. (If you're coming for the peace and beauty, check to see if a school group is booked.) The guide, daughter Sylvia Leslie, a former day-care teacher, helps visitors to see/find twenty kinds of butterflies on plants, under leaves, and—watch your step—on the red-brick walkway too. Some of the prettiest feast on the less-colorful plants. Some colorful caterpillars emerge as plain brown moths. Photographers welcome; no time limit!

An adjoining observation area with two picnic tables (bring your lunch) has display cases with butterflies and moths in various stages of development. The Leslie family dub themselves "dealers in anticipation." To that end, they sell hatching kits ($6–$14) with a guaranteed chrysalis that will grow its wings right in the box. The butterfly will live 1–3 weeks, then should be set free.

Charles River Dam 250 Warren Avenue, Charlestown 02129

Phone: 617/727–0488.

Location: *Walking?* Near the Charlestown end of the Charlestown Bridge. (Directions are on page 105.) *Driving?* For the duration of Central Artery construction, call for directions.

Tours: 1 hour, for groups with up to 30 people. Monday–Friday 9–3. Minimum age: 12.

For engineering students, the presentation is more technical. For schoolchildren, there's usually talk about the weather and its impact on the river. Perhaps the focus is on ecology or fish. How many boats go from the Charles River to Boston Harbor in a year? Visitors learn why the first dam was built and why this newer facility was needed.

Drop-in visitors appreciate the view and the very good self-explanatory twelve-minute multimedia show. (Please see page 105.)

Christian Science Center Boston 02115

Phone: 617/450–2000, tour information 450–3790.

Publishing tours: By appointment, year round. Weekdays except holidays. 1 hour. Minimum age: Grade 6.

Mother Church: Open 9:30–4. 30-minute tours on the hour November through mid-April; on the hour and half hour rest of year.

Guides at the **Christian Science Publishing Society,** One Norway Street, explain production procedures for publications. The publishing tour includes the pressroom for church periodicals. You are also taken into the *Monitor* newsroom, where international and national editors work. In the center of this room are desktop publishing computers that send copy via satellite to printing plants in Norwood, Massachusetts, and Phoenix, Arizona. Groups of no more than fifteen are taken into radio and television areas; studios are usually occupied and not part of the tour. Each tour is tailored for group size and needs and includes the Mapparium (page 120).

The tour of the **Mother Church of the First Church of Christ, Scientist** focuses on architecture. Carved stone walls, stained-glass windows, and a mosaic floor are in the Romanesque Original Edifice. In the domed extension—a wide open area with no supporting columns to block the view—is one of the largest organs in the Western Hemisphere. A carved stone portico fronts a magnificent entrance from Massachusetts Avenue.

DeRosa Florist, Inc. 212 West Central Street, Natick 01760

Phone: 508/653–6530.

Location: On left-hand side of Route 135, at Highlands Street, beyond Natick Square going into Framingham.

Tours by appointment: For any age, weekdays (but not around holiday time) 10–3. Several days' notice needed. 60–90 minutes, $35 for a group. (No charge for unguided visitors.)

A rare New England experience awaits visitors to the nine greenhouses of this wholesale business, which specializes in orchids grown and developed here under the eye and hand of Vincent DeRosa. A baker in the 1940s and now a recognized arranger as well as grower, Mr. DeRosa has learned everything he knows about flowers since asthma forced him to change careers. In great demand as a speaker as well as at the New England Spring Flower Show, he explains the breeding process; how pollens are crossed (white with lavender, for example); and how orchid plantlets are put in successively larger pots in the seven years (it used to be twelve to fifteen) they need to progress from pollen to the first flower. In February and March, the most colorful months, the show changes daily—with gorgeous magentas, yellows, plums, pinks, and oranges, and variegated blossoms too.

Federal Reserve Bank of Boston 600 Atlantic Avenue, Boston 02106

Phone: 617/973–3451.

Ⓣ: South Station on the Red Line.

Public tours by appointment: Year round, 45-minute program, one or two times a month. Call for schedule. Minimum age: 12.

Group tours by appointment: 90-minute program begins at 9 or 10:30 a.m. for groups of 20–35. Geared to age level (minimum age: 8) and interest, and can be combined with educational programs in check writing, money and banking, and career awareness. Four-week notice, please.

As you walk along the glass-walled viewing corridor, you find out how automation is responsible for transferring money from bank to bank and how bills are counted, sorted, and destroyed. You go by the computerized check clearinghouse and data storage systems. There are plenty of opportunities for questions, and even a souvenir—some shredded currency.

The art gallery, open weekdays 10 to 4, has rotating exhibits. And there's a free performance series in the auditorium on fall and spring Thursdays at 12:30. Check with the cultural affairs section (617/973–3454 or 973–3368) to see what's scheduled.

Nearby: Children's Museum (page 151), Boston Tea Party Ship and Museum (page 150), and Whit's End (page 125).

Harbor Sweets Page 90.

Hebert Candies 575 Hartford Pike, Shrewsbury 01545
Phone: 508/845–8051 or 800/642–7702.
Location: About 30 miles west of Boston, 10 minutes east of Worcester (museums on pages 174 and 177).
Tours by appointment: 45 minutes, for groups of at least 10. Year round, Monday–Friday, 9–3.
Directions: From Route 90 (Mass. Pike), exit 11A to Route 9 west, to Route 20 west into Shrewsbury. (Mansion is on left.) From Route 495, exit 24 onto Route 20 west to Shrewsbury.

Don a white paper hat, learn how chocolate is made, and see what's happening in the expanded stone mansion that was, in 1946, the first roadside candy store in the country. Grandchildren of Frederick E. Hebert are carrying on the seventy-five-year-old business, which produces more than 1,000 preservative-free items in this automated plant. In 1991 Hebert's, known for originating white-coat candies sometimes called white chocolate, introduced Chofu, a no-cholesterol chocolate.

You see the huge cauldrons where chocolate is melted before being poured into molds for solid pops or Easter bunnies. In the main kitchen, creams and chews and peanut butter logs are made. The candy bar room can produce 100,000 bars in one day, a million a week. When all the machines are in operation, it can be noisy. Always, it's aromatic. Yes, you leave with a tasty sample.

★ If you're having a birthday party for at least ten people in the ice-cream parlor (the former porch), the celebrant is given a free make-your-own sundae. Everyone gets balloons. Bring your own cake.

Not sure where the town is? Check the map on page 2.

Jonathan's Sprouts Vaughn's Hill Road, Rochester; mailing address, P.O. Box 270, Marion 02738

Phone: 508/763–2577 or 800/MY–T–BEAN.

Location: An hour southeast of Boston. Route 24 south to Route 195 west to Route 105 north for about 4 miles. Right on Vaughn's Hill Road.

Tours by appointment: 45 to 60 minutes, Sunday–Friday 10–3.

Requirements: 2 days' notice for groups of 4 or fewer; 2 weeks for student groups (educators required to purchase $3.50 curriculum for advance class orientation) and groups up to 20; 1 month for groups of 21–100. (For commercial groups, $1 per person charge.)

A big air-conditioned converted dairy barn along a winding rural road is the home of sprouting mung beans, alfalfa with radish, dill, or onion—all grown without chemical fertilizers, insecticides or herbicides. Depending on the variety, seeds are started in bathtubs or soaked overnight in rotating equipment that allows water to drain; or they are grown on shelves or inside stainless steel containers before the wispy "fields"—about fifty tons a week—are harvested and packaged. Everyone receives samples.

Where to from here? Plymouth and Cranberry World, pages 78 and 81, about a half hour's drive. Ten-minute drive to waterfront Ned's Point with lighthouse and picnic tables in Mattapoisett; five minutes to family-oriented, reasonably priced The Wave Restaurant on Route 105 in Marion. Six miles to Marion harbor.

A little lost? Check the map on pages xvi–xvii.

Logan International Airport Massport, Public Information Department, Boutwell 1, East Boston 02128

Phone: 617/561–1801.

Ⓣ: Airport on Blue Line; then airport bus to tour meeting place.

Tours by appointment: 1 to 3 hours (by age level). Weekdays at 10 a.m. year round; also at 1 p.m. fall through spring. May and June are busiest. Groups with special needs can be accommodated.

Requirements: 3-week notice. (Call for an appointment application.) Minimum age: Grade 3. Groups should be well supervised.

Tours vary depending on the size and age of the group, the day, and the weather. It may be possible to include a particular interest—customs, the flight kitchen, the inside of an airplane or cockpit, the weather bureau, the fire control unit, or a hangar. Visitors take a bus right onto the inner apron of the airfield for a close-up view of ground activity.

A Make-Your-Own-Tour (for younger children): If you take the water shuttle, page 233, or the Ⓣ, this could be an all-day excursion. If you must drive, park in the short-term lot ($3 first hour, $2 per hour thereafter) and plan to miss rush-hour traffic.

The **observation tower** on the 17th floor of the Tower Building, next to Terminal C, is open daily for an overview of the airfield. . . . Terminal C is the one with **Kidport,** a second-level carpeted play space located behind the ticket counters. Climbing structures built to look like an airplane, a baggage cart, and a fuel truck all have a view of the airfield. Seating is provided for parents. . . . Adjacent to Kidport are two huge glass cubes with mesmerizing, clever, and attractive **kinetic sculptures.** (All ages can spend long periods following the lacrosse balls and the moving parts.) . . . To the right and left of the ticket counters are giant **mirror sculptures** that reflect passersby in fragmented images. Also on the second level: an ice-cream parlor with an airfield view. Reminder: Terminals B, C, and D are connected, but it can be a long walk. The airport shuttle bus is free.

Massachusetts Envelope Company 30 Cobble Hill Road, Somerville 02143

Phone: 617/623–8000.

Ⓣ: Sullivan Square on the Orange Line; then a 5-minute walk.

Tours by appointment: ½ to 1 hour; year round, weekdays 9–noon and 1–3.

Requirements: 5-day notice. Group size: 6-10. Minimum age: 12.

Up to two million envelopes a day are produced with high-speed machinery. Before they come off the presses, there's work to be done in the art department and darkroom. You see all that and finish at the warehouse, where trucks are waiting at the shipping dock. Mary Ellen Grossman gives a personalized tour with sensitivity to group interests and backgrounds—often with career awareness in mind.

National Braille Press 88 St. Stephen Street, Boston 02115

Phone: 617/266–6160.

Ⓣ: Northeastern on the Arborway/Green Line.

Tours by appointment: 1 hour; year round, Tuesday–Thursday, 10–noon and 1:30–3:30 for groups of 5 to 30 people.

Books (for adults and children) and magazines are electronically transcribed onto braille zinc plates, printed, collated, and stitched, then shipped around the world. Visitors go into each area, where staffers (disabled and nondisabled) explain the work. There's also a brief discussion on the history of braille. If you'd like, you may leave with samples of braille materials, including alphabet cards.

From October through May, some of the candy is (still) hand dipped here

Phillips Candy House 818 Morrissey Boulevard (about 1½ miles from JFK Library), Dorchester 02122

Phone: 617/282–2090.

Tours: 20 minutes, Monday–Thursday, between 9 and 1:30. Year round except a couple of weeks before certain holidays: Valentine's Day, Easter, Halloween, Thanksgiving, and Christmas.

Requirements: Minimum age: 5. Maximum number: 10.

Maybe they are making caramel, coconut, nougatine, and cream centers (and coding the chocolate covering with the aid of a string)—or jellies or fudge—in the same way that Phillip Strazzula did when he began this business in 1925. Coating is done bottom side first, before the conveyor belt carries rows of pieces through a chocolate-fall. Turtles are a two-day process. All the nuts are roasted here. No preservatives are used.

Your guide, Mary Ann Nagle, the founder's granddaughter, carries on the family tradition with original recipes and with the help of a small staff who tend the copper kettles over open gas-fired stoves. They stir, funnel, fill molds (including 2½-foot-tall, five-pound hollow Santa Clauses), and hand cut. All these labor-intensive efforts are seen during the twenty-minute tour, which begins with an understanding of where chocolate comes from and culminates with "the freshest candy you'll ever taste"—right from the finish line.

Simpson Spring Company 719 Washington Street, South Easton 02375
Phone: 508/238–2741.
Tours by appointment: 45 minutes, Monday–Thursday, 9–12:30.
Requirements: 2-week notice. Group size: 6–60. Minimum age: 7.

White tile and stained-glass windows form the setting for the spring, the source of water for this 113-year-old bottling company. Visitors also see ingredients being tested in the lab and view the assembly-line bottling process. In the museum are bottles dating back to the 1800s and machinery used here at the turn of the century. Samples are offered at the end of the tour.

Symphony Hall 301 Massachusetts Avenue (corner Huntington Avenue), Boston 02115
Phone: 617/638–9390.
Ⓣ: Symphony on the Arborway/Green Line.
Tours by appointment (made at least 2 weeks in advance): Weekdays, September–June, when hall is available. Tours geared to various age levels.
Rates and requirements: $25 per guide for up to 15 people; minimum age is 9; maximum group size, 150. No charge for tours with Boston Symphony Orchestra Youth Concerts, page 39.

Even the most ardent symphonygoer and Boston Pops fan is surprised at the scope of this behind-the-scenes view, which begins and ends at the stage door on St. Stephen Street. In the basement there are organ bellows, cables, and a recording studio. Elevators transport the larger instruments, and there's a humidified room just for pianos. All tours enter the most acoustically perfect auditorium in the United States. Depending on rehearsal and concert schedules, you may be taken onto the stage. The tour is an anecdotal, historical look at the hall that's been the home of the century-old Boston Symphony Orchestra since 1900.

Trinity Church Copley Square, Boston 02116
Phone: 617/536–0944.
Ⓣ: Copley on the Green Line.
Tours: 30 minutes, Sundays at about 12:15, following the Sunday 11 a.m. service.

The church is open daily 8 to 6, but during the tour you hear about architect Henry Hobson Richardson and what is considered to be one of the most magnificent churches in the country. John La Farge was in charge of the painted interior decoration and executed most of the figure painting as well as four of the beautiful stained-glass windows. Trinity's altar and chancel were extensively remodeled in 1937.

U.S. Army Natick Research and Development Center Kansas Street, Natick 01760

Phone: 508/651–5340.

Tours by appointment: 90 minutes weekdays, for up to 30 people. Minimum age is 14. Individuals can join a scheduled group.

Research, often in cooperation with companies and universities, focuses on clothing, food, and protection of military personnel. Wash-and-wear shirts, freeze-dried foods, lightweight camping equipment, and crash helmets are among the items that have been developed in the laboratories. In light of environmental concerns, some items currently in an advanced stage of development are made of biodegradable plastics.

Not sure where the town is? Check the map on page 2.

U.S. Navy Ships Navy Office of Information, 408 Atlantic Avenue, Room 222, Boston 02110–3316

Phone: 617/951–2690.

Call to check on where visiting ships will be berthed and on the public hours for tours. Never a charge. Depending on the day of the week, the weather, and the ship, you may or may not have a wait. Aircraft carriers seem to attract the greatest crowds.

Wilson Farm 10 Pleasant Street, Lexington 02173

Phone: 617/862–3900.

Tours: 45 minutes, year round, Mondays and Wednesday–Friday 9–noon and 2–5. Heavily booked in April, May, June.

The greenhouse is always open, and the 30-acre vegetable farm can be seen May through October, but the poultry area is the big attraction. Yes, you see and hear thousands of chickens! As soon as eggs are laid, they're automatically collected in a tray and then graded. Although the grading machine, which requires four men, is operated at varying hours, it is sometimes turned on for visiting groups. Two cows, some rabbits, one llama, and "sometimes a pig" share the huge barn. Depending on the day, tractors may be plowing, harrowing, seeding, or cultivating.

   A fourth generation is running the farm (and garden center), which began in 1884. They no longer drive produce into Boston's Quincy Market by horse and wagon. Now, in addition to the Lexington farm, they grow much of their produce on a 250-acre New Hampshire farm, 45 minutes away, where horse-drawn hayrides are sometimes scheduled.

Favorable growing conditions, often near the coast, have encouraged the opening of about two dozen wineries in New England. Visitors are invited to taste (if over age 21) and to tour—see fruit ground and squeezed, and where wine ages and ferments. Often, you are welcome to picnic on picturesque grounds. The wineries below are an hour (more or less) from Boston.

Nashoba Valley Winery, 100 Wattaquadoc Hill Road, Bolton 01740
Phone: 508/779–5521.
Directions: Route 495 to Route 117 (exit 27) west 1 mile to Bolton center. Left at blinking light for ¼ mile to winery.
Open: Daily. 20-minute tours year round, Friday through Sunday, 11–5. $1 per person; under age 21 free.

Jack Partridge, a former city planner, started making wine as a hobby in the late 1970s. Now his winery is located in a rustic building built in 1982 on fifty-five acres with orchards and gardens. Sixteen varieties of wine—red, dry white, semisweet, and dessert—are produced from many fruits (some from cold storage in winter), but no grapes. During the 20-minute tour, equipment is usually turned off for safety and noise reasons.

In spring and fall the **picnic tables** fill quickly; bring a blanket. Sorry, no ball or Frisbee playing or kite flying allowed. Self-guided **orchard tour** (about 20 minutes) through old and new varieties of apples. **Pick-your-own arrangements**—sold by container, no scales here—for strawberries, purple raspberries, thornless blackberries, peaches, apples, and red raspberries. Bring hats! Very little shade. Call mid-June through October about availability. No charge for **festivals** with musical entertainment in February, May, June, July, and September.

Plymouth Colony Winery Pinewood Road, Plymouth 02360
Phone: 508/747–3334.
Directions: Take Route 44 from Plymouth (see page 78) 3 miles toward Route 58.
Open: April through December 24, Monday–Saturday 10–5, Sunday 12–5. December 26 through March, weekends and holidays 10–5.

Located in the middle of a 10-acre cranberry bog. Usually, late April is best time to view bogs in blossom. During cranberry harvest festival (maybe last weekend in September), see flooded fields and the fascinating process of shaking cranberries loose before they float and are corralled.

Tours and tastings are offered at this winery, which makes cranberry and cranberry blended wines from local fruit and grapes. Walk along bogs. Use the picnic tables.

Sakonnet Vineyards 162 West Main Road (Route 77), P.O. Box 197, Little Compton, RI 02837
Phone: 401/635–8486.

Open: Year round, daily, 10–6 for tasting, slide show, and sales. Tours, 20 minutes, May–December, Wednesday–Sunday, 11–6, every hour on the hour.

Award-winning wines are produced at the region's largest winery, established in 1975. The interesting slide show is about growing grapes, wine-making, and the winery. Great site for a picnic. Walk along pathway beside forty-five planted acres overlooking a reservoir.

Where to from here? Folks at the winery will direct you to **Adamsville** (ten-minute ride), a quiet historic village, Rhode Island's smallest. Adamsville has a general store, Stone Bridge Dishes (everything from china and pottery to paper fans and 25-cent beads), a millpond (if there hasn't been a drought) with ducks and herons, and Abraham Manchester Restaurant and Tavern (rustic, extremely reasonable prices, Italian menu, perfect for families). And then there's **Gray's Grist Mill,** a fun stop if Tim McTague is grinding. (Check: 508/636–6075. Operates year round, but open on weekends only.) Those huge granite stones have been turning out Rhode Island Jonnycake Meal since 1878. To this very day Tim uses the technique he learned from John Hart, who ran the mill for sixty years, with a 1946 Dodge truck that has wheels off and belt connecting car drive and mill shaft. No additives or preservatives in the meals, flours, and mixes.

Westport Rivers Vineyard and Winery 417 Hix Bridge Road, Westport 02790

Phone: 508/636–3423.

Directions: Route 24 to Route 195 east to Route 88 south (toward Horseneck Beach), left/east on Hix Bridge Road and across the river. (Eight miles from Sakonnet Vineyards.)

Open: Mid-May through early November, Thursday–Sunday, 12–5. Tours (20–30 minutes) Saturdays and Sundays, 12–5.

★ Reunions, luncheons, meetings, weddings.

You'll feel like a discoverer—of 110 scenic acres. The largest vinifera (European grapes) vineyard in the area is a family-run farm winery that opened to the public and sold its first bottles of chardonnay in 1991. The Russells purchased the farm in 1982 from the Smith family, who had worked the land since 1887.

Turn off the country road, drive by Hereford cattle, and arrive at the converted dairy barn, which is connected by a grape arbor to a wonderfully redone Victorian house. Here is the tasting room/gift shop (complete with crayons at children's table) plus a gallery featuring works by area artists and craftspeople.

Combination ideas: Literature available here includes a Wesport map with area attractions—farm stands, restaurants, Dartmouth Children's Museum, Lloyd Center for Environmental Studies, Demarest Lloyd State Park, antiques shops, and the village of Russells Mills.

More combination ideas: It's a 10-minute drive to **Adamsville** (see Sakonnet Vineyards above). Enjoy this bucolic countryside on two wheels (bring your own **bicycle**). Or, minutes away, visit **Driftway Meadows Horse Farm,** 540 Drift Road. From Westport Rivers Winery go back toward Route 88 along Hix Bridge Road, turn right on to Drift Road for about 2 miles.

At the farm, next door to Noquochoke Orchards (apple stand, recipes, no pick-your-own), Joanne and Scott Travers offer riding lessons. They train about forty horses and breed registered Dorset sheep. A couple of foals are usually romping in the spring. There's an outdoor riding ring, an indoor riding arena, and a half-mile jogging track (cart and harness sometimes used). The best time to stop by is between 11 and 4. You are encouraged to ask questions; average visit is an hour. Semiannual "open barn days" are held, with demonstrations including horseshoeing done by son Sean, a blacksmith. Year round it's a good idea to call ahead (508/636–8620 or 636–8864). A special place.

Calendar

Comprehensive weekly newspaper listings (page 3) show exact times and fees of the myriad activities and performances in the Boston area. . . . When the media highlight a particular place, it is "discovered" by everyone that weekend. Go the following week! . . . Herewith, a sampler.

January

First Night: New Year's Eve finds professional entertainment—folk dancing, classical music, poetry, theater, mime, a parade, something for all ages in dozens of locations throughout the city. Some free. Arrive early for events with limited seating. Phone 617/542–1399.

First Day Sail to Thompson Island: Public is invited to join Friends of Boston Harbor Islands. Warm-up place and hot beverage provided. Call 617/740–4290.

Outside: Feed hungry ducks (pages 28 and 188). Or walk along a beach, perhaps one you don't get to during the summer.

A garden tour: Have you ever been to Wellesley's Ferguson Greenhouses? What a treat (see page 204). Combine with the Jewett Arts Center on campus.

Bookstores: Particularly popular on lousy days. Attend talks or storytelling sessions (page 48). Or browse through the endless supply of new books at New England Mobile Book Fair, 82 Needham Street, Newton, where it's hard to "run in" or to leave with just one book. The selection, price, and helpful staff make the warehouse atmosphere most attractive.

February

Black History Month: Abundant special programming.

School vacation week: Call museum recorded-information numbers (page 149) for special plans. . . . Look for newspaper roundup articles about special events.

Boston Festival: Wide variety of concerts, ice carving, laser show, foods. Many events for children. Some are free. Discounted admission or none for $10 button (pass) purchasers. Phone 617/536–8152.

Valentine's Day: Chocolate-lovers' tour to area chocolatiers. A landmark excursion by a small personalized company known for its innovations, Uncommon Boston Ltd., 437 Boylston Street, 4th Floor, Boston 02116. Phone 617/731–5854. ★ Enquire about teddy bear birthday parties (minimum age: 8) or participatory culinary experiences with professional chefs.

Logan Airport: Where not to go the Friday at the start of school vacation or the Sunday when it ends. The expressway has added traffic tieups.

Sleigh rides: Weather permitting, at Old Sturbridge Village (page 77). Or book your own (page 242).

Chinese New Year: Ushered in with a dragon dance (driving the devil out to let good luck in) and firecrackers. Held at Beach and Tyler streets on a Sunday afternoon from 2 to 4.

Day seal hikes or cruises (in a pontoon boat): See seals and sea birds. Registration required. Massachusetts Audubon's **Wellfleet Bay Wildlife Sanctuary,** South Wellfleet (Cape Cod). Phone 508/349–2615.

March

New England Spring Flower Show: New Englanders are starved for greenery by this time of year. Lines start forming first thing in the morning for the magnificent displays and ideas. Special programming and demonstrations for children. School tours arranged. Children 5 and under are free. Phone 617/536–9280.

St. Patrick's Day Parade: On or close to March 17, in the afternoon, in South Boston. Floats, bands, and politicians galore in the ninety-minute procession.

March–April

Bird walks: This is the time of year, before trees leaf out, that birds are easy to find. Take your own walk in an open space area (pages 181–204), or call the Massachusetts Audubon Society (page 204) for scheduled walks. Beginners—and children—are welcome in many groups, but keep in mind that quiet is essential.

Maple sugaring: The season depends on the weather. Ideal sap-running days are cold nights followed by warm (40 degrees) days. There are about four hundred sugarhouses within a three-hour ride of Boston, and they vary in methods and facilities. Now, most use plastic lines that connect the trees from the top to the bottom of the hill. Everywhere you'll see sap collected and boiled down into maple syrup. (It takes forty pints of sap to make one pint of syrup.) Visitors are usually welcome at sugarhouses (no charge for watching) anytime, but it's a good idea to check the situation before leaving home. Dress in warm clothing and boots for the hike in the maple grove.

Local demonstrations are scheduled at many places, including several Massachusetts Audubon Society sanctuaries (page 204). One of the closest places to Boston: **Coolidge Farm** (400 taps), Berlin Road, Bolton. Phone 508/779–2716 or 779–6633. Many places are farther west; low-key **Cumworth Farm** (413/634–5529) in Cummington serves pancakes.

In New Hampshire, 60 miles from Boston: **Parker's Maple Barn Restaurant and Sugar House.** Uses 35,000 taps with pipeline and hundreds of buckets. Wood-fired evaporator. Free sugarhouse tours given throughout sugaring season, a period when you can expect a three-hour wait for the enormous Sunday morning breakfast. Blacksmith demonstrations. Antiques barn. Gift shop. Phone 603/878–2308.

April

National Library Week: Watch for special programs.

Fenway Park: Opening day.

New England Folk Festival: Usually at Natick High School on a weekend. All ages come from miles around for dance and music performances; participation in folk, square, and contra dancing (beginning to expert); and homemade ethnic foods. Activities inside and out. Phone 617/354–1340.

Herring Runs: This is the time (usually late in the month) when the fish spawn in lakes and ponds. Many do not survive the long, difficult journey. Those that do, come back year after year. (Survivors eventually go back to the ocean; young ones swim down in late summer or fall.) Watching fish by the thousands accept the challenge of the ladder is a memorable sight. To check if the season is on or for a nearby ladder, call the Department of Marine Fisheries at 617/727–3193.

Bournedale: One of the best and largest runs in the state is along **Cape Cod Canal.** Take Route 3 south to Route 6 at the Sagamore Bridge; then travel less than a mile to the parking lot. The herring come from the canal up the steps, then go under the road on their way to the herring pond. Later they retrace their swim.

Brewster: The prettiest productive run, about a two-hour ride from Boston on Cape Cod, at the **Old Grist Mill** on Stony Brook Road.

East Weymouth: Take exit 16B off Route 3. At first lights, left onto Middle Street, third lights onto Broad to second lights onto Commercial Street. Run is all along on your right. Viewing at (marked) **Herring Run Park.**

A major viewing place: The **Amoskeag Dam and Fishway Center,** just off I–293 at 1000 Elm Street in Manchester, New Hampshire. Learning and visitor center opened in 1988 with opportunities to view the turbines in the hydro plant. Slide shows explain the history of the Merrimack River, electric power and its use by the mills in the 1800s, the use of the ladder, and the habits of fish. The highlight: an underwater view of thousands of fish swimming by. Picnic tables provided along the river. Open to the public early May through mid-June, weekdays 1–6 and weekends 10–4. Free. Phone 603/626–FISH.

Patriots Day: Officially April 19. Celebrated third Monday of the month with activities at dawn, a march, and events in Boston, Concord, and surrounding towns. Reenactments include the famous William Dawes/Paul Revere ride "through every Middlesex village and farm." A uniformed horseman arrives near the Minuteman Statue in Lexington about 12, and a long wonderful parade follows at 2. While you're searching for a parking place, keep in mind that it takes about an hour for the parade to reach the Green from the official starting point.

The Boston Marathon: A 26-mile race, the country's oldest marathon, starts in Hopkinton at noon. Winners usually finish in downtown Boston at the Hancock Tower between 2 and 2:30. Much of the route includes Commonwealth Avenue, lined with cheering spectators. Phone 617/572–6452.

Ducklings Day Parade: In the Boston Public Garden on the last Sunday of the month. Kids are invited to dress in costume. $3 per person, $10 per family with advance registration. For this year's schedule: Historic Neighborhoods Foundation, page 126.

April–May

Big Apple Circus: Intimate one-ring circus with animal acts, acrobats, gymnasts, clowns. New theme and new hit every year. Every seat is less than 50 feet from ring. In fully heated tent. For schedule call Children's Museum, 617/426–6500.

May

Magnolias: Blooming on Commonwealth Avenue near the Public Garden. Nature's performance is difficult to time, but the spectacle is unforgettable.

Sheep shearing: Demonstrations at many places, including Gore Place (page 115) and Old Sturbridge Village (page 77).

Lilac Sunday: At Arnold Arboretum (page 183). More than six hundred kinds of lilacs—in seven color groupings, with single and double-flowering trees in each. Well publicized. Well attended. Go just before or after to avoid the throng.

Festivals. Everywhere. Art. Entertainment. Crafts. Demonstrations. Some are free. Some are for fund raising. Thousands participate in Kite Festival at Franklin Park, 617/725–4505. If you are inspired, try kite flying this month and next at area beaches (pages 213–221), without the summer crowds.

Apple blossoms: Late in the month. Drive through Stow (Routes 117 and 62) and Harvard (Route 110), or around Littleton and Groton (Routes 2A and 119). The countryside is a little hilly for young or inexperienced cyclists.

May–June

Boston Pops: For this Boston tradition, tables and chairs replace first-floor seats in Symphony Hall. Programs are a mix of classical, popular favorites, and novelties. Refreshments sold. The first floor is more social (and expensive); audio is better upstairs. Tickets can be reserved by phone (617/266–1492) with three weeks' notice.

Mountain climbing note: Black flies come to life in May, are at their worst in June, and supposedly taper off in July. They flourish in 72- to 94-degree temperatures. Recommended clothing: Long-sleeved heavy shirts, slacks, wool socks, and hats.

June

Militia Day: On the first Monday of the month, visiting delegations from the eastern seaboard join the Ancient and Honorable Artillery Company for a full-dress parade from Faneuil Hall to the Common. Ceremonies last until about 4:30. The spectacle, which seems to attract mostly passersby, includes a booming cannon and a drumhead election—where each ballot is cast on a huge, centuries-old drum. Phone 617/227–1638.

Boston Common Dairy Festival: Upholding an old law, still on the books, that says cows must appear annually on the Common. There's a variety of dairy breeds and some ducks, chickens, sheep, and calves. Staffers answer questions and let some onlookers try milking in late afternoon. Admission is free. School programs arranged for schools; call the New England Dairy and Food Council in early May at 617/734–6750.

Cambridge International Fair: Central Square. Petting farm. Storytellers. Dance. Music. Poetry. International performers. All free.

Copley Square Book Fair: (Free) readings by authors and children in the Boston Public Library. Outside, displays in tented booths by more than one hundred publishers and bookstores.

Summer Preview supplements: Special sections published by several newspapers. Worth keeping.

June–September

The Children's Theatre in Residence at Maudslay State Park: Performances for all ages, for young children, and for older children, Saturday and Sunday (May–October) in this gorgeous Newburyport setting. (See page 191.) $6 adults, $4 children. First performance of each show free. Phone 508/465–2572.

Agricultural fairs: Several of the big fairs are so much like carnivals that you have to look for the agricultural exhibits. Still, there are horse and oxen pulls, garden prizes, duck-calling contests, ecology exhibits, and cattle and sheep judging. For a list—major, community, youth, and grange—check with the Massachusetts Department of Agriculture, Department of Fairs, 100 Cambridge Street, Boston 02202, phone 617/727–3018.

Farmers' markets: Held weekly, all over—at twenty city locations and in many surrounding communities. For a schedule, call the Massachusetts Division of Agricultural Development, 617/727–3018.

Pick-your-own: Crops change from year to year. For this year's list send a self-addressed, stamped envelope to the Massachusetts Division of Agricultural Development, 100 Cambridge Street, Boston 02202.

Hints: Call before you go for hours, to know about availability, and to get directions. Children may or may not be welcome; if they are, please supervise! Containers (sometimes free) may be provided. Even if savings are small, the produce is fresh and picking is fun.

Strawberries: Late June into July. The beds are hotter than you think; bring a hat.

Blueberries: Mid-July through mid-August. It's slow going (it takes up to an hour to fill a quart). Pickers of the wild variety aren't eager to share their sources—you might try the Milton side of Blue Hills Reservation, page 192, but a sure giveaway is cars lined along the roadside. To car staples you might add buckets for berries, insect repellent for you.

Apples: Around Labor Day till they're all gone.

A variety of pick-your-own suggestions:

- **Bolton: Nashoba Valley Winery** orchard (tours, page 267). *Strawberries, purple (tart) and red raspberries, thornless blackberries, peaches, apples.* Phone 508/779–5521.

- **Concord: Verrill Farm,** Wheeler Road. *Strawberries, rhubarb, all kinds of vegetables* (some ready in June), *Oriental greens, herbs, and great array of flowers.* Plenty of grassy areas for sitting and picnicking. Phone 508/369–5952.

- **Framingham: Hanson's Farm,** 20 Nixon Road. *Strawberries and raspberries.* Just what you think a farm should look like. Low-key. Red barn. Produce stand. Bedding plants. Homemade pies and tarts. Fourth-generation farmers. Chickens, hens, geese. Phone 508/877–3058.

- **Ipswich: Goodale Orchards,** 123 Argilla Road. Two miles from Crane Beach (page 214). *Strawberries, raspberries, blueberries, and* (one weekend in fall) *apples.* Quintessential New England. Antique barn with "airplane" swing for kids, children's books (for reading here) by old flagstone working fireplace, play area, pies and cider doughnuts made (April–December) before your eyes. For sale: their own fruits, organic herbs and vegetables, hard cider, locally made cheese kept in seven old-fashioned refrigerators, and more. June Strawberry Festival. Hayrides on fall weekends. December Sundays, folksingers by fire. Picnic by small pond. Barnyard with sheep, goats, turkey, pigs, ducks, geese, horses, cats. "Bring a jacket; we're just two miles from the ocean." Phone 508/356–5366.

- **North Andover: Smolak Farms,** 315 Bradford Street. *Peaches, nectarines, plums, apples, pumpkins.* Beehive to view in farm stand. Pies, muffins, apple cider doughnuts made here. Walking trail around farm. Ducks and swans in pond. Goats, rabbits, pigs, chickens. **Hayrides** in fall. Phone 508/682–6332.

- **Northboro: Tougas Family Farm,** Ball Street. *Strawberries, raspberries, blueberries, blackberries, peaches, apples, pumpkins.* "Because we have three children, we built the barn with haymow in 1985." Slide, a place to jump in the hay, monkey bars—all bedded on hay. Farm kitchen with fruit sorbet, pies, shortcakes, ice cream, beverages, light lunch. Canning and jam supplies. Picnic tables. Phone 508/393–6406.

- **Peabody: Brooksby Farm,** Felton Street. *Strawberries, blueberries, raspberries, apples, pumpkins.* On dead-end street, beyond three Peabody Historical Society houses. Picnic areas with grills; one on hill with view of orchards and Salem Harbor. Huge stand heated by wood stove and solar heat. Bakery (doughnuts and pies) with window for watching. Beehives to see; incubator with eggs hatching too. Two-mile jogging trail. Free spring and fall festivals with entertainment. ★ One-hour **Hayride birthday parties.** Petting sheep and goat. Ducks, chicken, turkeys. Phone 508/531–1631.

- **Sharon: Ward's Berry Farm,** 614 South Main Street. *Strawberries, blueberries, pumpkins* at pick-your-own prices. (*Raspberries* expected in 1994.) Other crops at stand prices. Tour 200 acres that are highly managed—trellising, drip irrigation, fertility programs. Spread a blanket and picnic. Chartered tractor-drawn **hayrides** daily in summer, weekdays in June; $2 per person includes some pick-your-own crops. Free rides for strawberry pickers in strawberry season; no reservations. Phone 617/784–6939.

- **Weston: Land's Sake,** corner of Newton and Wellesley streets. *Organically grown strawberries, rhubarb, raspberries, "all kinds of vegetables and herbs"* at this nonprofit environmental education organization that is more than a farm. Some innovative programs involve Weston youngsters with the inner city. Weekend 20-minute **horse-drawn hayrides** (with talks about what workhorses are used for); custom hayrides for all ages. Maple sugaring. Strawberry and pumpkin festival. Group visits arranged. Phone 617/893–1162.

July

Harborfest: First week of month. More than one hundred events; many free, including concerts and fireworks. Boston chowderfest; fee charged. Annual turnaround of USS *Constitution* with twenty-one-gun salute off Castle Island, page 185. Phone 617/227–1528.

July 4 on the Esplanade: The Boston Pops and fireworks. Spectacular. Come the last minute and you'll hear; come very early (with blanket and picnic) and you'll hear and see. Free.

U.S. Pro Tennis Championships: The oldest professional tennis tournament in the country. At Longwood Cricket Club, 564 Hammond Street, Brookline. Day and evening sessions. Admission charged. Ⓣ: Chestnut Hill on the Riverside/Green Line. Phone 617/731–4500 or 731–2900.

Lowell Folk Festival: Three-day multiethnic celebration featuring nationally known folk artists, traditional dance parties, street parades, craft demonstrations, and ethnic foods. All performances are free. Special Ⓣ arrangements. Phone 508/970–5000.

July–August

Esplanade Concerts: At the Hatch Shell since 1929, when Arthur Fiedler, then a violinist with the Boston Symphony Orchestra, dreamed up the idea of playing classical music in a band concert setting. The Boston Pops continues to play here about twelve times during the summer, to enthusiastic crowds. Other 8 p.m. performances are given by local and internationally known dance, opera, and music groups. Ⓣ: Charles on the Red Line or Arlington on the Green Line. For a complete schedule phone 617/727–0460.

Tanglewood: This 200-acre estate in Lenox, where Nathaniel Hawthorne lived and wrote, is the summer home of the Boston Symphony Orchestra.

Families with younger children may be more comfortable on the lawn outside the music shed. (Under age 5 not allowed in shed; inquire about free admission to the lawn for children under age 12.) In addition to scheduled evening performances, open rehearsals are held Saturday mornings at 10:30. Picnicking (sometimes it's lavish) allowed. Lenox is 140 miles west of Boston via the Mass. Pike. Ticket sales and information from Symphony Hall, 617/266–1492. Early June through August: 413/637–1940.

Children's theater: It thrives in the summer at universities, at community and arts centers, and on tour. Check newspapers. See Maudslay State Park, Newburyport, page 191. The Boston Children's Theatre Stagemobile (page 39) performs at area sites.

Garden concerts: At Longfellow National Historic Site, page 113, at the Museum of Fine Arts, page 157, and in the amphitheater at DeCordova Museum, page 172.

City Hall Plaza concerts: Free. Some evenings and many weekdays at noon. Everything from local talent to internationally recognized companies.

International Folk Dancing by the Fountain: In Copley Square. Begun in 1970. The leaders have a special talent for getting large crowds involved. All ages come with or without partners and with or without experience. Free. Phone 617/491–6084.

North End Festivals: Just about every weekend on a different block of the small area (see page 141). Look for lighted arches and garland-strung poles where celebrations carry out Italian customs dating back hundreds of years. One of the largest is Saint Anthony's. The Fisherman's Feast (below) is a unique event. Time has brought changes—more vendors and people—but you can still see a statue of the Madonna being carried through the streets. The money taped to it goes toward expenses and neighborhood charities. Roma Band concerts can be heard from 8 to 11. Stands, most active from dusk on, sell stuffed quahogs, Italian sausage, fried dough, hot corn on the cob, slush, and pizza.

August

Moon Festival: In Chinatown when the moon is full. It's the Chinese Thanksgiving, with songs and dances, a parade, martial arts and crafts demonstrations. Free. The streets are closed off for activity from noon to 6. Phone 617/542–2574.

Fisherman's Feast: In the North End (page 141), the festival of Madonna del Soccorso (Our Lady of Perpetual Help). A highlight: Late Sunday afternoon, young girls dressed as angels stand on the balconies of North Street. At 5 p.m. (arrive much earlier for a viewing spot), one girl is lowered by a pulley into the street, where she gives a speech in Italian, and then pigeons are released from a decorated cage.

September

Whale watching: Ever been? See page 253.

Three Apples Storytelling Festival: Inside and out, on and around the Harvard, Massachusetts, town common. For preschoolers, for families, and specifically for adults too. Morris dancing, mimes, story-swaps. A major event. Early-bird specials, individual tickets, packages, and family rates available. Phone 617/864–3062.

Pick-your-own apples: At many orchards, from Labor Day through early October. To send for a full list of pick-your-own places, see page 277. Or watch for newspaper listings. Pick-your-own is very popular, more for fun than for savings. If the weather has been unkind, drops may be for sale. Always call to check picking dates. Go early on Sundays; afternoons can be very busy. Places that offer pony rides have a tremendous line a-waiting. Some suggestions (also see **Ipswich, North Andover, Northboro, Peabody,** pages 277–278):

- **Bolton: Nashoba Valley Winery,** page 000. Apple picking plus press-your-own cider (expensive but fun) possibilities. Phone 508/779–5521.
- **Harvard: Phil's Apples,** 24 Prospect Hill Road. Open weekends. Children are welcome to pick apples and turn the cider press. Homemade pies. One mile before Fruitlands Museum, page 173. Phone 508/456–3361. . . . **Doe's Orchards,** 327 Ayer Road. Family established orchard in 1915. Been entirely pick-your-own—"simply pick-your-own"—since 1980. Three generations of customers return to three generations of apple growers. Phone 508/772–4139.

Cider mills: Here and there, scattered through the countryside. Call about pressing times. List available from Massachusetts Division of Agricultural Development, page 277. Closest to Boston is in **Brookline: Allandale Farm,** 259 Allandale Road. Rustic barn in woods. Organic farm. Chickens. Maybe some cows named Ben and Jerry. Near Larz Anderson Park, page 188. Phone 617/524–1531. In **South Natick: Williamson Cider Mill,** 11 Rockland Street. Art Williamson started pressing in 1934. His former icehouse was moved from Dover years ago; it's an amazing old press in a three-storied building. Very near Broadmoor Wildlife Sanctuary, page 197. Phone 508/655–4521.

September– October

Cranberry harvest time: Spectacular. Colorful. Mesmerizing to watch. Catch the process, by chance, in the Plymouth/Carver/Middleboro area. (On bicycles, we seem to luck out.) Edaville Railroad, page 59, passes through bog land; see Plymouth Colony Winery, page 267, too.

October

Foliage: As soon as up-country peak is announced, weekend traffic is bumper-to-bumper. Think about a back road, or wait until the peak reaches Boston, usually a couple of weeks later, and visit Arnold Arboretum (page 183).

Columbus Day Weekend: More up-country traffic. It's the busiest weekend of the year in historic Concord (page 55) and in New Hampshire and Vermont.

Head of the Charles: The largest single-day rowing event in the world. Several thousand rowers from many countries in hundreds of shells cover the 3-mile course that starts at the Boston University Bridge and ends near Northeastern University's boathouse. A spectator sport for the cheering and picnicking crowds all along the shoreline.

The Greatest Show on Earth: The **Ringling Bros. & Barnum and Bailey Circus** arrives at Boston Garden. Call the publicity department, 617/227–3200, for exact time and route of circus parade in the North End.

Harvest Festivals: Country crafts, farm exhibits, and demonstrations— from bread making to cider pressing to wool dyeing (using native plants). Held weekends everywhere.

Halloween: Haunted Houses held in schools, museums, churches, or community centers. Nominal fees, often for fund raising.

Haunted Happenings: Last week in October, in Salem: haunted houses, storytelling at Essex Institute houses, spooky treasure hunt and mask tours at Peabody Museum, costume parade. Phone 508/744–0004.

Enchanted Forest: Candlelit hayride, 5–8 p.m., with dramatic scenes from classic children's stories along the trail in Franklin Park. By Boston Children's Theatre, page 38.

November

Enchanted Village at Jordan Marsh (in Boston): A wonderland. A Victorian village built to scale for a 4-foot 8-inch-tall person. Embellished with music, animation, and sound. Joyful. Free tickets issued on first-come, first-served basis. Mid-month until early January.

Thanksgiving: Special dinners at Plimoth Plantation, page 79, and Old Sturbridge Village, page 77. Reserve well in advance.

December

MIT Model Railroad Club open house: First or second Saturday, 2–5:30 and 7:30–10. About 5 miles of track with "plenty running" and lots of people to answer questions. In room that has been home of club since the late 1940s. 18 Vassar Street, Room 214, Building 20E. Phone 617/253–3269.

South Station train set display: In grand concourse. Track, buildings, trees, cars, tunnels, bridges. Look to your heart's content. Free. Phone 617/451–2266.

Ritz-Carlton Hotel Nutcracker scene: Fantasy come to life. A room decorated as a *Nutcracker* scene. Open 9–9. No charge. Make arrangements with Ritz-Carlton concierge, 15 Arlington Street, Boston. Phone 617/536–5700.

Alice in Wonderland Tea Party: At Boston Harbor Hotel, 70 Rowes Wharf. Scenes enacted by Boston Children's Theater, page 38. Phone 617/439–7000 or 617/424–6634.

Historic house tours: Wayside Inn (page 93) is decorated by local garden club.

Christmas trees: Cut down, or even dig up, your own tree. A list of farms is available from the Massachusetts Division of Agricultural Development, 100 Cambridge Street, Boston 02202. Phone 617/727–3180.

Hints: Check with the farm before setting out. Bring a tarpaulin to protect car finish. Bundle up, and wear heavy shoes or boots. Some Christmas tree farm possibilities:

- **Dudley** (75 minutes west of Boston): **Vernalwood,** Darling Road. Maybe hot cider, homemade cookies, chestnuts to roast at home. Skating if the pond freezes. Phone 508/943–5282.
- **Framingham: Baiting Brook Meadow Farm.** By appointment only. December weekends. Phone 508/877–7256.
- **Harvard: Doe Orchards,** 327 Ayer Road. Choose. Cut your own or they'll cut for you. Jay Doe, wearing Santa's hat, will carry it on a trailer to your car. Phone 508/772–4139.

- **Southborough: Wolf Hill Christmas Barn,** Jericho Hill Road. Thursday through Sunday. Hot cider in barn shop that sells wreaths, greens, roping. Phone 508/485–5087.

Music: Everywhere. Check the newspapers.

Family performances: Represent a broad scope of the arts. Among Boston's traditions:

- **Black Nativity:** A gospel song-play by Langston Hughes that tells the Christmas story from a black perspective. For all ages. At several locations in the Boston area. Call National Center for Afro-American Artists, 617/442–8614.

- **Festival of Light and Song:** Theater, songs, storytelling, dance from American, European and Jewish traditions. Phone 617/232–6760.

- **Christmas Revels:** A celebration of the winter solstice, the shortest day of the year. Join in song and dance. Cast of Morris sword dancers, children (who steal the show), mummers, and much more. Held in a perfect setting—Harvard's Sanders Theater. Phone 617/621–0505. Direct mail-order tickets are the least expensive. To receive a three-month notice of audition and rehearsal schedule—for children and adults—request a place on the mailing list.

- *The Nutcracker:* By several companies. The acclaimed Boston Ballet's production is lavish, with exquisite sets and beautiful costumes.

- *A Christmas Carol:* By several companies, including Huntington Theatre, page 42.

New Year's Eve: First Night (page 273). Many afternoon events for young children and families followed by hours more of good entertainment for all ages throughout the city. Laser light and sound show. Fireworks over Boston Harbor.

Phone Directory

Here's a thumbnail outline of frequently called local numbers. Looking for a category? Check the index, page 291.

Airport Water Shuttle, 800/23–LOGAN

American Youth Hostels, 617/731–5430; 617/730–8294 (recorded tripline)

Amtrak, 617/482–3660, 800/USA RAIL; TDD 800/523–6590

Animal Rescue League of Boston, 617/426–9170

Appalachian Mountain Club, 617/523–0636

Arnold Arboretum, 617/524–1718; 617/524–1717 (recorded)

Blue Hills Trailside Museum, 617/333–0690

Bostix, 617/723–5181

Boston Ballet, 617/695–6950

Boston Bruins, 617/227–3200

Boston By Foot, 617/367–2345

Boston Celtics, 617/623–3030

Boston Children's Theatre, 617/277–3277

Boston City Hall, 617/635–4000 (Boston phone book blue pages list specific departments)

Boston Garden, 617/227–3200

Boston Harbor Islands State Park, 617/740–1605

Boston National Historical Park Visitor Center, 617/242–5642

Boston Park Rangers, 617/522–2639 or 725–4505; TTY 617/715–4006

Boston Parks and Recreation Department, 617/725–4505

Boston Public Library, 617/536–5400

Boston Red Sox, 617/267–1700

Boston Tea Party Ship and Museum, 617/338–1773

Charles River Museum of Industry, 617/893–5410

Charles River Wheelmen, 617/325–BIKE

Charlestown Navy Yard (National Park Service Visitor Center), 617/242–5601

Children's Hospital Emergency Room, 617/735–6611

Children's Museum, 617/426–6500; 617/426–8855 (recorded); TTY 617/426–5466

Children's Museum in Easton, 508/230–3789

Computer Museum, 617/426–2800 (live); 617/423–6758 (computer message)

Dartmouth Children's Museum, 508/993–3361

DeCordova Museum and Sculpture Park, 617/259–8355

Discovery Museums (Acton), 508/264–4200; TTD 508/264–0030

Drumlin Farm, 617/259–9807

Faneuil Hall Marketplace, 617/523–3886

Foxboro Museum of Discovery, 508/543–1184

Franklin Park Zoo, 617/442–2002

Garden in the Woods, 508/877–7630 or 617/237–4924; 508/877–6574 (recorded)

Gardner Museum, 617/566–1401, 617/734–1359 (concert information)

Greater Boston Convention & Visitors Bureau, 617/536–4100

Greyhound, 617/423–5810 (Boston); 617/969–8660 (Riverside)

John Hancock Observatory, 617/247–1977

Harvard University, 617/495–1000; events, 617/495–1718; Information Center, 617/495–1573; Art Museums, 617/495–9400; Natural History Museums, 617/495–1910

Higgins Armory, 508/853–6015

Historic Neighborhoods Foundation, 617/426–1885

Information Center for Individuals with Disabilities, 617/727–5540

Institute of Contemporary Art, 617/266–5152; 617/266–5151 (recorded)

John F. Kennedy Library and Museum, 617/929–4567; TTD 617/929–4574

Logan International Airport, 800/23–LOGAN

Lowell National Historical Park, 508/970–5000

Massachusetts Audubon Society, 617/259–9500

Massachusetts Office of Travel and Tourism, 617/727–3201

Massachusetts Society for the Prevention of Cruelty to Animals, 617/522–5055

Massachusetts State Parks and Forests, 617/727–3180

Massachusetts Turnpike winter road conditions, 617/237–5210

MBTA (Ⓣ), 617/722–3200, 800/392–6100; TDD 617/722–5146

Minute Man National Historical Park, 508/369–6993

Museum of Afro American History, 617/742–1854 or 723–8863

Museum of Fine Arts, 617/267–9377

Museum of Our National Heritage, 617/861–0729

Museum of Science, 617/723–2500; TTY 617/227–3235

Museum of Transportation, 617/522–6140

National Center of Afro American Artists, 617/442–8614

National Park Service, 617/242–5642

New England Aquarium, 617/973–5200

New England Patriots, 800/543–1776 (tickets)

Peter Pan Trailways, 617/426–7838 (Boston); 617/965–7040 (Riverside)

Phillips Drug (24-hour pharmacy), 617/523–1028

Poison Information, 617/232–2120

Puppet Showplace, 617/731–6400

Skywalk (Prudential Tower), 617/236–3318

Sports Museum of New England, 617/78–SPORT

State House, 617/727–3676

Steamship Authority, 508/540–2022

Swan Boats, 617/522–1966

Symphony Hall, 617/638–9200

Time and temperature, 617/637–1234

USS *Constitution* Museum, 617/426–1812

Weather (Boston), 617/936–1212

Wheelock Family Theatre, 617/723–4760 (box office); TTD 617/731–4426

Index

FOR THE NEXT EDITION

Want to share your impressions? Discovered a new place? A combination of places? A new activity? A new resource? Readers' comments and suggestions are welcome and helpful.

Something new: Calling all photographers (no minimum age)! If you have captured some magic moment and would like to have the shot considered for the next edition of *In and Out of Boston with (or without) Children,* write to me for information. All submitted photographs will be nonreturnable. It is planned to give the entire submitted collection to the Boston Public Library archives.

Bernice Chesler

The Globe Pequot Press
P.O. Box 833
Old Saybrook, CT 06475-0833

New England Travel

Here are some other fine books on New England regional destinations. All Globe Pequot travel titles are published with the highest standards of accuracy and timeliness. Please check your local bookstore for other fine Globe Pequot Press titles, which include:

Daytrips, Getaway Weekends, and Vacations in New England, $16.95
Recommended Country Inns™ New England, $14.95
Bed & Breakfast in New England, $16.95
Guide to Nantucket, $12.95
Guide to Martha's Vineyard, $12.95
Boston's Freedom Trail, $5.95
Blue Laws, Brahmins, and Breakdown Lanes, $9.95
Guide to Cape Cod, $10.95

Off the Beaten Path™ series:
Connecticut: Off the Beaten Path, $9.95
Maine: Off the Beaten Path, $9.95
Massachusetts: Off the Beaten Path, $9.95
New Hampshire: Off the Beaten Path, $9.95
Vermont: Off the Beaten Path, $9.95

To order any of these titles with MASTERCARD or VISA, call toll-free 1-800-243-0495. Free shipping for orders of three or more books. Shipping charge of $3.00 per book for one or two books ordered. Connecticut residents add sales tax. Ask for your free catalogue of Globe Pequot's quality books on recreation, travel, nature, gardening, cooking, crafts, and more. Prices and availability subject to change.